Ferryman of Memories

Ferryman of Memories

The Films of Rithy Panh

DEIRDRE BOYLE

Rutgers University Press

New Brunswick, Camden, and Newark, New Jersey

London and Oxford, UK

Rutgers University Press is a department of Rutgers, The State University of New Jersey, one of the leading public research universities in the nation. By publishing worldwide, it furthers the University's mission of dedication to excellence in teaching, scholarship, research, and clinical care.

ISBN 978-1-9788-1464-6 (cloth)
ISBN 978-1-9788-1466-0 (epub)

Cataloging-in-publication data is available from the Library of Congress.
LCCN 2022021986

A British Cataloging-in-Publication record for this book is available from the British Library.

References to internet websites (URLs) were accurate at the time of writing. Neither the author nor Rutgers University Press is responsible for URLs that may have expired or changed since the manuscript was prepared.

♾ The paper used in this publication meets the requirements of the American National Standard for Information Sciences—Permanence of Paper for Printed Library Materials, ANSI Z39.48-1992.

rutgersuniversitypress.org

Manufactured in the United States of America

For all the wandering souls

The poet is the ferryman of all that forms
an order. And an insurgent order.

RENÉ CHAR, *À une sérénité
crispée* (1951)

Contents

Preface

The title for this book is inspired by a statement from the Franco-Cambodian filmmaker and genocide survivor Rithy Panh: "I am a ferryman of memory in debt to those who have disappeared." The ferryman is, of course, a reference to Charon, Greek god of the underworld, whose job was to transport the dead to their proper resting place. There was just one catch: the dead had to be properly buried to be able to make the crossing. Nearly two million souls died during the Khmer Rouge regime, most of whom were tossed into mass graves or abandoned by the roadside, unburied, deprived of religious rituals and mourning, left to aimlessly wander without hope of rebirth. Rithy Panh, who lost most of his family during that terrible time, took upon himself the seemingly endless task of conveying the memories of the dead to history and their souls to peace. As Panh ages he resembles Charon more and more, insomniac son of the goddess of night and god of darkness, tireless worker preoccupied with ferrying Cambodia's souls to rest.

Over the course of more than thirty years, Panh has written five books and directed and written over twenty feature-length films—both fiction and documentary—winning numerous awards for his work. He is best known in the English-speaking world for his documentary films about perpetrators and survivors of the Cambodian genocide. His film about his own journey surviving Democratic Kampuchea, *The Missing Picture*, was nominated for an Oscar for best foreign language film, but there is so much more to Panh's creative portfolio. This book draws attention to the breadth of his feature films, particularly the interrelation between his fiction and documentary works. It focuses on his cinematic methods as well as the intellectual and artistic sources that have influenced him.

My first encounter with Panh's films was at the New York Film Festival in 2003 where I saw his groundbreaking documentary *S-21: The Khmer Rouge Killing Machine*. I wrote an essay about it that questioned whether genocides since World War II demanded culturally relevant forms for telling the story of what happened and should not be measured against the rubrics established for Holocaust films. Panh's film presented traumatic memory in a way I had only read about. My essay proved controversial—I quoted Janet, not Freud, and I approached the representation of traumatic reenactment as a clinician, not a theoretician. (I had just completed a degree in clinical social work focused on trauma, grief, and loss.) My essay was included in a book and reprinted in a film journal, and without intending this, it launched me into a new chapter of my life and work. When Panh's memoir, *The Elimination*, was published in English in 2012, I learned more about his experiences as a boy evacuated from the Cambodian capital to the hinterlands to work in labor camps where he endured starvation, disease, overwork, and indoctrination sessions in Khmer Rouge ideology. He witnessed the deaths of all but one of his family during the nearly four years he was a captive of Democratic Kampuchea. I realized it was not enough to write about his films one by one as I had been doing. I wanted to see them all. I wanted to understand how his films were linked together to better appreciate his cinematic achievement in remembering the Cambodian dead and archiving a past the Khmer Rouge tried in vain to erase without a trace.

When I first viewed *S-21: The Khmer Rouge Killing Machine*, I knew nothing about Panh, but I did know something about the undeclared war the United States had waged on Cambodia during the Vietnam War. I graduated from college in 1970 and wore a white armband on my academic gown in solidarity with those killed a week earlier at Kent State University, gunned down by the national guard for protesting the U.S. invasion of Cambodia. I later saw Roland Joffé's *The Killing Fields*—the film that introduced moviegoers around the world to the horrors committed during the Khmer Rouge regime.

I enrolled in the first American graduate program in media studies, which was dedicated to an understanding of the equal and inextricable relationship between theory and practice. I learned a little audio, photography, film, and video production and read the major theorists of the day; I specialized in documentary and wrote film criticism and video history. My interest in Holocaust films was rooted in my past: my childhood playmates were the offspring of concentration camp survivors; my beloved doll was a gift from one of the mothers who survived Auschwitz. Over the years I viewed many films made about the Holocaust, supervised my students' thesis work on such films, and engaged in animated debates about the legitimacy of staging and reenactment in documentary and the ethics and aesthetics demanded when representing atrocities. All of that changed for me with Panh's *S-21* when I saw a former prison guard, tongue-tied and hesitant, begin to reenact his everyday actions tormenting people shackled to the floor before sending them to their next torture session. The past became present as the guard relived his experience as a perpetrator: the memory of his body unleashed words that narrated his behavior. Suddenly my interests in trauma, death, history, memory, and documentary all came together resoundingly.

I began work on this book in 2015. I traveled widely as my research broadened and deepened, inspired by Panh's films and his wide-ranging intellectual interests. The French Revolution, trauma theory, *baksbat*, totalitarianism, stateless refugees, Lazarean art, postcolonialism, Marguerite Duras, Holocaust memoirs, Buddhism and death, the poetry of René Char—there was so much to discover, to read, to learn from. Part of the endless appeal of Panh's art for me has been the fact that each work finds its own form, and as a result, they are full of surprises, innovations, risks, puzzling genre combinations, and the unique contributions of his repertory company of superb collaborators. Panh's determination to find the right form for each film inspired me to experiment, and this is why the structure of this book is unconventional, an eclectic mix of different forms—part memoir, part history, and part film analysis and criticism. It took time and effort for me to understand the historical context for so much of what happened in Cambodia, and I thought it helpful to provide a short introduction to that history for readers as unfamiliar with it as I was at the start. I knew that it would be challenging researching what had been written about Panh's work in French and would demand reactivating dormant language skills that took me back to my youth long before Google Translator was invented when I was a student in Mme. Marzi's classes. Her family helped shelter the poet Max Jacob during the Second World War until the Gestapo seized him and sent him to his death. It was her love of French history and culture that inspired me to take on the task of translating superb French criticism about Panh's films. Happily, I also discovered that some of the best thinking came from critics and scholars writing in English. I have tried here to identify the contributions of authors whose cultural, generational, or disciplinary differences have led to new and imaginative analysis of his films. I am sure there are mistakes and imprecisions here, but I hope this book will serve as a helpful introduction to Panh's cinematic work.

I believe *Ferryman of Memories* will interest readers curious about the impact of colonialism, the Cold War, globalization, and genocide in Southeast Asia. Panh is treated with great respect in the Francophone world that welcomed him as a political refugee in 1979, but he remains little known in U.S. film circles despite his many awards and the attention given him by media superstars like Angelina Jolie, whose film about the Khmer Rouge, *First They Killed My Father*, was produced by Panh in 2016. As he has wryly noted, his films are unlikely to win more Oscar nominations because he has no money to launch ad campaigns for them or, as he jokes, even pay for a cocktail party for critics. Panh's "poor means" apply not only to support for his films but to the Bophana Audiovisual Resource Center in Phnom Penh, which he cofounded in 2006 to preserve Cambodia's film and photography heritage. The Bophana Center has taught a new generation the art and craft of filmmaking and attracted international directors to Cambodia to shoot films with skilled technicians and actors and at affordable prices. It is an essential archive of Cambodian audiovisual records, much of which would have perished without the labors of archivists and the gifts of donors. The scope of this book does not allow me to explore all the many roles Panh still juggles. This book ends with his last single-channel film, *Graves without a Name*. I have yet to see *Irradiés*, which premiered at the Berlin Film Festival in 2020, where it won the prize for best documentary film just before the pandemic called a halt to its theatrical distribution. His latest film, in postproduction as of this writing, is a documentary titled *Everything Will Be OK*. I hope to be able to write about both films by the time this book is in your hands.

One of the reasons I felt compelled to embark on this project had to do with feeling myself a guilty bystander who had done nothing—beyond wearing a white arm band—to halt more U.S. bombs dropped on Cambodia than on Japan during World War II. Were it not for those bombing runs, some historians have argued, farmers would not have been driven into the ranks of the Khmer Rouge, and the scourge of the Pol Pot regime might never have come to such devastating power or lasted as long as it did. The United States was not solely responsible for setting in motion what would culminate in genocide. French colonialism, Marxism, and Maoism along with age-old warring among Indochinese states were significant factors. But I could not shake a sense of responsibility for what my country had contributed to the deaths of so many. I felt compelled by the souls of the dead to help tell their story by writing and teaching about the films of the artist considered by many to be the conscience of Cambodia.

I hope the mix of personal and objective voices here proves engaging for general readers as well as scholars. Chapters are arranged in loose chronological order more or less following the films' release dates, and they are grouped around some underlying concerns. There is a chapter on Panh's background and another on Khmer Rouge history. There is a prologue, an interlude titled "Dark Tourism," and an epilogue, each of which conveys my experiences in Cambodia while interviewing Panh, attending the genocide tribunal, and visiting relevant Cambodian sites from Angkor Wat to the S-21 prison. And there are the chapters that explore nineteen of his feature-length films one by one. The book ends with two appendices that include previously published interviews I conducted with Panh. Please note that Cambodian names when Latinized are often spelled differently. For example Houy is written as Huy in other texts. For non-Khmer speakers, it is difficult to determine which name is the surname of a Cambodian, and the gender of an individual is not always evident from the name. Given all this, if I have made mistakes in any of these particulars, I beg the pardon of these individuals.

Ferryman of Memories

Prologue

The Bophana Audiovisual Resource Center is located in the middle of Street 200 in central Phnom Penh. My hotel was, according to the map, right around the corner, but I wandered about in circles unable to find my way. Maybe it was the result of jet lag. Or maybe it was Phnom Penh playing tricks with me. The streets were pockmarked with ruts, and the sidewalks were packed with parked bikes, food vendors, and workers pruning the overhanging trees. Everywhere traffic was a chaotic flow of motorbikes, *tuk-tuks*, taxis, and trucks crammed with people. Traffic lights were rare, and crossing the street seemed to require an act of faith or desperation. Finally I found Street 200, memorizing the beauty parlor on the corner as my landmark. I headed in what I hoped was the right direction.

I was early for my appointment when I saw the red and white banner fluttering over a solid, colonial-style, two-story building somewhat hidden by tropical plants clustered to provide shade and privacy to the wide-open ground floor. I looked into the entry where Rithy Panh stood. He glanced at me, smiled briefly, and continued to focus on the children who were scurrying across the red and white tile floor. I walked over, and he gruffly announced he needed to be sure the children were taken care of first. I noticed then that all of the children hurrying into the theater were disabled. The last boy was a teenager, slim and long limbed. He flew across the floor, propelling himself with his hands and arms, looking remarkably like a crab scuttling sideways in his rush to see the movie about to begin.

I was a crab too, astrologically speaking, and crabs play critical roles in two of Panh's films—*Rice People* and *The Sea Wall*. There are no coincidences. No symbol is wasted on those who choose to look and see. I shed my shell many times in the process of researching and writing this book, and I discovered new levels of personal vulnerability thanks to Rithy Panh and his films. The writer Nick Paterniti warned me before I left home that his experience in Phnom Penh researching the genocide tribunal had left him reeling for months after. I foolishly thought I was too well prepared for that to happen to me. I continue to struggle with the enormity of what I learned and what I experienced. Like the boy scuttling across the tile floor of the Bophana Center, Panh also had to maneuver with hands and arms, unable to walk for a year, after accidentally wounding himself with a pickax that he drove into his foot while working in a Khmer Rouge field. For a long time after, he experienced phantom pains. There are no coincidences, and pain comes back to haunt one when it will.

I wondered if Panh saw me as a crab, an alien invader storming the barricades he has created to protect himself from unwelcome pests. When he failed to answer my emails confirming he would be in Cambodia when I planned to arrive, I fell into a state of depression weeks before my departure. I knew I was at the end of a long line of others who had more urgent claims on him and his attention. I rallied, reminding myself that with or without him, I had plenty to do in Cambodia during my two-week stay. There was viewing all the films he has made that are not available in the United States, many in French or Khmer without any translation into English. And there were the genocide sites that I had seen in his films and that I knew I needed to visit. There was the genocide tribunal, which is what most people call the Extraordinary Chambers of the Courts of Cambodia, or ECCC, where I would witness the appeals hearing in Case 002. And finally there was Angkor Wat, the site of ancient Khmer power and artistic achievement in the heart of the country, the inspiration for some of the most insane ideas of agricultural reform hatched by Pol Pot, ideas that would work people to death to realize impossible goals. So, I told myself, if Rithy Panh was not in Phnom Penh or was unavailable to talk with me, I was not going to let it stop me from flying halfway around the world. Whatever happened, I knew it would become a part of what I would write. And so I flew to Phnom Penh, landed at midnight, and rode through the steamy city to my hotel. Before doing anything else, I opened my computer and read this email: "Mr. Panh will see you tomorrow at 2:30 P.M."

It did not take long for him to confirm my suspicion that his neglect of my emails was calculated to put me off, a tactic that had succeeded with other nuisances. That I did not get the message or chose not to accept it was never spoken about directly. Once I was there, he seemed resigned to making the best of a bad situation, or so it seemed.

In person Rithy Panh looks very much like the small clay figurines he fashioned to tell the story of his early life in *The Missing Picture*. With his compact body, receding hairline, and astounding energy, he willfully propels himself from one project to the next. I do not know when I began to see him as a Napoleonic figure, a diminutive commander of Cambodian film troops, a dynamo exerting his will either through fear, charm, sulky insistence, or skillful persuasion. He reminded me of the multiheaded Buddha statues at Bayon, one of his favorite Angkorean temples—a man of many faces and just as dominant as those larger-than-life statues. Each day I went to see him, I was unsure which Rithy I would meet: the shyly beguiling child-man, the overworked director-producer, or the sleep-deprived survivor grappling with the traumatic memories he was materializing on camera next door. Everything I had read—in English and in French—all the interviews, the books he had written, the films themselves, had not prepared me for this unpredictable and deliberately impenetrable individual. Each day I spent in his company proved unlike the other, whether we were meeting in his office at the Bophana Center or I was chasing him down on the roof of the Cambodian Film Commission, where his crew worked on the film set. Sometimes I failed to find him, hesitating to open closed doors to see if he was catnapping or curled up with his cell phone surfing the internet and posting images on Facebook.

One afternoon I arrived looking for Rithy and found him standing on the roof, looking out over the city and munching a roasted ear of corn. He turned around and walked toward me. He asked if I would like some, and I politely declined. I think I asked if he wanted me to come back later or the next day. I cannot recall what I said because I was thinking about his observation that he avoids stairwells, terraces, precipices, unobstructed views, cliffs: "Falling is easy. . . . If I'm on a balcony, I can't help myself. I calculate how many seconds I'd fall before hitting the ground. But I don't give in."

I surfed the web and found plenty of photos of him taken over many years, from the young student with brooding glance and generous mop of hair to the world-renowned director attired in haute couture accepting an award. His various personas were captured in these photos. I hoped the months I had spent translating his books from French to English, researching scholarly essays about his work, exploring the history of Cambodia and "Pol Pot time," and writing about his films would stand me in good stead. Much as I might have dreamed of conducting the kind of interview François Truffaut once conducted during fifty hours with his idol Alfred Hitchcock, this was not going to be like that orderly career interview. All the questions I had compiled, all the theories I had formed and wanted to test, had to be tossed aside. When my question about casting a film he shot ten years earlier inspired no interest, he simply changed the subject. He was the director, not me. I was often frustrated and even angry, but eventually I realized that what Panh was telling me was maybe more important than what I had hoped to learn. I started listening carefully to what he wanted to tell me. I continued showing up, intimidated by the large brown cigar stuck in his mouth, those sunglasses shielding eyes that had not slept the night before, and whatever mask he wore that day. But slowly, slowly a kind of rapport developed between us that would extend past Cambodia to other encounters in New York, Geneva, and Toronto. It would change course many times, sometimes leaving me blindsided and speechless. But invariably there was the compelling need to understand the films and the man behind them.

1

Uncle Rithy and the Cambodian Tragedy

Works of art always spring from those who have faced the danger, gone to the very end of an experience, to the point beyond which no human being can go. The further one dares to go, the more decent, the more personal, the more unique a life becomes.

RAINER MARIA RILKE in a letter to his wife Clara, *Letters on Cézanne*[1]

Rithy Panh is a storyteller. He has always been a storyteller, even as a child, even in the Khmer Rouge labor camps where he told tales about ghosts and witches and moon landings. Being a storyteller won him a better job in the kitchen and saved him from death by exhaustion in the rice fields. But his stories also proved dangerous and were branded as lies, imperialist propaganda, and a betrayal of the revolution. After public self-criticism ordered by the Khmer Rouge, the thirteen-year-old storyteller within was forced to surrender, and the worker went back to the rice fields. Yet somehow, Rithy Panh endured along with the storyteller inside him. Over the past thirty years, he has made more than twenty feature-length films—both documentaries and fictional narratives—and he has written five books, inspired by the Cambodian genocide and its aftermath.

Rithy Panh is a powerful agent of memory and his nation's leading filmmaker. His is a cinema of witness and critical inquiry into the mechanisms of genocide. What makes men perform acts of evil, acts of violence? How did Cambodia become a killing field? How did intellectuals become torturers intent on destroying innocent people? Why does the corruption that arose out of such terror linger on to this day? Using the most subtle means, exploring language and silence, creating original cinematic forms to express intolerable memories, his fiction films, documentaries, and books all serve to keep alive the history of what happened during the Khmer Rouge regime. It would be a mistake to think that his filmmaking is concerned only with the Cambodian genocide, since his work also concerns the predicament of refugees, migrant laborers, and sex workers, otherwise invisible and silent, and the persistence of colonial forces that continue to exploit them in a new age of globalization. Panh is neither an "Asian" filmmaker nor a "French" filmmaker, and efforts to question the authenticity of his filmmaking as one or the other shed little light on its complexity. Panh is an exile who shuttles between East and West, North and South, and his films belong to the world.

Panh has wryly said he has made only one film, part jest, part truth. His films have won prizes at major festivals around the world, including the prestigious Un Certain Regard at Cannes and the Berlinale's award for best documentary. He has been nominated for Academy Awards, including Best Foreign Language Film, the first Cambodian filmmaker so honored. His memoir has been compared to the books of Primo Levi and his films to those of Claude Lanzmann. He is far better known in his adopted country, France, where he was trained to become a filmmaker, than in the Anglophone world. He attracted international attention with his first fiction film, *Rice People*, which was awarded a prize at Cannes in 1992 for best film script adaptation. His work achieved breakthrough global attention with the release in English of his documentary film *S-21: The Khmer Rouge Killing Machine* in 2002 in which survivors confront their torturers in the hellish prison where it is estimated 17,000 men, women, and children were interrogated, tortured, and executed. His book *The Elimination*, written with the novelist Christophe Bataille, offers a beautifully written and multilevel account of the making of

Duch, Master of the Forges of Hell, an extended interview with the commandant of the S-21 prison, whom Panh interviewed while Duch prepared for his
trial for crimes against humanity in the Extraordinary Chambers of the
Court of Cambodia. *The Elimination* interweaves the backstory of the making of this film with Panh's memories of childhood, when his world changed
overnight. Panh crafted an ingenious method to make the film he had been
wanting to make for twenty years: an autobiographical film of his own survival that would not require anyone to reenact the horrors he had experienced.
The Missing Picture won Panh international recognition as one of the most
creative and powerful filmmakers of our times.

Rithy Panh was born in Phnom Penh on April 18, 1964. Actually, he is
uncertain whether it was in 1962 or 1964. The ambiguity seems to suit him.
He is the youngest of nine children. His mother was a peasant from the
Mekong delta of Vietnam, formerly known as French Cochinchina. His
Cambodian father, Panh Lauv, was also of peasant origins, but he was the
only child in his large family to be educated. He worked as a primary school
teacher before becoming deputy to Cambodia's minister of education and
ultimately a senator. Rithy's happy childhood revolved around his parents,
siblings, extended family, and friends. His paternal grandparents died before
he was born, but the family returned often to their village because his parents never wanted to forget their origins. There he learned to fish and to appreciate rural life, which was difficult but not harsh. On the contrary, he
perceived it as magical and marvelous. Most days, though, his life revolved
around the family at home in the Tuol Kouk quarter of Phnom Penh. Listening to his father's voice reciting poetry after dinner laid the ground for Rithy's
enduring love of poetry. His mother was an exceptional cook and resourceful housekeeper, who was often left to keep the home fires burning and raise
the children on her own while her husband was abroad inspecting the educational systems of countries like France, Yugoslavia, and the United States.
His older sister was a curator at the National Museum and sometimes took
him with her to work. There he came to love the magnificent sculptures that
embodied the spirit of the ancient Cambodian culture. His oldest brothers
were educated in French and studied abroad in subjects like medicine and law.
Panh laughingly suspects his father intended to sire enough children to lead
Cambodia into a progressive future in all major areas of learning. As a child
Rithy dreamed of becoming a pilot or an astronaut. He has said he also
thought of becoming a musician, a writer, or a painter. He often spent his
free time on the film sets where his "uncle" worked. "Uncle" is here used as
an honorific term, one that Panh also bears as mentor to many young

Cambodian filmmakers. As a child, he enjoyed watching films being made, but he never thought of becoming a filmmaker himself. By the time he began school, the educational system had changed, and Khmer, not French, had become the language of instruction. There he found science and mathematics captivating. Rithy idolized his older brother Hiran and saw him as a real artist. He wanted desperately to wear his hair long, take up an instrument, and win the affection of young girls as his brother did, ambitions all discouraged by his mother. Rithy looked up to his siblings and loved his two nephews and a niece. Within six months of the Khmer Rouge take-over, he would begin mourning their deaths.

On April 17, 1975, the Khmer Rouge entered Phnom Penh and plunged the country into heightened turmoil that would last nearly four years. Everyone was ordered to evacuate the city. As the family joined thousands on the road, Hiran turned back home in search of his guitar; he disappeared and was never heard from again. Rithy believes he turned thirteen years old the day his family began their arduous trek into rural Cambodia. They were deported to Chrey, a village in the middle of nowhere, and as "new people," they would be "reeducated" through hard work, indoctrination sessions, and increasing privations in the elusive goal of becoming acceptable members of the revolution. Life as he had known it was over. Now fishing meant catching fish for sustenance with his bare hands, something he was initially incapable of doing. He learned how hard it was to work the land, harvesting rice in the mud for hours with the sun on your back and the temperature 35 degrees Celsius (95 degrees Fahrenheit). He passed from early adolescence into adulthood overnight.

The Khmer Rouge wanted everyone to become members of one of three classes: workers, peasants, or soldiers. The "old people" or "base people" were peasants living in rural areas and were considered loyal to the revolution. The "new people" were urbanites, who were de facto suspected of harboring antirevolutionary inclinations. They were not just intellectuals but anyone who could read and write as well as all foreigners, ethnic minorities, and clergy, including Buddhist monks and Christian priests. Even people who wore eyeglasses were suspect and could be put to death for that offense.

At first the Panh family was allowed to stay together. But the Khmer Rouge were intent on breaking down all forms of bourgeois life, including the traditional Cambodian devotion to family. Soon all families were divided, with boys sent to separate dormitories from girls and married couples allowed to retain only very young children and finally none at all. Rithy's mother was strong and resourceful. She kept the family together, using what little she was able to bring from their home in Phnom Penh to barter for food, miraculously retaining an ax that she used to build a structure for them to live. His father exerted a moral influence on the family. They lived in a traditional dwelling built a flight above ground, and at night villagers loyal to the Khmer Rouge huddled underneath and spied on them. When they heard his parents talking about Pol Pot and Ieng Sary, whom Panh Lauv knew because of his work within the Education Ministry, they were frightened and abandoned plans to kill the family. Panh Lauv had been guardedly optimistic about the family's ability to weather the storm of revolution because he believed that the Khmer Rouge leadership, most of whom had been educated in France, would support a strong educational system. He was sadly mistaken; one of the first acts of the Khmer Rouge was to dismantle the schools, destroying a system that provided basic education for everyone in society. Panh Lauv's ultimate response to what was happening was to assert his dignity by refusing to eat the meager food they were given, food he considered unfit for human beings. And so he starved to death. At first Rithy was angry with his father for abandoning the family, but he later came to admire his father's last act of freedom, an act of rebellion against the regime.

Rithy went to work in the rice fields and was sent far from family members, stealing back to see them infrequently, invariably discovering their numbers dwindling as they died of malnutrition, exhaustion, and untreated disease. Eventually his mother followed his fifteen-year-old sister, lying down beside her corpse in the mockery of a village hospital staffed by untrained "doctors." Rithy also fell ill and lived in the hospital for a time, becoming a de facto nurse's aide, removing dead bodies each morning, burying them in mass graves, and wondering when he would join their number. But like his mother, he was strong and with help from others managed to survive. In the chaos of civil war, as the regime was collapsing, he escaped and miraculously found one of his sisters still alive, and together they set off for Thailand. After weeks dodging the Khmer Rouge and being beaten by Thais, Rithy and his little band of refugees were found by a journalist who told the Red Cross about them. That is how they came to be rescued when so many others disappeared without a trace. When they arrived at the Mairut refugee camp on the Thai border, their photos were taken, and they were given medical care. As soon as he reached the camp, he stopped fearing for his life but experienced profound sadness. It seemed to him that his life lay behind him and belonged to the years of struggle for survival. Fortunately, four of his brothers were studying abroad when the Khmer Rouge entered Phnom Penh. Two were in France, one in Germany, and one in Algeria. And so, thanks to France's family reunification law, he and his sister were able to claim political asylum in France.[2]

His relatives in Grenoble welcomed the traumatized boy. Suddenly transported from the tropics to a cold country where he could neither speak nor understand the language, he was silent and withdrawn. He wanted to forget everything about his nightmarish past, including the Khmer language. He wanted to live another life in another world, believing it was possible to begin again as if he had just been born. But the past would not let him go.

Rithy told his relatives little of what he had experienced. He wrote about what he had endured and then destroyed the text:

> I didn't want to talk about any of that.... I had been uprooted and I felt somehow incomplete, torn between forgetting and remembering, between past and present, always ill at ease. I lived with memories of my relatives, with the anxiety—the certainty—that the same tragic story would repeat itself. It was burned into my flesh forever, as if with a branding iron, that this is what the world is like: a place where there's a lot of indifference and hypocrisy and little compassion.[3]

Like the Italian writer Primo Levi, who survived Auschwitz, Panh struggled with survivor guilt: "You feel others have died in your place, that we're alive because of a privilege we haven't deserved, because of an injustice done to the dead. It isn't wrong to be alive, but we feel it is."[4]

For Panh, life after genocide was a terrifying void. Contrary to what he had believed, to revive was also to reconquer his memory and his speech. It would take years before he recovered his ability to imagine, to laugh, to dream again, and more years before he could express what he knew about the crimes he had witnessed committed by the Khmer Rouge.

The troubled teenager tried to find his way in school. He began to paint, to sketch drawings of barbed wire and skulls and men in striped clothes. He took up the guitar. And he tried to write, but nothing seemed to satisfy him. One day at school, as he recounts in *The Elimination*, a boy hit him in the head and was rewarded with the laughter of his friends. Thus encouraged, the boy struck his head repeatedly as Rithy pleaded with him to stop because the head in Cambodia is the most sacred part of the body. Suddenly Rithy lashed out, and soon the boy was lying on the ground with blood all over his face, and Rithy was breathing hard, trembling. Fearing reprisals after his outburst, Rithy carried a metal pipe for months in his schoolbag. He had discovered violence within himself and thought: "The evil done to me is inside me. Present and powerful. Lying in wait."[5]

It was an art teacher who saw the promise in him and gave him a Super 8 film camera to experiment with. He began by making a short Chaplinesque film that elicited a hilarious response from his viewers. He then made shorts inspired by popular films like *La Boum* (*The Party*), a popular teen romance film, as well as Hitchockian horror films and a silent film inspired by a Jacques Prévert poem. He had finally found a medium he could use to express himself. And when he had no money for film, he took photos. The director of a film center in Grenoble helped him synchronize his images with sound and told him his films were "Bressonian." Panh had no idea who Bresson was then, but he thought that making films was what he should do.[6] He had originally been headed for a vocational program in carpentry, but his teacher recommended he take the admissions test for the national film school, l'IDHEC (L'Institute des hautes études cinématographique, now called La Fémis). He sat for the entrance exam in 1985 and passed. "I chose film, which shows the world, presents beauty, and also deals in words. I figure it keeps my fists in my pockets."[7]

When he was accepted into France's most prestigious school for filmmakers, he thought cinema would allow him to pursue the memory of the past, a difficult choice but one he now felt compelled to embrace. He was interested in making documentary films, but the multiyear training program at l'IDHEC afforded only four months' focus on documentary versus three years on narrative fiction. Frustrated, he went ahead with the program, availed himself of the school's vast film library, and found two professors who shared his interests. On the plus side, he was exposed to world cinema and came to appreciate the cinema verité of Jean Rouch and the direct cinema of Fred Wiseman. Mostly he was influenced by cinematic giants like Andrei Tarkovsky, Alain Resnais, Chris Marker, Yasujiro Ozu, Satyajit Ray, and Roberto Rossellini, among others. He had seen few films before he began his studies at l'IDHEC, where watching Tarkovsky's *Andrei Rublev* was a revelation: "Everything that I wanted to make comes from that, this way of filming the will and effort of a man."[8]

His thesis film, *Le passé imparfait* (*The Imperfect Past*), was the first film in his long career, but it was, in hindsight, a catastrophe according to Panh, who claims he destroyed it. He had made all kinds of errors, he says. It would take time for him to develop his own aesthetics and ethics of filmmaking—how to make a film *with* people and not *about* them. These ideas applied to his documentaries as well as his fiction films, which rely extensively on the participation of nonactors. But one important thing did happen when making his thesis film: he worked with a young friend, an expat American composer living in Paris, named Marc Marder. Marder's music for this film was the start of a long and productive creative collaboration that continues to this day. Marder has become more than a creative partner; he is like a brother to Panh, who knows well the importance of brothers.

By the time Rithy Panh graduated from l'IDHEC in 1988, he knew he wanted to return to make films about Cambodia's past and his own. As a student he had developed a treatment for a documentary on refugees living on the Thai-Cambodia border, people like him who had escaped one form of terrorism for another, forced to live in a gulag, dependent on precarious support from major aid organizations, and at the mercy of an often corrupt and inhumane infrastructure. In 1988 his return to Cambodia became possible, although the political situation remained unstable. It took him two years to raise money, technical support, and permission to shoot on the Thai-Cambodian border. It took even more time before anyone made good on their promises to give him access to a camp. He chose Site 2, which was the largest refugee camp at that time. He thought it was the best place for him to find individuals who could tell the story of refugees whose lives had been displaced and forever changed by the overthrow of the Lon Nol government, five years of civil war, four years of terror and deprivation under the Khmer Rouge, and ten years of Vietnamese occupation. With this first feature-length documentary, he began the long and demanding task of uncovering one of the worst genocides of the twentieth century. He found a path that has kept him busy and creatively engaged ever since.

Today Panh splits his life between Paris, where he lives, and Phnom Penh, where he works. There he founded a center for the archiving of Cambodian film and photography; for the training of a new generation of filmmakers and technicians; and for the screening of films that otherwise would never be seen in Cambodia. Panh has stepped down as director of the Bophana Audiovisual Resource Center but continues to work there on a volunteer basis and without salary. He also helped set up the Cambodian Film Commission, which attracts international filmmakers to the region to shoot their films and build up an industry that is slowly becoming an important resource for filmmaking in Southeast Asia. He produces films in Cambodia with major international figures like Régis Wargnier (*Indochine*, *The Gate*) and Angelina Jolie (*First They Killed My Father*). Much of the time he shoots his own films there. He has invested nearly all his money in getting the Bophana Center

FIGURE 1.1 Panh films *The Land of Wandering Souls* © John Vink / MAPSimages

established and functioning, and despite the success of his films, he still struggles to get funding for them as well as for the center. People think getting nominated for an Academy Award means you are "in the money," Panh bitterly observes, but it seems to make it harder to raise funds because people think you already have whatever you need and more besides. He earns his money teaching. "I teach everywhere—whoever pays me best," he says and laughs.

Panh leads a double life: sometimes the globe-trotting sophisticate gamboling on the Croisette at Cannes, a trickster with a Cheshire cat grin on his chubby face; sometimes a scowling dervish in sandals and loose-fitting clothes stomping about the corridors of the Bophana Center. The worldly European cineast is also Uncle Rithy, father figure to forty workers at the center and the many film professionals and budding filmmakers who owe their opportunities to this pathfinder. He has begun to work in new media forms—installation and multimedia work like the project *Exile* he designed for the International Film Festival and Forum on Human Rights in Geneva—and directing the theatrical work *Bangsokol, Requiem for Cambodia*, which included a triptych film he designed that accompanies the music composed by Him Sophy. Will he continue to work in expanded forms, like the three-part film *Irradiés* that won the award for best documentary at the Berlin Film Festival in 2020? Panh will doubtless continue to devise original forms for whatever he creates.

During the pandemic, he finished shooting a new film in Cambodia in 2021, *Everything Will Be OK*, which builds on the original style he created with Mang Sarith for *The Missing Picture*. He called the effort a "fight" but one that he won. It earned him a silver bear award at the Berlinale in 2022.

Panh has many faces. He is at times brooding and sullen, arrogant and dismissive, penetrating and incisive, seductive and wistful. He can be suddenly childlike in his enthusiasms but more often impenetrable and impassive. In rare unguarded moments, he reveals exceptional flashes of vulnerability and fear and then switches into the most disabling sarcasm, a single word delivered with withering intonation. He is, as he insists, complicated. He is a director. He likes to be in command. He lets few people see beyond whichever mask he is wearing. And when he does allow a glimpse of what lies beneath, he rapidly regroups and resumes the impenetrability he has fashioned for himself. I see him with his signature large Cuban cigar planted firmly in his mouth, a graceful hand propping up his head, and shaded glasses veiling his eyes as he looks out and reveals nothing of what is going on within. It is a mask that he probably first crafted when he had to defend himself from "reeducation" sessions by the Khmer Rouge. When asked how he managed to keep them from brainwashing him, he paused to reflect, looking off to the side, and then said softly, "I used to go into the forest afterwards and sing songs."

2

The Return

Discovering the Gaze

> It is one of the tragedies of writing about tragedy that the weight and texture of words matter unduly, for suffering needs a measure of grace to be bearable to others.
>
> **JONATHAN SPENCE**[1]

Rithy Panh did not want to begin his career by making personal films. He was more interested in doing something about collective destiny, but there was no way of escaping his own past. He had written a film treatment while he was still a student in Paris. In "Aux abords des frontières" (Near the borders),[2] he proposed observing Cambodians living in the refugee camps along the Thai-Cambodian border, an idea that evolved and became his first feature-length film, the documentary *Site 2*. In 1988 he returned to Asia to revisit the experience of being a refugee. The political situation in Cambodia made it difficult for him to film there then, so he traveled to the largest Cambodian refugee camp in Thailand to find someone who epitomized the struggle to recapture life after years of being displaced. The film he made clearly relates to the international plight of refugees today. *Site 2* exists beyond time and place and is able to address some of the most urgent issues we are confronted with now.

After the Vietnamese invaded Cambodia in December 1978, the Angkar ("the organization") began to unravel, and thousands headed for the border with Thailand, among them Rithy Panh. En route to freedom, he was reunited with his sister, and they set off chased by Thais, Vietnamese, and Khmer Rouge. After a long and arduous journey, they reached the Mairut refugee camp, which housed 5,200 refugees in July 1979. Panh and his sister were able to take advantage of the French family repatriation act and secured visas to travel to France, where two of their brothers lived. Panh arrived at Charles de Gaulle airport in Paris on September 13, 1979. He had avoided relocation to the largest camp at that time, Sa Kaeo Refugee Camp, which housed at its peak 185,000 people who lived in the most appalling conditions of squalor, beset by a host of diseases and the attendant problems related to starvation and exhaustion. Many Cambodian refugees were forced to live in such horrific conditions for years.

Ten years later, the living situation for Cambodian refugees had improved, but many were still living a marginal existence without land, adequate food, or hope and hugely dependent on the support of charitable and nongovernmental organizations. *Site 2* offers, among other things, a glimpse at what Cambodian refugees experienced at that time. It is a reality that has not changed for the better today, when the predicament for global refugees has become as urgent and compelling as it was after World War II and, many would argue, even more critical given the crisis of the "nation-state" and waning compassion in the West, which increasingly and aggressively bars the stateless from crossing their borders to find asylum. The United Nations' 1951 Convention Relating to the Status of Refugees defined a refugee not as a person who is entitled to rights that she or he has been denied but as one who can demonstrate that she or he lives in fear for her or his life. Hannah Arendt, herself a refugee and a theorist of statelessness, wrote of the bitter irony that the human person appears in the law just as her human rights are withdrawn. Rithy Panh, like Arendt, refused to consign the refugee to the position of a quivering supplicant before the law. His own experience had led him to champion the refugee as a human being with human rights, which included the right to speak.[3]

Speaking up was not easy for the young Panh when he arrived in France. At first he tried to forget his native language in an effort to bury his memories. "When I arrived in France, after four years under the Khmer Rouge regime, I wanted to live very simply and forget everything, including my mother tongue. The past no longer existed. Nothing at all. I behaved as if I had just been born."[4]

As Arendt points up, such loss means not only to lose one's linguistic anchorage to nation and tradition but to lose the "naturalness of reactions, the simplicity of gestures, the unaffected expression of feelings"[5] that are available through one's mother tongue. Like many refugees, Panh thought he could forget his suffering by immersing himself in a new language and culture. Suspended between Khmer, a language of pain, and a still to be mastered French, Panh embraced another language where linguistic grammar, syntax, and vocabulary ceased being obstacles and free expression was directly accessible—the language of images, of cinema.[6]

Panh's principal language today is French. Although he is at ease when speaking French, he remains curiously insecure about his writing in it, which may explain why he has chosen to work with a collaborator on nearly all his writing projects, from funding proposals, screenplays, and film narrations to the books and essays he has written during his career. But he never wavers in his certainty when using his language of choice, cinema.

When Panh returned to Asia, he knew that he needed to reconnect with his mother tongue to be able to engage with the people in the camps. He quickly realized that he also needed to work with a production crew that could speak and understand the language of the people being filmed. At the start this was impossible, and he had to rely on a professional crew of French colleagues who could help him train native crews who would eventually take over all the roles required to make his films in Cambodia.

Panh decided to shoot his first documentary at the refugee camp known as Site 2, which was four kilometers from the Cambodian border. It was the largest Thai refugee camp at that time and for several years the largest camp in Southeast Asia. It had been opened by the Royal Thai Government in January 1985 during the Vietnamese dry-season offensive against guerrilla forces opposing Vietnam's occupation of Cambodia. The camp was 2.9 square miles (5.6 square kilometers). Records indicate 180,000 individuals were jammed together with few resources and little security. The Thai government collaborated with the United Nations Border Relief Operation (UNBRO) and other UN agencies to resettle people displaced from eight smaller refugee camps destroyed by military activities.[7] Available programs were limited to basic support services: medical care, public health programs, sanitation, construction, and skills training. At first, education for the children was not provided following the Thai policy of "humane deterrence," which discouraged permanent programs and services that would attract refugees who could not find relief in Cambodia. Eventually primary schools were set up, and literacy training was given to adults. Services were provided by an international array of NGOs and charity organizations, including Médecins Sans Frontières, the International Committee of the Red Cross (ICRC), the Japan International Volunteer Center, and Catholic Relief Services, among others, all coordinated by UNBRO, which was responsible for the distribution of food and water.

The plight of Cambodian refugees consigned to border camps like Site 2 would be studied by scholars for years. The anthropologist Lindsay Cole French conducted her research at Site 2 around the time Panh made his film. She wrote poignantly about the post-holocaust suffering of Cambodians who had endured four years of horror under Pol Pot followed by ten years of civil war after the overthrow of the Khmer Rouge regime. For survivors, arriving in a refugee camp like Site 2 literally locked them into another experience of dysfunction and despair, which would affect the rebuilding of social organization in Cambodia for years to come. In the camps, economic relations, political power, family relationships, and spiritual beliefs and practices all converged under the influence of local, regional, and international forces. Everything was subject to change. This uncertainty, added to the trauma of surviving a genocide, made it difficult for refugees to believe in the possibility of a future worth living.[8] Panh's film offered an unprecedented view of the situation in 1988, a reality that unfortunately has not changed much for refugees today—except for geography, language, and nationality. Then as now, refugees fleeing from the oppression of civil wars and other catastrophes were locked into camps where they could barely survive with their human dignity or their lives.

What makes Panh's film so relevant now is his decision not to focus on rampant corruption in the administration of this refugee camp. Rather than trying to expose the complex web of political and economic interests at stake in holding refugees in a state of indefinite detention, he focused on the refugees themselves, more precisely on one woman and her family.[9] He was interested in the refugee as a human being and what it was like to live as a virtual prisoner within this system. Site 2 was the ideal place to explore how individuals who had survived civil war, genocide, and foreign occupation still had to struggle to retain their dignity and face an uncertain future.

Site 2 (1989)

Panh explains what happened when he arrived in Thailand:

> I wanted to go to Site 2 but the Thai military didn't want me to go. They kept
> me outside the camp for months. Every two or three days, I went to see the
> military in Bangkok. They refused me again and again. I was very naïve. I
> believed in the UN. I went to see the UN, and I said, "Help me, please, you are
> the UN." I was really naïve. They didn't help me. They just sat me in a chair,
> "Wait here. We will help you," but nothing ever happened.
>
> One day I was very angry because I had run out of money. I went back to see
> the Thai official and said, "Maybe I will not make the film, but I will see you.
> You will be my neighbor. I will see you one day." I went out, and the guy came
> after me. "I give you three days." Three days to make *Site 2*.
>
> I went to Site 2. I didn't have a ride to go back. I went to the camp and . . . I
> could not go inside. When you closed your eyes, you could hear the murmuring
> of the city. There were 180,000 people . . . small place, big town. You cannot see
> the camp, but you can hear the murmuring. I started to make the film with
> these sounds, to imagine how people lived.
>
> When they gave me the possibility to go back to Site 2, we only had three
> days. The first day, I did not shoot. It was a situation where I knew I should not
> do that, but I was young. I did not shoot the first day, but I told my team, "You
> can use three boxes of film, 12 minutes each, but shoot something that is
> interesting for you, that you have never seen or something that you can see
> people fighting to survive or to protect themselves or something like that."[10]

While his crew began to shoot, Panh went searching the camp for someone
who could serve as principal character. On the third day, he noticed a woman
napping and sensed that she could become a central character. He woke her
up. She was not very happy at that, but when he shared his own story with
her, Mme. Yim Om agreed to allow him to follow her daily life and hear her
story. "I think she had waited for me for five, six years already," Rithy observed.
"I started to make the first take with her, and this became the first scene of
the film. And we went on like that, and the story kept coming, coming, coming, coming."[11]

Panh went back to the Thai military and reported that the light had been
too strong, that he had completely ruined all the film he had shot, and so he
would need more time. That is how he finagled another two days, and he spent
that entire time shooting with Yim Om and her family. He followed her about

her daily activities, and in the evening, he would go over with her what they had done. He filmed ordinary gestures, all the little things one does without which a human being would be reduced to a caged animal. She showed him her life down to the smallest details. He considered her participation in the film a political act: throughout, she demonstrated how she had maintained her character and dignity despite all she had been forced to endure.

Panh described his process making the film: "I realized the film instinctively, without really reflecting, urgently, and it has become the matrix of my work—where one finds it certainly through work on memory but also the search for the right physical distance with people, the decision to leave speech to others without adding explanation, the desire to film a unique territory."[12]

The film opens with a close-up of Yim Om talking in a soft monotone, telling how she came to be in this refugee camp. She has a broad face, shoulder-length hair, and an unselfconscious presentation of self. She is middle-aged and wears a traditional sarong skirt and a T-shirt as she goes about her daily work. Her story is one of perpetual flight since 1970 when her family was expelled from their land during the Lon Nol coup that unseated King Norodom Sihanouk. Once the Khmer Rouge seized power, Pol Pot ordered the execution of her father, and later her brother was killed. When life did not improve during the Vietnamese occupation that began in 1979, she joined the throng who escaped and sought refuge in Thailand. Fleeing from further persecution, she and her husband gathered up their children and little else to begin a long journey from one refugee camp to another, in search of food, shelter, and safety, continually forced to move on, menaced by thieves and thugs, grenades, bombs, and land mines. The family had nothing but each other. They migrated within ten different camps, and one day after they had arrived at yet another camp, their youngest son was run over by a truck. She explains all this simply, without self-pity, with all the clarity of a schoolteacher explaining a lesson. She then moves about their tiny home to show how they live on meager food rations and other supplies provided by international aid organizations. From a respectful distance, Panh films their private spaces, elevated rooms carved out with woven bamboo, wooden scraps, and cheap cloth.

Yim Om explains that a family is only entitled to a kilogram of dried fish each week; her husband's salary of two cans of sardines supplements the weekly food allotment. Only two or three times a month does the family get a small amount of meat and fresh produce. Food is administered by an incredibly complex bureaucratic system that sucks the life out of the people who are dependent on it. Small amounts of rice are exchanged for other staples, and what is not consumed is sold to acquire such luxuries as fish sauce or basic condiments. She tells all this looking straight into the camera, and Rithy Panh listens to all she has to say.

He focuses in long takes on her mundane gestures—where she places her salt and rice for cooking, how she sweeps their sleeping quarters. His montage alternates between close-ups of her talking to tracking shots of the camp and scenes of her at work. The sequences of the camp are observational and detached passes along a stream that borders the ramshackle dwellings on the scraps of land given each family. The camera tracks down the narrow alleys where children play, women prepare food, the elderly rest, and the constant restless activity of people crammed together runs its daily course. Yim Om's voice often floats over these traveling shots, speaking of her past and of her dreams in which her father and mother welcome her back home only to disappear on waking each morning. She speaks about the only thing she can give her children—not land or money but an education and, with it, the hope that they may be able to better themselves. "Only knowledge can't be stolen," she tells him. As she speaks we see children in the camp lining up, marching into bamboo classrooms where they learn geography and mathematics from energetic teachers. Her two older daughters are frequently seen running errands in the camp—carrying two jerricans of water balanced on a long pole and transported over the long stretches between the main distribution site and their home. The trucked-in water provides for what is needed for drinking, cooking, and washing. There is no source of water within the camp. The camera lingers on the earnest face of the younger girl, dressed in green, and follows the graceful older one as both girls help their mother prepare the family meal. Yim Om confides to Panh her regret that her children do not know where rice comes from. "They think it comes from UN trucks," she says wistfully. She wants them to know how to cultivate the rice that always has been the Cambodian people's staff of life.

The film, so simple on the surface, contains the seeds of Panh's mature aesthetics and ethics. "It really put me on the path and the way in which I approach my subject," he states.[13] Panh asks questions and listens, paying close attention to what people have to say. He patiently waits for them to reveal themselves, always focusing on the ordinary gestures in which so much can be revealed and understood. He respects the "threshold" and rarely crosses the line between his place and the intimate space of others. This is most apparent when Yim Om shows him her daughters' room and lifts a flap of cloth to show where they stow their belongings. The camera remains outside the space. This attention to where the camera can and cannot go will serve him in good stead in later films where the ethics of camera placement could make or break the film.

After Yim Om demonstrates the complex system that determines how much food is allotted to each family, we follow her to the Thai and Cambodian markets to buy clothing for the children and offset her family's meager food rations with some meat. Everything she does is labor intensive; she does it efficiently yet with an unmistakable melancholy. In her gestures, whether she is arranging rice on a shelf or bending over to speak to a child, Yim Om expresses both love and deep resignation. She tells the story of the poorest children who cannot afford school and must support themselves by taking on dangerous jobs, foraging for vegetables and wood in the minefields outside the camp or collecting and recycling plastic bags to sell to merchants or serve as fuel because of their petroleum base.

The camera observes some of the little joys of childhood here: we follow her son hurrying to watch a titanic fish fight in a glass water jar, and we watch an older boy meticulously construct a kite with bits of stick and a leftover plastic bag. He flies it high in the sky, attached to a magnificent coil of blue string that anchors it, a vivid metaphor for the soaring dreams perpetually out of reach for these refugee children. A few nighttime shots show the pitch dark in which people huddle at their doorways in hope of a breeze. Nighttime is the most dangerous time in camp—all the aid workers leave before sunset for their own safety, leaving the refugees to contend with roaming thieves, AWOL soldiers, and various gangs who move about freely under cover of darkness. Stitching all of these elements together is Yim Om's soft, understated voice and the music of Marc Marder, who plays the contrabass—now bowing, now plucking its strings and alternating between sounds of mourning and unnerving edginess—both of which communicate the ever-present uncertainty of life in Site 2.

At the time the film was being shot, there was talk of peace in Cambodia, but little was reported about the lives of its displaced people. Reports by the UN stated that refugee women suffered from depression, but in reality, many lost their minds and committed suicide. "Imagine 180,000 people living in a few kilometers without any vegetation," Rithy reflected. What struck him about the running of the camp was how much like the Khmer Rouge labor camps it resembled. People—strong, proud, and resilient—were forced to crouch on the ground to get their allotment of rice, humiliated without any reason. And the process was often accompanied by blaring music from loudspeakers that uncannily resembled Khmer Rouge reeducation assemblies. Panh's film crew was not always supported by the NGOs working in the camp; they did not trust Panh and his crew, fearful they might reveal that Khmer soldiers illicitly left the front at night and stole into the camp to be with their families.[14]

What Panh discovered in making his first film was the power of a voice when that voice is sincere and the audience knows it. He would go on to use this technique in many of his documentaries. It was in sharp contrast with the prevailing norm, particularly in French made-for-television documentaries, where a voice of authority spoke over the words of the film's protagonists. He found in making *Site 2* what would become the hallmarks of his documentary style—an ethic of staying close to the person he was filming, usually an arm's distance away, so as to make films *with* people, not *about* them, and an emphasis on ordinary gestures that unlock the reality of a person and what he or she is trying to communicate. He was interested in what people had to say for themselves, not the opinions of experts.

Panh kept in touch with Yim Om for two years after the film was made and then lost contact with her. During the time he spent with her, he gave her a new feeling of liberty: "I was a link to the world outside the camp. And she taught me a lot: the maturity of the glance, respect for the other, generosity, compassion, poetry. Every morning I took her somewhere outside the barbed wire: for food, for news, for an image. There were a lot of other things I could have done and could have avoided. I had to respect the territory her speech sketched for me. It was in that camp, with her that I found my way of looking [*mon regard*]."[15]

The idea of creating a voice-over soundtrack (*travelling sonore*) came from the speech of Yim Om. She revealed the basic elements of home, earth, and water. In Asia, water is everywhere except in the refugee camps. "At first the film team didn't understand what I wanted to achieve. They didn't speak the language and so they discovered the situation in the camp through what Yim Om had to say. I wanted them to hear the rhythm that enveloped everything, in words and for the senses, what makes the poetry," he explained. "It was her speech that guided our understanding of the political and social situation. And it is Yim Om who directs the rhythm of the film."

Alain Freudiger writes about the importance of the threshold—*le seuil*—and the way Panh always stays at a polite distance in Yim Om's home, most notably when she is in her daughters' bedroom. This private space is respected by the camera's gaze, which does not pry or lean in voyeuristically to see what is hidden. Panh demonstrates a sensitivity to the boundaries that mark not merely one's possessions but one's integrity and sense of self, what Freudiger terms the humanity of the person on the screen.

From the start of the film, the voice of a woman leads us into the life of real people. Panh observes how everything is said in the first person present because for Yim Om there is no palpable future, only a tenuous present. She grounds us in the reality of her present life. The absence of any dreams for the future, apart from securing an education for her children, is one of the most revealing features of her monologue.

Marc Marder has composed for all of Panh's films and also writes music for the films of Panh's Cambodian students and protégés. His family was affected by the Holocaust, and, like Panh, he bears psychological effects of genocide. Their creative collaboration is like a faithful marriage albeit an unorthodox one. Marder watched the edit of *Site 2* several times, without subtitles, before writing anything. Not knowing the Khmer language, he translated Yim Om's speech musically using the sounds of the contrabass. "It was another language, a translation of Yim Om in another tongue," observes Panh.

Site 2 received the Grand Prix Documentaire at the Festival International d'Amiens, the Grand Prix from la SCAM for best documentary in 1989, as well as a Special Mention at the Festival du Réel at Nyon. Not bad for a first film by a refugee from one of the former colonies. These awards drew attention to the arrival of a serious young filmmaker on the French cinema scene. The success of *Site 2* would help open doors for future backing from television channels like Franco-German Arte and French Canal +.

Back to Cambodia

When Panh returned to Cambodia in 1990 the first thing he needed to do was create a studio to train Cambodian filmmakers. Memory had been systematically destroyed by the Khmer Rouge—the temples destroyed, schools transformed into detention centers, the towns emptied, and people evacuated. The young had no memory of what had happened before, and those who had survived were devoid of memories repressed as a matter of survival. Cinema in Cambodia in 1990 consisted of two hundred productions, unreal, fabulous, or sentimental stories that revolved around men with Mercedes cars who cheated on their wives, stories no one could identify with. Panh set out to create a platform where documentaries about real life and Cambodia's memory could be made. With advice from Jacques Bidou, who produced *Site 2*, Rithy went to l'Atelier Varan (the Varan Studio) in Paris, a film production house created by the renowned anthropologist-cum-filmmaker Jean Rouch to train aspiring filmmakers. Varan subsidized the start of a studio in Phnom

Penh, and from 1994 to 1995, Panh was in charge of training documentary filmmakers there. The idea was to have French technicians—cinematographers, sound specialists, editors, and the like—not only work on Panh's productions but also train a new generation of Cambodians eager to make films. Although the studio could not be sustained financially beyond its start-up, it marked the beginning of a new era of independent cinema in Cambodia and laid the foundation for what would become a more sustainable enterprise—the Bophana Audiovisual Resource Center, which Panh would launch in 2006 with Ieu Pannakar, the former director of the Center for Cambodian Cinema.

Television documentaries at that time were made with authoritative commentary spoken over the scenes. Panh had seen such films about Africa edited in a style particular to the developing world. One would see a peasant discussing something with a journalist but never hear what the man had to say, only what the journalist chose to summarize in voice-over, what has been disparagingly called "the voice of God." "One was informed about everything and saw nothing," according to Panh. If Cambodian memory had been stifled, and if the people were now rendered mute, what could one do? So Panh became one of the first to work with direct sound in Cambodia, and his students later were all taught to use a boom microphone. He encouraged them to get closer to their subjects, to stick close to them and not resort to camera zooms to do so.

The making of *Site 2* set in motion a process that Panh followed at the start of his career: a cycle that consisted of two or more documentary films followed by a culminating fictional work. Panh saw himself as a documentary filmmaker concerned with facts, but he thought at the time that fiction allowed him greater freedom to express his own opinions. Panh produced two television documentaries after *Site 2*. The first was a made-for-television portrait of the Malian director *Souleymane Cissé* (1991). A year later Panh made an hourlong documentary, *Cambodia, Entre Guerre et Paix* (*Cambodia, between War and Peace*), prompted by the signing of the Paris Peace Accord that called a halt to Cambodia's war with Vietnam and the return of Norodom Sihanouk to Cambodia as its monarch. The conclusion to this cycle of films was his first feature-length fiction film, *Rice People* (*Neak Sre* or *Les gens de rizière*, 1994).

Souleymane Cissé (for *Cinéma de notre temps*) (1991)

Although a portrait of the great Malian filmmaker Souleymane Cissé seemed an unlikely subject for an up-and-coming Cambodian cineast, Panh was nonetheless an obvious choice given the essence of both men and their films. Cissé, who was born in Bamako in 1940, was widely known as a leader of the social realism movement in African film. He had recently won the Jury Prize at the 1987 Cannes Film Festival for his film *Yeelen* (*Brightness*), an Oedipal story adapted from an oral Bambara legend dating from the thirteenth century. Since he was the first African filmmaker honored at Cannes, he was clearly a candidate for a profile for the popular French TV series *Cinéma de notre temps* (Cinema of our times). Although he was roughly twenty years older than Panh, they discovered they had much in common when they met through their editor, Andrée Daventure.

Both artists shared similar aesthetic and political values. Both had been trained as filmmakers far from their native lands and at two of the best institutes available—VGIK[16] in Moscow for Cissé and l'IDHEC in Paris for Panh. They were committed to using the language of film to explore the complicated history and sociocultural, economic, and political issues facing their postcolonial homelands.

Cissé had been a passionate cinephile from childhood. He began his film career as an assistant projectionist for a documentary on the arrest of Patrice Lumumba, which convinced him that films could make a difference. After his training in Moscow, he returned to Mali and worked as a cameraman for the Ministry of Information for several years, eventually producing two films of his own, including *Den Muso*, about a girl who has been raped and is rejected by both her family and the rapist-father of her baby. His focus on women and the injustices visited on them would be yet another bond between the two filmmakers. Because of its taboo subject, *Den Muso* was banned, and Cissé was arrested and thrown into jail for accepting foreign funding to make the film. Cissé persevered and began to define an approach to filmmaking that emphasized working with nonactors and using the natural elements of earth, water, and sky to express the complexity of his characters' lives along with the political and social tensions of modern Africa. His luminous camera work and unlikely protagonists coupled with plots that mixed folk traditions with contemporary problems would be echoed in Panh's fiction films, beginning with *Rice People*.

Panh's portrait of Cissé mixes interviews with him along with clips from his major films. Cissé explains on camera and in voice-over the power of ordinary gestures to convey more than words. Panh seamlessly cuts scenes from Cissé's films within this extended interview to reveal the metaphoric power of Cissé's imagery, beautifully evoked in the scene that Panh chose to close his film, which is drawn from *Yeelen*. It presents a young woman standing in a river in a wide shot that shows her as part of the environment. She bends over and lifts up one of two large wooden bowls. She raises it up and then pours the milk in it over her head and body. The camera moves in for a close-up as the milk mingles with the water, eddying among the green shoots at her feet. Slowly the discarded bowl glides gracefully toward the other, gently tapping it like a stolen kiss, and then drifts away. It is a moment of exquisite awareness that manages to express Cissé's feelings for time, place, and the feminine and offers a poetically resonant finale to Panh's portrait of him and his work.

Cissé narrates the film much like Yim Om did in *Site 2*. There is an obligatory on-camera interviewer, in this case the African film scholar and documentary filmmaker Manthia Diawara, who says little but seems to satisfy existing expectations for what a TV documentary should provide. But it is Cissé who is the "authority" speaking, whether in a *vérité* interview as he takes Panh to see his father's compound in Bamako or in a more ruminative scene, floating in a dugout canoe headed toward a distant shore where tall trees are backlit by a setting sun, an exquisite image that anticipates the lush watery landscapes that will beguile viewers in Panh's *Rice People*.

Mali received its independence from France in 1960; Cambodia was liberated in 1953. Both filmmakers had to confront the diverse and often horrifying consequences of decolonization, including a rocky road to democracy punctuated by insurgent revolts and brutal repression. (When this film was made, Mali was ruled by the dictator Moussa Traoré.) Panh was curious to see what postcolonialism looked like in Africa. Cissé told Panh he was particularly angry at the way French filmmakers had treated Africans as animals, not as human beings, and explains that his films are motivated by a desire to challenge such lingering attitudes. He believed in making films of *dama* (which translates as "grace" or "soul" in the Bambara language), and grace is a concept that Panh will refer to in describing his own films throughout his career. Cissé also believed in the power of earth and water to convey all that is essential to life, and he uses these elements and ideas in all his films. They are vital components in Panh's work, and they recur strikingly in his films about farmers and migrant laborers and most spectacularly in his memoir film, *The Missing Picture*.

Watching Panh's affecting portrait of Cissé, one senses an understanding between two filmmakers who share similar aesthetic and social values. It is hard to know how much Cissé may have influenced Panh and what was already rooted in the young Cambodian's outlook on filmmaking and life. Both are technical perfectionists, and the seemingly effortless simplicity of both men's films arises out of scrupulous attention to detail and an aesthetic standard equal to if not surpassing that of most Western filmmakers. One critic noted that "paramount to Cissé's work is his use of feminine themes to evoke the symbolic sense of the feminine in Africa."[17] Panh also focuses on the role of women in Cambodia in his films, often reprising the figure of the "madwoman" who embodies the toll that war, corruption, revolution, hard labor, and genocide have taken on women during Cambodia's recent history. Both filmmakers are independent men critical of the devaluation of human lives, and both refrain from revenge. It is remarkable the parallels between them and in their determination to champion a subtle sociopolitical analysis. Fittingly, it was during the postproduction of this portrait that Panh first worked with a woman who would become one of his best long-standing collaborators, the editor Marie-Christine Rougerie, who here served as assistant editor. This is the first time Panh relies on his much-loved poet René Char for the film's final words: "Les yeux seuls sont encore capable de pousser un cri" (The eyes alone are still capable of crying out).

Cambodia, between War and Peace
(Cambodia, entre guerre et paix) (1992)

Cambodia, between War and Peace was also made for French television and is a stylistic hybrid, combining archival footage of life under the Khmer Rouge, interviews with survivors, vérité shots of classes where little girls are trained in the ancient arts of Cambodian classical dance, and press conferences with the commanding figure of the returning Norodom Sihanouk. Woven throughout are interviews with a range of Cambodian people—from academics to elementary school teachers to illiterate farmers—who discuss Cambodia's past and speculate about its future. Some knew Cambodia before Pol Pot while others grew up knowing only the tyranny of terror. Many of the most affecting interviews come from young people who witnessed their families' suffering when the Khmer Rouge controlled every aspect of life.

One young woman tells how her father helped her catch a frog to eat when they were starving. A Khmer Rouge cadre caught him in the act and accused them of stealing from the commune. Her father was sentenced to death and buried in the sand, without food or water, and left to die in the hot sun over several days until he was eaten alive by ants. His little daughter's punishment was being compelled to watch this spectacle, and as she tells the story, she

FIGURE 2.1 Student dancer in *Cambodia, between Peace and War* © RPanh / droits réservés

strokes a palm frond, her eyes darting about without a place to rest. She says that until then she did not know what a massacre was. Another young woman, a student surrounded by books in a library, tells how, "under the regime of Pol Pot, they killed all the books, all the spirits, all the thoughts of men."

This hour-long film is densely packed with such stories and contains many of the issues that Panh revisits at length in subsequent films. While he was shooting a sequence of the film at S-21—the notorious prison where men, women, and children were interrogated, tortured, and executed by the Khmer Rouge—Panh met one of the prison's few survivors, the painter Vann Nath. He agreed to speak on camera and, in his quietly commanding voice, described his near-death experience and how his ability to paint portraits of Pol Pot saved his life. While speaking, he touched canvases that bear witness to what happened there; many now hang on the walls of the prison that is now known as Tuol Sleng Genocide Museum. Panh quickly bonded with Nath, and their friendship later launched what would become one of Panh's most celebrated documentaries, *S-21: The Khmer Rouge Killing Machine*.

For anyone unfamiliar with the recent history of Cambodia, this documentary offers a succinct summary of the issues facing the newly liberated country at the end of war and foreign occupation. Of particular cinematic interest is the opening montage. It begins with a classic view of Angkor Wat in vivid color, which dissolves into a hallucinatory stream of black-and-white archival images of people herded together in the night, guarded by gun-toting Khmer Rouge cadres, and thrown into labor camps where they were worked mercilessly. Accompanied only by Marc Marder's music, this powerful opening captures some of the experiences that haunted the thirteen-year-old Panh, starkly presented in this brief wordless montage, drawn from the elusive cinematic record that Panh would set about to collect, study, and preserve for generations to come.

Rice People (Les gens de la rizière, Neak Sre) (1994)

After filming *Site 2*, Panh began to imagine a documentary about the seasons of rice cultivation on four continents. Rice is life for Cambodians, much as bread has been for the French. Mostly, though, he was inspired by his meeting with Yim Om, who told him that what symbolized freedom for her was the possibility to choose for herself what she would cultivate on her plots of land.[18] Panh knew that it would take time for refugees like Yim Om, who had been separated from the land for decades, to be able to live and work on the land again once they were able to return to Cambodia. While researching this documentary project, he came upon a novel by Shahnon Ahmad, a prominent Malaysian writer and literary critic who experimented with integrating dream, fantasy, and magical elements as well as stream-of-consciousness techniques in his narratives. The novel was *Ranjau Sepanjang Jalan* (1966), which was titled in French *Le Riz* (The rice) and in English as *No Harvest but a Thorn*. It was an example of the father-oriented novels then popular for Malay writers and a belief that literary expression arises from a specific place and people. Panh found Ahmad's story about a family struggling to maintain their rice paddies in the face of implacable forces compelling, probably because he found resonances in the novel with his own life. He quickly abandoned the idea of making a documentary in favor of adapting the novel as his first fiction feature film. He met with Ahmad and bought the rights,[19] knowing that it would require recasting a narrative originally set in Muslim Malaysia for Buddhist Cambodia. His focus would shift from the father to the mother, and he would eliminate Ahmad's religious theme and stylistic use of repetition but conserve his dramaturgy. Panh decided early on to name the mother in the story after Yim Om because her attachment to the land had inspired this film. The film chronicles the story of the rice farmer Vong Poeuv and his wife, Yim Om, and their seven daughters. Sylvia Blum-Reid in writing about the film suggested the chief character is actually the rice field that rules the entire village.[20]

Panh knew he would never be able to produce the film in Cambodia without the help of European producers.[21] He turned to Jacques Bidou,[22] who had produced *Site 2*. Bidou saw Cambodia as "a martyred land, toward which, because of our colonial past, we [French] have a latent feeling of guilt," but Bidou knew that guilt alone would not be enough to get the film fully funded. "It was necessary to have a scenario sufficiently solid to bring support for the production. . . . Rithy is someone who is very clear about his needs and his limits. He has an immense ambition but also an absolute humility which he knows to put in the service of his exigence."[23] Bidou raised 350,000 francs for the writing of the script, which took nearly two years. Panh worked with the French scenarist Ève Deboise to produce a three-hundred-page script that had to be cut by a third. The result won him the prize for best film adaptation at Cannes in 1992. The screenplay was published in an issue of *L'Avant-Scène Cinema* that was dedicated to the film; it demonstrated the mastery of Panh's vision and his intelligent transformation of a Malaysian novel into a classic cinematic work about Cambodia.[24]

Panh found the location for the film roughly 30 miles from Phnom Penh in the village of Kamreang. Khmer Rouge guerrillas were stationed along the borders of the fields, and so cast and crew had to work without thought to the dangers that surrounded them.[25] Panh hired ten film professionals from France; their contract specified they would not only shoot the film but also train the local crew because it was essential that the film not just be *about* Cambodians but made *with* them. Production design, makeup, and casting—among other creative responsibilities—were assigned to Cambodians. Panh chose people whose skills were on the periphery of what was needed—for example, an architect directed the set decor—and in so doing he began training people for cinema.[26]

Panh needed more than Cambodian film technicians. "Rice paddies are everywhere, in Thailand, in Vietnam, in France, in Portugal. However, if you choose to film Cambodian rice paddies, it is not the rice paddies that matter, it is the people in the rice paddies," Panh told interviewers.[27] After the Khmer Rouge destroyed the Cambodian film industry, only a handful of actors remained. So Panh had to look for nonactors who could speak Khmer.[28] He needed to train them once he persuaded them to participate in the film. "For them cinema means action films from Hong Kong or Indian melodramas," he explained. "So we had to talk to them, give them the script, convince them of the honesty of our intentions."[29]

Casting the film proved a challenging process because everything depends on the audience's belief in this family of two adults and seven children. He had to find people who could express their characters, people with "grace." The villagers were played by professors of dance, singers of Ayaï, bike guardians, shopkeepers, housewives, and traditional musicians.[30] For the principals, he got it down to five or six persons who auditioned for each role, asking them on video to speak about their lives, looking to see how well they could shift from joy to sadness. He found for the father the artist Mom Soth, who was respected for his work in theater and the sole "professional" in the film. For the mother, it was clear Peng Phan was right for the role. She had done many things in her life, including work as a TV announcer, but when he met her, she was selling coconuts in the market. Panh found the seven daughters in the Beaux Arts school. Only one proved a problem, Chhim Naline, who plays the oldest, Sokha. She was relatively easy to convince, but her mother would not hear of it. She feared for her daughter's reputation, that she could not marry her daughter because in the film she has a fiancé and presses up against him. She pushed Panh to make revisions and obliged him to be clear about his ethics. "It was an unbelievable lesson in morality," he recalls. "After choosing all the actors, I had them spend all their afternoons together.... I had them call each other by their character's first name and the children called the adults 'papa' and 'maman.' ... The oldest sister began to exercise a real moral authority over the others, coming each day to make the meal for the little ones or give them their baths. The oldest girls went to the rice paddy each day to work together.... A family like that is not improvised, it's created.... My role was not to direct but to facilitate the real rapport created among them."[31]

Next to that, there was the enormous work of collective reading of the script. Panh wanted each actor to be conscious of what the other family members were feeling. He explained each scene for the children so that the youngest children understood that what they played was "false," so the story of the film would not disturb their real lives.

Panh wanted the cast to live their roles, not play them. And to create a similar esprit de corps among the crew, he had them work together to build the house where the shooting would take place.

Because there is little dialogue, the film depends on gestures and glances, privileging the emotion in each instant. And to stay close to the people, the camera had to follow them. Panh filmed in 16 mm to gain maximum flexibility, and he shot nearly five hours.

FIGURE 2.2 Daughters harvesting in *Rice People* © RPanh / droits réservés

The film follows the natural cycle of rice culture from planting to harvesting, interrupted by natural cataclysms that alter the family. Tragedy hovers from the outset when a cobra threatens the mother and is killed by the father. Vong Poeuv's actions propel the narrative, because it is dangerous to kill a snake, and this act bears ramifications in the spirit world. Nicole Biros, French translator of the novel, knowingly observes, "Among living beings, the borders are blurred and the passage between the living and the dead takes place. This explains their familiarity with one another."[32] It also explains the fluidity with which the mother moves between the real and surreal. When the father, Poeuv, steps on a poisonous thorn, infection sets in that will eventually cause his death. The agony of the father and the subsequent madness of the mother underscore the effect the spirits have in taking possession of her mind.

The only reference to the Khmer Rouge in the film comes in a nightmare the ailing father has. In it he is being rounded up and beaten as firebombs fall and houses burn. Sensing his end nearing, Vong Poeuv gathers his daughters together—encouraging them to be like seven sticks that, when held together, will not break. When Poeuv dies, his eldest daughter, Sokha, assumes the Buddhist funeral role of the oldest son and then performs an animist ceremony to take away the evil spirits.

Grief-stricken at the loss of her husband and partner, Yim Om loses her grasp on reality and begins to talk with her dead husband. She wanders out of the village and drinks alcohol given to her by scornful men who insult her by lewdly proposing marriage to her in her drunken state. As a result of her scandalous behavior, she becomes the target of public humiliation in the village, and children follow her and cast stones at her. The village leader's response is to lock her up in a bamboo cage inside the family home, partly for her own protection but also for the peace of mind of the villagers. Restraining her in this way is justified by the paramount value of saving the rice crop. Because Yim Om cannot do what is needed to save her own fields, her oldest daughter, Sokha, must take over. The village ultimately sends Yim Om to a hospital for treatment, but this proves ineffective, and on her return, drugged and lethargic, she is again locked in a cage. But Sokha can no longer subject her mother to such confinement. She leads her mother out to the paddies as the camera follows her in a long take. We see Yim Om caressing the plant stalks, jumping up and down in the field, and screaming to chase away imaginary birds. Her cries end the film along with Panh's dedication, "To my family 1975–1979."

Panh was clearly inspired by the real-life story of Yim Om, and there are various traces of her in words and gestures in this film: for example, we see Poeuv sweeping the floors of their house much as Yim Om did in her spartan dwelling in *Site 2*; as Poeuv is dying, he borrows her poetic expression to express his feelings: "I am no different than a floating plant, carried by the water current." But fictional Yim Om lacks the stability of her namesake; her descent into madness serves as a metaphor for Cambodia in the aftermath of so much death and political insanity, and more particularly, it points to all the women who lost their reason as a result of the Khmer Rouge's degradations. Panh laments women's losses here, and this concern will animate many of his films throughout his career. His early proposal for "Aux abords des frontières" makes this preoccupation clear: "Khmer women have lost the value, place and respect granted to them by culture and religion. If war and resistance concern men who fight with weapons, women are the ones who have to endure the consequences. . . . They are stripped of everything that made their strength: land, house, and a stable family life."[33]

Yim Om is confined to a cage much as her namesake was confined to a miserable home in the refugee camps, a bitter sanctuary from war and the devastation visited upon them by the Khmer Rouge. This story becomes, on one level, an elaborate metaphor for life before and after the revolution. It reveals, however subtly, that the younger generation must take up the task of carrying on, reconnecting to the land and to sacred values, if they are to survive.

Panh is adamant about asserting that he deliberately chose to avoid dating the film. It is set in an indeterminate time, neither before, during, nor after Pol Pot: "The film is stronger if one is suspended outside of time. As for the dream scene, for me there are three interpretations possible. One can consider the dream a premonition and that the film is situated before the Khmer Rouge. One can believe that it is a dream born of memories and that the film is happening now. One can also interpret it as the fear that the nightmare may one day become reality again, that it is not an aberration: seeing the poverty of the population, such an anti-capitalist discourse could very well rediscover resonance."[34] The film lovingly portrays the land, the rice fields, the sunsets, the familial altars to the ancestors, and the all-consuming labor required to harvest the rice. It celebrates the labor of women by acknowledging the heroic efforts of the seven daughters and their mother to hold onto their land.

Bidou raised nine million francs for production, working with a diverse group of partners from Switzerland, Germany, England, and France. When it was screened in Cambodia, it was well received among peasants and teachers, but city people had a harder time understanding it. Compared with the films being screened in Cambodia at the time—American, Hong Kong, and Indian big-budget productions—Panh's film disturbed the apparently "peaceful surface of a nation of people that only 'want dreams.'"[35]

It was released in eight Parisian theaters and stayed eleven weeks.[36] Reception of the film in Europe was overwhelming. The French press was ecstatic and reached out to find comparisons with the work of Souleymane Cissé, Ken Loach, Lino Brocka, and Abbas Kiarostami (*Le Soir* claimed that Panh cited them as his masters) as well as John Ford, Ermanno Olmi, and Akira Kurosawa. François Forestier writing for *Nouvel Observateur* noted that *Rice People* recalled 1949 when neorealism arrived on the Croisette with the now classic film *Bitter Rice*. The critics were smitten with the self-sufficiency of people who lived on the edge of annihilation. But mostly they were struck by Panh's subtle style, which emphasized materiality, the ordinary gestures of work, the simplicity and purity of unaffected characters, and the power of nonactors to communicate an authenticity of life lived close to nature.[37] It was called a film of pastels that registers the levels of life in major and minor tones. Some were impressed by Panh's decision not to turn this into a political tract, restricting all reference to the Khmer Rouge to the nightmare that disturbs the dying Vong Poeuv, a single but vivid scene that called up horrors Panh knew well.[38]

Adaptation

Although Panh observes the narrative arc in Shahnon's novel, his award-winning adaptation recasts the novel and makes it very much his own story. In his hands, the drama has shifted from the story of the father to that of the mother. The most graphic and goriest aspects of the novel, which revolve around the father's decline as infection ravages his body and pus and blood oozes out of every bodily orifice, are gone. Panh refrains from such disturbing images and refocuses on the dignified suffering of Poeuv as he becomes weaker from the poisonous infection that will take his life. His stoic suffering and resignation prevails. This allows for greater dramatic impact when Poeuv descends into the nightmare that begins with a flaming bomb dropped from the sky onto homes burning and people rounded up at gunpoint. This is the only reference to the Khmer Rouge era in the film, but it is what decisively turns the Malaysian novel into a film about Cambodia. The other unmistakable Cambodian detail is when the oldest daughter, Sokha, who must carry on in the place of her father and mother, not only takes over the work of harvesting the crops and caring for the children but also performs Buddhist mourning duties as if she were the eldest son. In this ritual, her head is shorn, a moving scene that surprised the lovely actress whose tears were sincere as she watched her beautiful hair drop to the ground.

In Shahnon's novel, there are frequent references to Allah, who knows what is best and who is in charge of the future. None of the novel's characters blame Allah for their harsh fate; rather, they pray to him for help. Panh substitutes Buddhist rituals that are part of Cambodian tradition and culture, but religion does not play an important role in the film. In both film and novel, the headman of the village does his best for the family, but his wisdom is limited. The involvement of a healer does little to cure either the father or the mother, and neither does Western medicine save Yim Om's sanity. The madness she experiences is beyond the reach of anyone's medicine.

Panh significantly alters the ending of the novel for his film. Yim Om returns, still ill and frailer than before. Ahmad closed his novel with her being locked up in the cage again; her madness is the last thought the reader is left with. Panh is less despairing in his conclusion: he has Sokha tell her mother that she should never have allowed her to be sent away, and she will not keep her caged. She leads Yim Om out into the rice paddies. Yim Om acts as before, running about and shrieking, but we, like Sokha, have arrived at a different understanding of the roots of her illness and her need to be close to her land and her rice. She is bewildered in the paddy, but she gently strokes the fertile plants, an image that will recur in Panh's later films, and in the last shot, she becomes an integral part of the rice field once more.

Ahmad's novel is moving and possesses a starkly repetitive style that seems well-suited to the illiterate but deeply human individuals who inhabit his story, but from a cinematic standpoint, his writing lacks visuality. This is what Panh's script rectifies so beautifully. Throughout we are treated to glorious landscapes of a changing growing cycle, dazzling sunsets, and torrents of rain beating down on the sisters as they struggle to salvage the rice. The screen is a space populated with enigmatic, poetic images—the ominous owl who foretells separation and loss, a figure that appears in later films as well, and a staircase going nowhere in the middle of a paddy. Panh builds on and arguably improves on Shahnon's story in his adaptation. Shahnon positions the death of the father midway through the story. Panh dispatches him at forty-five minutes, one-third of the way through his film, which allows the balance of the film to tilt toward the consequences of this loss for the family. Panh moves briskly through events that propel the plot—the sighting of the cobra, the damage from the thorn, Poeuv's rapid decline—and adds both subtle and bold additions to the narrative to establish Cambodia as its location. Whereas Ahmad lingers over certain events, drawing out the father's decline, Panh concentrates on the mother's escalating madness after his death. Small details suggest possible readings of when this is happening: the villagers are largely clothed in black, remnants of the uniform demanded of everyone by the Khmer Rouge, so when Yim Om puts on a beautiful shirt and sarong, it may not be just a sign of her madness so much as an act of rebellion or nostalgia for an irretrievable past. Panh leaves this for viewers to decide.

With cinematographer Jacques Bouquin, Panh frames the family's view of their paddies from the terrace of their home as if it were through a proscenium arch. It is through this classical vantage point that we see their tragedy unfold. The film crew spent days shooting in the rice paddies, which was risky in 1992 since the political situation in Cambodia was quite unstable. Khmer Rouge soldiers were present and sometimes fighting along the periphery of the paddies. The French crew also ran afoul of the Cambodian crew whose religious practices and beliefs they did not understand. Bidou wrote: "An assistant director was convinced that he had the evil eye during the shooting of the film because we had shaved the head of the older daughter, who is in mourning in the film, while in reality, nobody in her family had died. When people from the Cambodian team, that we know are cultured, schooled and intelligent, come and tell us: 'If we don't burn incense tomorrow we won't be able to shoot the scene,' one enters a world of the irrational that only Rithy, as a Cambodian, was able to understand."³⁹ "Irrational" is Bidou's word for their behavior, but it was less irrational than a cultural difference that was tough to surmount without an intermediary like Panh, who could appreciate both perspectives. Throughout the process of making this film, Panh served as mediator between worlds—East and West, the living and the dead, innocent youths and wounded survivors.

Freed from conventional cinematic expectations, *Rice People* is a sensuous and tragic story of individuals at the mercy of natural forces, which are also complicated by unexpected interventions—some benign and well meaning, some horrific and destructive. A few Western critics faulted the film for a lack of dramatic elements. What they seemed to quarrel with most was a different sense of time and montage. "It is a very intimate film; one must take time and respect time," Panh explains. "I take frames that last two and a half minutes. If you accept to enter this rhythm, you will like the movie. If you refuse this rhythm, you cannot like it."⁴⁰

One wonders at the cultural blinders of Westerners who can apply only one standard of dramatic flow when confronted with a story of peasants whose literacy lies in their mastery of the land, not language. The film offers subtle evidence of the emotions of the principal characters, notably Poeuv (played by Mom Soth), Yim Om (played by Peng Phan), and Sokha (played by Chhim Naline). The younger daughters are not well-developed characters—as is true in Ahmad's novel—and they have little to say or do, with the exception of Sophoeun, whom we see left behind when her mother is carted off, who brings the razor to her father, and who is positioned as a silent eyewitness to the family tragedy. But all the children seem entirely natural as performers—a testimony to Panh's direction—and they lend their innocence and curiosity to the uncertain realities that engulf this large family. On the screen they are more dimensional than in Ahmad's novel.

Peng Phan makes her first appearance in Rithy Panh's films here and will reappear in later Panh films, including *One Evening after the War*, *The Burnt Theater*, and *The Sea Wall*. She is excellent as the devoted wife and mother whose mad scenes are believable because viewers come to understand her character and her pain. Mom Soth matches Peng Phan's performance strength for strength: he is loving with the children, pensive about the future parceling of the land to his many daughters, and stoic in preparing for his impending death. Rithy Panh effectively directs Mom's understated performance to contrast with Peng Phan's near-Shakespearean hysteria.

Part of what makes this film so resonant is Panh's experience, which seems to fuel the screenplay. Panh knew what it was like to plant and harvest rice in blistering sun and torrential rain. He also knew what it was like to injure his foot in an accident he suffered while clearing land with a pickax. He nearly died of the infection, but his life and foot were saved because his mother was able to acquire a tablet of penicillin, which she crushed and rubbed into the wound. As he explains in his memoir, *The Elimination*, he could not walk for a year and had to propel himself about on his hands. He experienced phantom pains long after the wound had healed. So Ahmad's novel must have struck a deep chord within him because of such experiences. Ahmad dwells on the moans and groans and grossness of Poeuv's infection, but Panh keeps such details to a minimum, focusing instead on Poeuv's emotional state and character rather than on the physical aspects of his rapid decline. One wonders how this scene was influenced by the drama Panh witnessed as a boy, observing his father die of starvation in a final act of protest against the regime. Rithy's mother was no madwoman; she was strong, resourceful, and determined until she too succumbed to exhaustion, starvation, and disease. Yim Om is drawn from the emotionally damaged Cambodian women Panh encountered in the refugee camps, many of whom were suffering from PTSD and chronic severe depression.

Among the nonactors who play the villagers, it is worth noting the older woman who plays Voen, who shaves Sokha's head and calms Yim Om when she is being taken out of the cage to go to the hospital. Her womanish wisdom exists in sharp contrast to the male "healer" who spits betel juice on Poeuv, takes his fee, and accomplishes little good. Such healing plays a minor role, but it contributes to an understanding of the limited resources available to poor villagers and the importance of compassion over medicine, whether traditional or modern.

Panh takes village gossip about the mother in Ahmad's novel further. In the novel, children taunt and torment her as a widow with many daughters, throwing stones at her and suggesting her roaming is an effort to get herself and her daughters husbands to work the land. Panh creates the scene where the otherwise sober Yim Om drinks with men and flirts out of her loneliness, grief, and despair over being left on her own to manage the family fortunes. This scene is more disturbing than the meanness of the children in the novel and offers up the contempt and cruelty of adults who should know better. The villagers want her put away for their convenience and to assuage any responsibility they might feel for her predicament. Panh's depiction of her decline after being hospitalized is more nuanced than Ahmad's. Yim Om is the first of a series of madwomen who will compel viewer sympathy over the course of his films.

With *Rice People*, Panh completed a "cycle" of films that were interconnected despite the apparent differences in their subject matter. There is a sense of buildup from one film to the next. The cycle begins with *Site 2* and the introduction of a character whose strength prevailed over the emotional and material assaults of life. Then with the Cissé portrait, we discover the ideas and issues that mark not only Cissé's films but Panh's. And we discover the aesthetics that will be a Panh hallmark—a sensuous feeling for light, for landscape, for an intimate connection with characters who are at home in their environment. In *Cambodia, between War and Peace*, we encounter many of the issues that will absorb Panh—the importance of remembering and giving testimony about what happened during the Pol Pot years; the challenge of healing a nation ravaged by terror, trauma, and corruption; the huge task of rebuilding Cambodia's culture, traditions, and political systems; and guarded hope for peace and progress for a new generation after years of civil war and foreign occupation.

One final thought: *Rice People* contains a curious foreshadowing of one of Panh's later films. When Yim Om is being led off to the hospital, her youngest child comes up to her and offers her mother her clay doll. This tender object, which appears fleetingly in only one scene, prefigures the clay figurines that Panh will rely on to tell his own story of survival in *The Missing Picture* in 2013. The child's clay doll represents an uncanny thread of continuity in Panh's work, which depends so often on his vivid memories of childhood. Inspiration arises ineffably when Panh most needs it and comes often through the eyes of a child.

3

The Khmer Rouge

Three Years, Eight Months,
Twenty-One Days

> The official silence is another form of
> appropriation. It prevents public witnessing.
> It forges a secret history, an act of
> political resistance through keeping alive
> the memory of things denied. The
> totalitarian state rules by collective
> forgetting, by denying the collective
> experience of suffering, and thus creates
> a culture of terror.
>
> **ARTHUR AND JOAN KLEINMAN**[1]

The Cambodian genocide was a life-changing event for Rithy Panh. To understand his films it helps to know something about Cambodian history and, in particular, the Khmer Rouge, the radical communist organization determined to create an agrarian utopia which, in the process, destroyed roughly one quarter of the Cambodian population. Nearly two million people died during the three years, eight months, and twenty-one days the Khmer Rouge ruled the country they renamed Democratic Kampuchea. This chapter offers a brief summary of that history. It is reliant upon the research, insights, and conclusions of historians, journalists, area specialists, eyewitnesses, and survivors.[2]

Early History of Cambodia

Some historians believe the earliest influence shaping the Khmer Rouge was the Khmer Empire, which dated from the ninth to the fourteenth centuries, an era when great achievements in administration, agriculture, architecture, hydrology, urban planning, and the arts revealed Cambodia's creative and accomplished civilization. Proof can be found today in the ruins of the magnificent Hindu-Buddhist temples of Angkor Wat, the largest religious monument in the world. Reclaiming Cambodia's early glory inspired Pol Pot, head of the Khmer Rouge, who said: "If our people can make Angkor, we can make anything."[3]

Practically speaking and of more immediate influence was a century of French colonization that began in 1863 when the king sought France's help in withstanding frequent incursions into Cambodia by its long-standing adversaries, Vietnam and Thailand. Cambodia became a French Protectorate, but quickly became a *de facto* colony. What was protected was not Cambodia, its monarch or its people but France's economic interests. They defended themselves as fulfilling their "civilizing mission." (See chapter 6 for additional background on France's role in Cambodia.)

During World War II, France's Nazi-aligned Vichy government introduced the rule of xenophobic European nationalism, introducing the abolition of all elected bodies, the violent dispersal of peaceful protests, the internment of Cambodian activists, and a crackdown on press freedoms.[4] When Japan occupied Cambodia during the war, Prince Sihanouk—who had been put in power by the French—declared the country free of French control, renamed the kingdom Kampuchea, and deftly engineered his coronation. For nearly a century, the French had benefited from Cambodia's natural resources and held its populace in check with economic and political controls increasingly managed by French-speaking Vietnamese, all of which contributed to the rise of Cambodian nationalism and animosity towards the favored

Vietnamese. When the Second World War in Asia ended, the Free French attempted to reclaim their Asian colonies, but the Viet Minh, Vietnam's anti-colonialist independence movement, fought back and waged a successful guerrilla campaign against France in the First Indochina War (1946–1954). France formally granted Cambodia independence in 1953. Independence, however, meant little to a people who continued to pay taxes to finance an unresponsive government that was now, at least, Cambodian.

Sihanouk proved to be a skillful strategist and emerged as a popular and influential political actor who held both pro-American policies and leftist sympathies. Politics in Cambodia between 1955 and 1970 was characterized by Sihanouk's monopoly on power and prosperity. As historian David Chandler has observed, Sihanouk's grip on the political process postponed the apocalypse that overtook his country in the 1970s. But by treating Cambodians as his children and his opponents as traitors, Sihanouk set the stage for the chaos of the Khmer Republic, the horrors of Democratic Kampuchea, and the single-party politics of the post-revolutionary period.[5]

On Genocide

Raphael Lemkin, Polish-born Holocaust survivor and human rights lawyer, coined the term "genocide" by combining "genos" (race, people) and "cide" (to kill). In his foundational text, *Axis Rule in Occupied Europe,* Lemkin defined genocide thus:

> Generally speaking, genocide does not necessarily mean the immediate destruction of a nation, except when accomplished by mass killings of all members of a nation. It is intended rather to signify a coordinated plan of different actions aiming at the destruction of essential foundations of the life of national groups, with the aim of annihilating the groups themselves. The objectives of such a plan would be the disintegration of the political and social institutions, of culture, language, national feelings, religion, and the economic existence of national groups, and the destruction of the personal security, liberty, health, dignity, and even the lives of the individuals belonging to such groups.[6]

Lemkin believed that war and genocide are almost always connected.[7] Social scientists today argue that ethnic cleansing and genocide tend to follow state collapse, regime changes, and civil war whereas historians emphasize that certain kinds of polities—such as communist-party states like the Soviet Union, the People's Republic of China, and Cambodia under the Khmer Rouge—are capable in times of peace of killing large numbers of their own citizens as a matter of deliberate policy.[8] Regardless of one's perspective, two wars preceded the Khmer Rouge genocide: the American war in Vietnam and the civil war in Cambodia.

The American or Vietnam War

In 1963, Sihanouk rightly suspected the United States had a hand in the coup that toppled South Vietnamese president Ngo Dinh Diem and resulted in his murder. Sihanouk broke away from U.S. economic and military aid, a decision prompted by his desire to stay out of the Vietnam War, gain control of his economy, and maintain good relations with members of the communist bloc. Sadly, turning his back on the United States did his nation more harm than good.[9] He secretly allied himself with the North Vietnamese, allowing their troops sanctuary in Cambodia in exchange for recognizing Cambodia's frontiers and the promise to leave civilians alone. When Sihanouk severed diplomatic ties with the United States in 1965, his bid to keep his country out of war backfired and turned Cambodia into a "sideshow" of the Vietnamese war.

Sihanouk appointed General Lon Nol to launch a crackdown on the Cambodian left. The conservative, pro-Western general had risen quickly, holding a succession of Cambodia's top ministries. When he was elected prime minister in 1966, Sihanouk welcomed him. Unfortunately, he misread Lon Nol's political aspirations, thinking he was loyal to him. At the time, Sihanouk was more interested in pursuing his private passions than in addressing Cambodia's worsening economic, infrastructural, and social problems. Instead of monitoring growing civil unrest in the country, he turned over more and more power to Lon Nol, devoting his energies to producing and directing films that demonstrated how much out of touch he was with the Cambodian people. Meanwhile, the crackdown on leftists sent intellectuals far from the capital including leaders of a secretive communist organization that by then had built their power base in the eastern forests of Cambodia under the protection of the Vietnamese communists operating there. In May 1968, Sihanouk denounced them and dubbed them Red Khmers, the Khmers Rouges (KR).[10]

The Original Khmer

Their commander was a man named Saloth Sar who would become known to the world as Pol Pot. He was born to a prosperous farming family with close ties to the royal court where he spent much of his childhood. An indifferent student, he studied in a Buddhist monastery and a Roman Catholic primary school; attended a middle school imbued with Vichy values; and was admitted to Phnom Penh's oldest colonial high school, Lycée Sisowath. He was one of Cambodia's elite, educated in the French colonial school system with its emphasis on great eighteenth-century European thinkers and on the French Revolution. When he failed his exams, he went to a technical school for carpenters. This downward spiral ironically allowed him to successfully compete for a government scholarship to study in France. Once Saloth Sar arrived in Paris in 1949, he became part of a Marxist student circle and came to admire the writings of Marx, Stalin, and Mao. He loved nineteenth-century French poetry but told an interviewer the book that most influenced him was *The Great Revolution* by Russian anarchist Pëtr Kropotkin. According to biographer Philip Short, Pol Pot took away from this book three core principles: revolution requires an alliance between the intellectuals and the peasantry; it must be carried through to the end, without compromise or hesitation; and egalitarian principles of the French Revolution are the basis of communism. These ideas would stay with him throughout his life.[11]

Saloth Sar's approach to Marxist-Leninism admitted no need to study Marxist classics or translate them into Khmer. According to Marx, the industrial proletariat represented progress, the peasantry backwardness. Class was determined by a person's economic activity. Saloth Sar turned these ideas on their head. Class was a mental attribute—all that was needed was "proletarian consciousness." Cambodian communist party leaders identified with the middle-class because none of them had working class backgrounds or any experience of working-class life. Whenever problems arose, say in a factory—they blamed "enemy agents" for mistakes made by the party, a habit that proved disastrous once the Khmer Rouge began to rule the nation.[12]

In Paris, Saloth Sar met up with other alumni of the Lycée Sisowath, who would later become influential figures in the government he would forge. Saloth Sar left Paris after three years without finishing his studies. On his return to Cambodia in 1953, he taught high school students and joined the underground communist party, a rural, grassroots movement that emerged within a nationalist struggle for independence from France.[13] When leftists were forced out of the capitol Phnom Penh, Sar took refuge with Vietnamese communists on the eastern border who were promoting their idea of revolution throughout Indochina.[14] Living among them for eight years, he came to resent the Vietnamese largely because they took him to task for his party's unwillingness to subordinate Cambodia's interests to Vietnam. They also assigned him menial tasks rather than the leadership roles he felt fit his experience and abilities. A trip to China where he was warmly welcomed led him to transfer his loyalties to new patrons and a more inspiring revolutionary model.[15] Cambodia's traditional view of the utility and virtue of farmers and rural life was receptive to the Maoism about to engulf China and soon Cambodia.[16] Although the Vietnamese had taught him much, his animosity towards them was part cultural, part experiential. It led to his conviction that Cambodian revolutionaries needed to strive for "self-reliance, independence, and mastery. The Khmers should do everything on their own."[17] "Self-reliance" was code for a Marxist idea of autocratic development in the Third World, economic independence by a rejection of capitalism and international integration.[18]

Coup d'état and Civil War

In March 1970, when Sihanouk was out of the country, Lon Nol staged a successful coup, toppling the 1,168-year-old Khmer dynasty and replacing it with a republic. Lon Nol's declared intention had been to rout the communists and overturn corruption in government, but the abundance of U.S. military aid that poured into his pro-American regime only worsened the corruption, which further alienated the peasantry and helped fuel five years of civil war. On one side were Lon Nol and the United States and on the other, the Vietnamese communists and Khmer Rouge along with political and military support from China. Although Sihanouk's authoritarian rule initially turned the Khmer Rouge against him, Lon Nol's government led them to an about-face: the Khmer Rouge embraced Sihanouk as their figurehead leader in an unlikely coalition. It was a shrewd move that earned them the support of millions of Cambodians who trusted Sihanouk. Doubts arose about whether Sihanouk really spoke for the Khmer Rouge, but he held fast. "I do not like the Khmer Rouge and they probably don't like me," the prince said in 1973. "But they are pure patriots. . . . Though I am a Buddhist, I prefer a red Cambodia which is honest and patriotic than a Buddhist Cambodia under Lon Nol, which is corrupt and a puppet of the Americans."[19]

Although Richard Nixon had campaigned for the U.S. presidency in 1968 promising an end to the war in Vietnam, once in office he plotted with his national security advisor Henry Kissinger to secretly expand the war across South Vietnam's border into Cambodia. Over four years—between March 1969 and August 1973—the United States dropped 540,000 tons of bombs on Cambodia, three times as many bombs as they had dropped on Japan during World War II. These raids in an undeclared war killed tens of thousands of Cambodian civilians. Inflation soared, roads and bridges were reduced to rubble, and with the local economy dysfunctional, Cambodia was almost totally reliant on U.S. aid. Meanwhile, between 1970 and 1975, the Khmer Rouge grew from about 3,000 guerrillas to about 30,000 largely in response to fallout from the U.S. intervention.[20]

In early 1968, when U.S. troop presence in Vietnam peaked at 550,000, growing U.S. opposition to the war was fanned by significant troop losses during the successful North Vietnamese Tet offensive, media coverage of the MyLai massacre conducted by the U.S. military, and outrage over American use of napalm and defoliants like Agent Orange. In April 1970, the U.S. ground invasion of Cambodia began—an effort at "cleaning up" North Vietnamese strongholds in Cambodia. The invasion proved to be a turning point for the American anti-war movement's actions against the Nixon administration. On May 4, 1970, students at Kent State University were demonstrating against the invasion of Cambodia. The governor brought in the National Guard complaining that the demonstrators were worse than "Brown Shirts . . . the communist element and also the nightriders and vigilantes."[21] Four students were killed and nine others injured. Massive protests spread across the country, and public opinion against the Vietnam War gained added force. Political observers believe the Vietnam War's "incursion" into Cambodia was a contributing factor in Nixon's downfall.

The United States spent $1.85 billion propping up Lon Nol's regime.[22] His repressive, corrupt, and incompetent government stripped citizens of basic freedoms and suspended parliament. Cambodians fought each other in a brutal civil war and rarely took prisoners. Younger and younger boys were drafted into Lon Nol's army while the Khmer Rouge grew stronger. Mao endorsed the Khmer Rouge's drive for military victory in Cambodia. Meanwhile, efforts to restore Sihanouk's government failed.

When the final Khmer Rouge insurgent offensive started in 1975, thousands of Cambodians had been killed and thousands more made homeless. Lon Nol saw what was coming and fled the country with his wealth and family, settling into early retirement in the United States.[23] For most Americans the fall of Saigon was a tragedy; the fall of Phnom Penh and the butchery that followed barely even registered.[24] Cambodia, the small, largely forgotten casualty of the war in Vietnam, was headed into one of the worst chapters in the history of the twentieth century.[25] The Khmer Rouge take-over coincided with the Cambodian New Year. The Khmer Rouge named it Year Zero.

There are many accounts of what happened on April 17, 1975, when the Khmer Rouge entered Phnom Penh and the Cambodian Army surrendered. Rithy Panh's representation of his experience on that day appears in *The Missing Picture* (see chapter 7). Although Panh is decidedly not a fan, the best-known film about the Khmer Rouge take-over is British director Roland Joffé's film *The Killing Fields* (1984), which was based on the story of Dith Pranh, the Cambodian fixer for *New York Times'* journalist Sydney Schanberg. It introduced global audiences to the terrible suffering of Cambodians under the Khmer Rouge.[26] It also inspired a striking account of the era by performance artist Spalding Gray, who played a small role in Joffé's film. He later offered this view of what began on April 17 in one of his signature monologues, *Swimming to Cambodia*:

> In marched the Khmer Rouge in their black pajamas and Lon Nol's troops threw down their guns and raced to embrace them, thinking that the country would then be reunited. The Khmer Rouge did not smile back. . . . They emptied a city of two million people in twenty-four hours . . . and then the mass murder began. . . . Eyewitnesses said that everyone who had any kind of education was killed. The only hope was to convince them that you were a cab driver, so suddenly there were a thousand more cab drivers than cabs. . . . Little kids were doing the killing, ten-year-olds, fifteen-year-olds. There was very little ammunition left so they were beating people over the head with ax handles or hoses or whatever they could get hold of. . . . It was a kind of hell on earth. . . .
>
> It was better to kill an innocent person, the Khmer Rouge said, than to leave an enemy alive. It was nothing like the methodical, scientific German genocide. They were tearing apart little children like fresh bread in front of their mothers, gouging out eyes, cutting open pregnant women. And this went on for four years. Two million people were either killed outright or starved to death. And to this day no one knows exactly what happened. Oh sure, it's easy to research what happened in Germany because we can speak German, and Hitler's dead or living in Argentina. But Pol Pot is recognized by the United States government. And he's still out there, waiting. . . . Maybe a cloud of evil did land and the people simply went mad.[27]

Year Zero

Journalist William Shawcross was the son of Britain's chief prosecutor at the Nuremberg trials of Nazi war criminals, which may explain his curiosity about the relationship between the Holocaust and the Cambodian genocide. In the introduction to his book *The Quality of Mercy: Cambodia, Holocaust and Modern Conscience,* Shawcross wrote why he felt that Cambodia above all other nations deserved international attention. "I think Cambodia has an importance beyond itself, because there in its fragile heart paraded, throughout the 1970s, many of the most frightful beasts that now stalk the world. Brutal civil war, superpower intervention carelessly conducted from afar, nationalism exaggerated into paranoid racism, fanatical and vengeful evolution, invasion, starvation and back to unobserved civil war without end."[28]

The reality was a reign of terror. Behind acts of genocide was "a small handful of intellectuals, a powerful ideology, a rigorous organization, an obsession with control and therefore with secrecy, total contempt for the individual, and the status of death as an absolute recourse," wrote Panh in his memoir. He continues:

> This is the reason why I dislike the expressions "suicide of a nation" and "autogenocide" and "politicide" so profoundly. . . . A nation that commits suicide is a unique body, a body cut off from the greater body of nations. Such a nation is enigmatic, impenetrable. It's a sick nation, maybe even an insane one. And the world remains innocent. The crimes committed by Democratic Kampuchea, and the intention behind those crimes, were incontrovertibly human; they involved man in his universality, man in his entirety, man in his history and in his politics. No one can consider those crimes as a geographical peculiarity or historical oddity; on the contrary, the twentieth century reached its fulfillment in that place.[29]

The Khmer Rouge (KR), the armed wing of the Communist Party of Kampuchea (CPK), controlled Democratic Kampuchea between April 17, 1975, and January 7, 1979. The CPK was secretive and kept its agenda concealed and their identities hidden under the overarching name of the "Angkar," the Organization. During the Seventies, when outsiders had no access to the country, only official propaganda was released that portrayed not the reality of what was happening but the ideals of the revolution. Films by the Khmer Rouge promoted the political propaganda of collective labor and communal spirit, projecting idealized images of people building a new nation. "A Khmer Rouge film is always a slogan,"[30] Rithy Panh observed. "We understand the Khmer Rouge by watching their footage. In films . . . the harvest is glorious. There are these calm, smiling faces, like in a painting, a poem. At last I see the revolution so promised us, it exists only on film."[31] This dubious cinematic reality was challenged by refugees who confided their traumatic experience of life under the Khmer Rouge to François Ponchaud, a French missionary to Cambodia, who was evacuated in May 1975 and later conducted hundreds of interviews with refugees who fled to Thailand, Vietnam, and France.

In his book *Cambodia Year Zero,* Father Ponchaud was one of the first to document what was told to him by those who escaped the Khmer Rouge takeover:

> On April 17, 1975, a society collapsed . . . Individualism and chaotic license have been replaced by radical collectivism and perpetual conditioning. Using class inequality and racial animosity as tools, a handful of ideologists have driven an army of peasants to bury their entire past. To learn a new art of living, many of the living have died. . . . . in this new regime, in which all possessions have been abolished and knowledge confers no privilege, the one thing that is not shared is power: it remains wholly concentrated in the hands of a very small number.[32]

It would be years before fierce opposition to such evidence, mounted by leftist supporters of the Khmer Rouge revolution in the West, gave way to judgment that the refugees' testimony was true.[33] By then, whatever efforts could have been taken to abort further massacres were too late.

Claiming that over two thousand years of Cambodian history had ended with the revolution, the Khmer Rouge did away with money, formal education, religion, private property, clothing styles, and freedom of movement. They closed schools, hospitals, banks, libraries, markets, and monasteries. Everyone wore black, their hair was cut short, and their shoes were cut from rubber tires. The system deprived Cambodians of three of the most cherished features of their lifestyle: land, family, and religion. Children were separated from parents, husbands from wives. The Khmer Rouge believed individualism and "feudal" institutions stood in the way of progress, and they monitored every step of the revolution and the lives of "base people" and "new people." The "base people" were the farmers who had always worked the land and had suffered most from bombing raids. The "new people" were the educated city dwellers, professionals, government bureaucrats, and soldiers who

FIGURE 3.1 Khmer Rouge propaganda in *Duch, Master of the Forges of Hell* © RPanh / droits réservés

had fought in the civil war; they were suspect because they were capable of questioning the new regime that became ever more hierarchical and totalitarian. In crushing their enemies, Khmer Rouge cadres relied on agricultural metaphors like "pull up the grass, dig up the roots" and announced that the "new people's" bodies would be used for "fertilizer."

Two million Cambodians were driven into the countryside. Several thousand died as a result of the evacuation, which added to the estimated five hundred thousand deaths inflicted during five years of civil war. Evacuation from the cities was explained to the populace as necessary to protect them from further bombing raids by the United States, which was untrue, but it motivated people to gather a few belongings for what would become a long march into a shocking future. There was too little food in Phnom Penh to provide for the numbers that had come seeking refuge in the capital during the civil war, so lack of provisions was one reason for the evacuation. Add to that motivation the difficulty of administering so many people and the Khmer Rouge's fears for their own security. Sending urban dwellers to remote villages as agricultural workers was deemed the only way Cambodia could grow enough food to provide for all members of society and produce surplus stock that could be exported, netting necessary income to finance industrialization. The Khmer Rouge believed that removing literate people from the cities, blamed as the breeding ground for counter-revolution, would help in breaking down entrenched social hierarchies and loyalties.[34]

The "new people" or "April 17 people" were forced to work tirelessly in labor camps. Many were unused to manual work, and they succumbed to the grueling regimen of 10- to 12-hour days, 12 months a year, without rest, adequate food, and access to family, health care or material rewards. Hundreds of thousands were driven to the northwest where the most productive rice fields around Battambang and Pursat were located. The "new people" were constantly reminded of their negligible value with oft-repeated KR slogans such as: "Keeping you is no profit; losing you is no loss." They suffered greatly, and when they died, their bodies were tossed into unmarked graves or left by the side of the road. One in four people died from overwork, malnutrition, disease, or execution. As David Chandler notes, "On a per capita basis, and considering the short lifespan of Democratic Kampuchea, the number of regime-related deaths in Cambodia is one of the highest in recorded world history."[35]

Language of Terror

The Khmer Rouge began by assassinating words, according to Panh. Eventually every word was attached to a dream or a nightmare. To manipulate the peasants, they needed a very keen sense of language and knowledge about the origin of words. In the registry books at S-21 prison, there are frequent references to *kamtèch*. This does not signify *to kill* but *to destroy, to reduce to dust*. To replace "to kill," "to execute," with words more imaginative like "to reduce to dust" helped the peasants to kill. This is how adolescents became murderers. The Khmer Rouge also replaced "to execute" with "to smash," then "to abandon." This language uses the images and methods of poetry, all relating to horror. To speak of enemies, the word "*khmang*" designates someone whose every trace must be erased. The Khmer Rouge's language followed three models: the language of the French revolution, that of the Chinese Cultural Revolution, and finally ancient khmer, which allowed them to attach the revolutionary project to a national mythology. They forged a rhetoric that introduced a new sonority in the language, very strange and easily understood. This rhetoric had a function: to infuse an obsessive hatred that allows a peasant to commit difficult acts of killing. The language with which one thinks, unique to each people, to each culture, is also the one with which one resists. Without a penetrating awareness of language and what it signifies, words can be manipulated and with them, the power to think and resist. The language of terror is a language of hatred.[36]

Rule by Terror

Robespierre's France and Stalin's Russia, the two revolutionary pillars of the Marxist Circle in Paris, afforded no room for sentimentality. Khmer Rouge leaders agreed that humane feelings were a sign of weakness and should be ruthlessly suppressed. Saloth Sar's inspiration was Chairman Mao and his Great Leap Forward, only the Khmer Rouge tried to outstrip Mao by achieving far more in far less time. Mao, who presided over a greater scale of slaughter than Pol Pot, did not glory in the destruction caused by the Chinese revolution. For Mao, it was a necessary evil, not a revolutionary virtue. For Pol Pot, bloodshed was cause for exultation.[37]

The Khmer Rouge indoctrinated people in the right way of thinking and being, engaging them in hours of self-criticism and lectures designed to convert them into revolutionaries who had given up not only all their material possessions but their spiritual possessions as well. Hunger, lack of sleep, and long hours of labor were the tools of mental control. Laurence Picq, a French woman, returned to Cambodia with her children to be with her husband, a cadre close to Foreign Minister Ieng Sary. Picq compared her experience to membership in the Moonies. She wrote in her memoir that "when political education drips into minds emptied by hunger and weariness and cut off from the outside world, the effects are prodigious." The diet of thin soup and moldy bread improved during the twice-yearly seminars held by Ieng Sary. Fruit and fresh-water crayfish, vegetables and rice, when combined with indoctrination and good treatment had, according to Picq, "a psychological impact that was frightening. . . . It acted on collective attitudes and behavior with such power that the participants emerged feeling they were capable of anything."[38]

According to Philip Short, the aim of indoctrination was to demolish the personality, "that hard, tenacious, aggressive shell which in its very essence is counter-revolutionary," as one Khmer Rouge cadre described it. The ultimate goal was to have no personality at all. To achieve this, the Khmer Rouge attacked the individual's most vulnerable point—his family relationships or educational background or ties with a foreign country—to decondition him, liberating his behavior from acquired reflexes of his former life, before building a new personality on the basis of revolutionary values. The process was repeated until a new person emerged who embodied loyalty to Angkar and non-reflection. The ideals of the French Revolution, the practices of Maoist China, the methods of Stalinism, all played their parts.

Hannah Arendt, writing about Hitler's Germany and Stalin's Soviet Union, anticipated Cambodia under the Khmer Rouge when she described how complete rule by terror operates. First the regime must destroy all organized opposition. Then the people must become "atomized," separated from each other and forbidden normal ties and relationships. Then they must be policed by spies and informers. Children inform on parents, neighbors on neighbors, to save themselves. The result, according to Arendt, is a regime where no one can be trusted. In this environment, economic progress is doomed because terror produces paralysis. Waste of human lives and human production is the natural product of terror. Eventually the regime is consumed by its quest for enemies. She concluded: "Terror turns not only against its enemies, but against its friends and supporters as well, being afraid of all power, even the power of its friends. The climax of terror is reached when the police state begins to devour its own children, when yesterday's executioner becomes today's victim."[39]

In Cambodia, cultural and religious minorities had to abandon their identities and assimilate as worker-peasants or face death. Everyone had to give up traditions and live a uniform, cooperative way of life. This was demanded in defense of purification of the worker-peasant revolution. The CPK continued their practice of hunting down and murdering ethnic Vietnamese in Cambodia. They also targeted other ethnoreligious groups, including Buddhists, Christians, Muslims and in particular the Chams, an ethnic Chinese Muslim minority one third of which died between 1975 and 1979. Khmer Rouge leadership employed biological metaphors that suggested the threat of contamination from these "pests" much as Nazis had talked of Jews as "vermin."[40]

Democratic Kampuchea

Democratic Kampuchea can be divided into four phases. The first began with the capture of Phnom Penh and lasted until early 1976 when Democratic Kampuchea was formally announced, a constitution proclaimed, and a new wave of migration was set in motion from the unproductive central and southwest zones to the rice-growing areas of the northwest. During this period unnamed enemies and traitors were identified as lurking within and outside the country, but no genuine or imagined enemies surfaced.[41] The constitution of Democratic Kampuchea, promulgated in January 1976, guaranteed no human rights, few organs of government, and effectively banished private property, religion and family-oriented agriculture. It said nothing about Marxist-Leninist ideas but instead made the revolution sound uniquely

Cambodian with no connection to the outside world. Representation was based on "class" not territorial constituency. A faux election was held, and "new people" were not permitted to vote. Few others actually did vote. The national assembly met once to approve the constitution and never played another significant role in the country. In March 1976, Saloth Sar, under his *nom de guerre* Pol Pot, was announced as prime minister. The people who would play key roles in the government, members of the Central Committee, were a mixture of French-educated intellectuals—such as Ieng Sary, Sary's wife Ieng Thirith, Khieu Samphan, Khieu Ponnary (Pol Pot's wife), and Son Sen—and older members of the Indochinese Communist Party like Nuon Chea (Brother Number Two) and Ta Mok, (The Butcher).[42] Pol Pot (aka Brother Number One) would rely on the Central Committee for advice and support.

Pol Pot with his colleagues drafted a four-year economic plan "to build socialism in all fields," but it was never formally launched. The goal of tripling the rice harvest was to be achieved by extensive irrigation, double and triple cropping, and longer working hours. Historians would later compare the plan to "war communism" in the Soviet Union in the early 1920s and the Great Leap Forward in China in the 1950s. The plan said nothing about testing soil and water conditions to see if they would sustain such growth or if the infrastructure was in place to achieve these goals. By early 1976 food was in short supply and would worsen to famine in 1977 and 1978. One way of meeting surplus goals was reducing the amount of rice given laborers. The party eventually reduced the rations in many areas to 180 grams—the equivalent of approximately 230 calories—every two days. Thousands died from malnutrition along with malaria and overwork.[43] Rather than re-examine policy goals and their feasibility, the Khmer Rouge viewed starvation as the result of mismanagement and treachery by cadres responsible for food distribution. They arrested cadres, interrogated them, and put them to death.[44]

The second phase lasted until the end of September 1976. Zhou Enlai, Chinese prime minister and friend of Prince Sihanouk, died in January 1976. Without Zhou in power, the CPK decided it no longer needed Sihanouk. It was time for him to "retire." Although Sihanouk with his wife lived in relative comfort under guard in a villa on the grounds of the royal palace, he lived in fear for his life.

The third phase of Democratic Kampuchea was marked by waves of purges and a shift toward blaming Cambodia's difficulties and counter-revolutionary activity increasingly on the Vietnamese. Enemies of the state varied at different times, including the middle-class, soldiers who fought for Lon Nol, members of the CPK when it was guided by the Vietnamese or those who had been exposed to the influence of foreign countries. By 1978 targeted enemies included high-ranking CPK members, military commanders, and officials associated with the eastern zone.

Pol Pot, ever distrustful of the Vietnamese, interpreted Vietnam's signing a treaty of cooperation with Laos in July 1977 as a plan to encircle Cambodia and reconstitute what had been French Indochina.[45] The third phase ended in late September 1977 when Pol Pot announced the existence of the Communist Party of Kampuchea, probably at the insistence of the Chinese, and named himself as its heretofore unknown leader. His aim was to unite the party against the Vietnamese, attack Buddhism, and minimize Sihanouk's role. As a result, Pol Pot received additional support from China for Democratic Kampuchea's confrontation with Vietnam. The Khmer Rouge secretly purged military officers and CPK cadres and executed several hundred at S-21 prison. One who escaped this purge and found refuge in Vietnam—Heng Samrin—later was installed by the Vietnamese as head of the post-Khmer state, the People's Republic of Kampuchea.

S-21

S-21 was a secret prison located in Phnom Penh and used initially for the interrogation of upper-level party members suspected of disloyalty. It became the epicenter of the horror of the Khmer Rouge regime. S-21 was one of a network of security sites across the country, but its purpose was the most sinister. Approximately 17,000 men, women and children were brought there, interrogated, and tortured, often forced to confess to unlikely membership in the CIA or KGB, and then taken for execution to the nearby killing fields of Choeung Ek. To be suspected, a person had to be mentioned in three confessions. Thousands who were arrested were probably innocent, but everyone arrested was considered guilty. There was no juridical procedure, no judge, no trial, no sentencing, only arrest followed by coerced confession and death.

S-21 could hold a maximum of 1,500 prisoners. Over four thousand dossiers of those held at S-21 remain, with hundreds of pages of confessions dictated by the interrogators. Only 200 prisoners entered S-21 in 1975, more than ten times that many (2,250) arrived in 1976. Another five thousand were taken there in 1977, and roughly the same number were condemned in 1978. It was long believed that only seven survived S-21, but archival research suggests 23 lived, five of whom were children; some of them are missing or do

FIGURE 3.2 Vann Nath painting of S-21 torture © RPanh / droits réservés

not want their identities known as Tuol Sleng survivors. Among the known survivors, five had their lives spared because they were visual artists—painters and sculptors like Vann Nath, Bou Meng and Im Chann—who were needed to produce idealized photorealist paintings or sculptural busts of Pol Pot for propaganda purposes.[46] S-21 had been a school before being transformed into a prison. Workers at a nearby factory in Phnom Penh, who knew about the building but not its purpose, called it "a place of entering, not leaving."[47]

Most survivors of the regime remember 1978 as the harshest year when rations fell below the starvation level of 1977. Vietnam and Democratic Kampuchea began a long and costly struggle that played into the hands of larger powers. Through miscalculation and stupidity, according to *Washington Post* journalist Elizabeth Becker, the Khmer Rouge transformed what they imagined would be a useful border dispute with Vietnam into an all-out war. All Cambodians were ordered by Pol Pot to kill 30 Vietnamese, an official statement of genocidal intent.[48] Having created and massacred their "enemies," the KR thought it would prove they were the ultimate nationalists and saviors of Cambodia and thereby solidify their regime. Becker countered that, having destroyed their society in order to save it, they were in fact "marching toward an apocalypse."[49]

In 1978 Democratic Kampuchea tried to open itself to the outside world, inviting sympathetic journalists and foreign radicals to visit. A group of Yugoslav filmmakers came and made a film that thinly veiled their distress over what they observed. They found few adults and only children working in the fields, running factory machines, and working on fishing boats. "It was like an absurd film. It was like a nightmare."[50] In the final days of December 1978, two Americans and a Scottish Marxist academic travelled to Cambodia to observe how the revolution was faring. Elizabeth Becker and Richard Dudman, who covered the Vietnam War for the *St. Louis Post-Dispatch*, had worked in Cambodia in the Seventies and were the first non-socialist writers to visit Democratic Kampuchea. Malcolm Caldwell, unlike them, had been a longtime and enthusiastic supporter of the revolution. All three were closely monitored during their stay. On the last night, after interviewing Pol Pot, the group was attacked, and Caldwell was killed in his hotel room by armed Khmer assailants. It was unclear who was behind this. Several days later Vietnamese forces numbering more than one hundred thousand attacked Democratic Kampuchea in the northeast and encountered little resistance. They then decided to capture Phnom Penh, and the city fell to the Vietnamese in 1979 as roughly fifty thousand bureaucrats, soldiers, and factory workers fled the city.

The Khmer Rouge had thrown their people into a perpetual revolution based on forced labor and engaged in an ethnic and territorial war against Vietnam. Pol Pot escaped the arrival of the Vietnamese in a jeep and drove to Anlong Veng, on the border between Cambodia and Thailand, where he lived until his death nearly twenty years later. It was a humiliating defeat for Brother Number One and his utopian dream of an agrarian paradise.

Vietnamese Occupation

The Vietnamese occupied the re-named People's Republic of Kampuchea until 1989. Not surprisingly, most Cambodians initially welcomed the Vietnamese invasion and the end of Pol Pot's rule. But survivors of Democratic Kampuchea's reign of terror were mistaken in thinking they would be able to resume their prerevolutionary lives.[51] Violence, confusion, hunger, and suffering lingered and hindered the nation's attempts to recover. Thousands of Khmer Rouge died in combat and from malaria and malnutrition in the exodus. Hundreds of thousands of liberated people took to the roads headed either for home or to refugee camps on the Thai border, only to die in the chaos that ensued. In Phnom Penh, Hanoi installed a "puppet government" of the People's Republic of Kampuchea (PRK) headed by Heng Samrin and staffed by former CPK members who defected to Vietnam in 1977 and 1978. The new regime dismantled some of the most offensive aspects of Democratic Kampuchea, reestablishing markets, schools, hospitals, freedom of movement, and family farming. In 1980 Buddhism and money were reintroduced. Most Cambodians were too preoccupied with reconstructing their lives to notice. Those opposed to the Vietnamese occupation escaped to Thailand, while others grudgingly worked alongside the Vietnamese to bring Cambodia back to life. The wider world was slow to accept the stories of the atrocities committed by the Khmer Rouge, finding them so outlandish that they were initially dismissed as Vietnamese propaganda.

The decks remained stacked against Cambodia. The PRK was ineligible for development assistance because Democratic Kampuchea retained Cambodia's seat in the United Nations, the only government-in-exile to do so. Support for the Khmer Rouge given by the United States, China, and other powers hostile to Vietnam continued to punish Cambodia materially, and it was the people who suffered once more.[52]

The Khmer Rouge retreated to the northwest and formed a guerrilla army in the 1980s. Their leaders, including Pol Pot, remained in command of the resistance throughout the 1980s and 1990s. Their presence was often violently announced by the detonation of landmines concealed by them in the rice fields, markets, and paths to villages throughout Cambodia. They killed or maimed thousands. Pol Pot was indifferent to the suffering of innocent people. The Khmer Rouge continued to enjoy support from their powerful and prosperous patrons who shared Pol Pot's hostility toward Vietnam.[53]

A "show" trial in absentia for Pol Pot and Ieng Sary, organized by the People's Republic of Kampuchea in 1979, was held. Both men were condemned to death but to no effect. In the 1980s human rights activists in the West tried repeatedly to bring Pol Pot to justice at the International Court of Justice in The Hague but invariably failed because the Thai were unwilling to hand him over.[54] When information about Pol Pot's years in power spread in the 1980s, he became an embarrassment to the United States, according to David Chandler, but they lacked the courage to abandon him.[55] Spalding Gray reflected on the criminal absurdity of the situation. "Roland Joffé said to me 'My God, Spalding, morality is not a moveable feast.' But I keep seeing it moving all the time."[56] Only Pol Pot's death in 1998 and the surrender of Khieu Samphan and Nuon Chea the following year brought an end to the Khmer Rouge regime's direct threat to the Cambodian people.[57]

4

Perpetrators and Survivors

The S-21 Trilogy

> Those who can make you believe
> absurdities, can make you commit
> atrocities.
>
> **VOLTAIRE**, *Questions sur les miracles*
> (1765)

S-21 was the code name for the secret prison created in 1975 by the Khmer Rouge to incarcerate, interrogate, torture, and execute top figures of the Communist Party of Kampuchea (CPK) who were suspected of being traitors. Its purpose expanded to eliminate the old guard, which included army officers, civil servants, aristocrats, and "new people" who lived in cities suspected of remaining loyal to the old regime. The first victims were the mentally ill and physically impaired. Then the religious, homosexuals, and intellectuals were all targeted to be "smashed." Over four years, more and more people were arrested and brought there, and of the estimated 17,000 men, women, and children who were incarcerated, only 23 survived.[1]

There were different explanations offered for what the term *S-21* designated. Ing Pech, one of the first directors of the S-21 genocide museum, told Panh that *S* stood for "security" and *2* for "second bureau." Today everyone knows that S stood for Santesok/santebal/security and 21 was the prison's radio communication line. The code name was created by Comrade Duch, the prison director.[2] The compound originally housed a school and consisted of four whitewashed concrete buildings three stories high with balcony corridors running along each floor. A fifth building split the grassy courtyard in two. The high school had taken the name of the district, Tuol Svay Prey ("hillock of the wild mango"), and an adjoining building, which housed a primary school, was called Tuol Sleng ("hillock of the *sleng* tree"). The Tuol Sleng Museum of Genocidal Crimes was the name chosen by the Vietnamese to designate the entire compound when they decided to create a genocide museum on the site, choosing it perhaps because a sleng tree bears poisonous fruit.[3]

To be a prisoner at S-21 was to be guilty and slated for execution. There was no juridical procedure. Forced "confessions" were extracted through torture and were largely fabrications dictated by interrogators.[4] Their goal was not the gathering of information so much as the denunciation of suspected enemies who then would be arrested, tortured, and forced to denounce more human sacrifices for Pol Pot's paranoiac state.[5] When the Vietnamese invaded and occupied Phnom Penh in 1979, they found over the gate to S-21 a red placard that read: "Fortify the spirit of the revolution! Be on your guard against the strategy and tactics of the enemy so as to defend the country, the people, and the Party."[6] Wordier than "Arbeit macht frei" but no less chilling. They also found corpses shackled to metal beds, blood on the floor, assorted instruments of torture including ammunition boxes filled with human feces, and thousands of identity photos of Cambodians photographed on their arrival. The historian David Chandler thinks S-21 was probably the most efficient institution in all of Cambodia during the Khmer Rouge reign. "When I have immersed myself in the S-21 archive, the terror lurking inside it has pushed me around, blunted my skills, and eroded my self-assurance," he observed. "The experience at times has been akin to drowning."[7] Like Chandler, Panh's experience there culminated in his own feeling of drowning, an image that would appear repeatedly in his subsequent autobiographical film, *The Missing Picture.*

When Rithy Panh returned to Cambodia, he intended to visit the archive at Tuol Sleng Genocide Museum, but it took time before he could steel himself to the task of searching for evidence that his uncle had died there.[8] While conducting his research, he read the case file of Hout Bophana. It was the largest file in the S-21 archive. In it lay the story of a woman who became Panh's muse, the heroic embodiment of all those anonymous victims who died during the Khmer Rouge regime. While making his film about her, *Bophana, a Cambodian Tragedy*, Panh realized he could bring together perpetrators with S-21 survivors to question them about how they became cold-blooded killers. It took three years to find and persuade some staff to agree to participate in *S-21: The Khmer Rouge Killing Machine*, an unprecedented documentary that would bring Panh international attention and the film special selection at Cannes. The only person missing from the film is the man mentioned at every turn by guards and survivors alike, Comrade Duch, director of S-21, the sophisticated interrogator, ingenious torturer, and consummate bureaucrat, who kept the prison running according to the dictates of the Khmer Rouge Central Committee. Duch was missing because he was awaiting trial as the first defendant accused of crimes against humanity before the Extraordinary Chambers of the Courts of Cambodia. Panh tried repeatedly to get permission to interview Duch without success until 2008 when he was unexpectedly allowed to visit him in prison, where he filmed three hundred hours of interviews with him. *Duch: Master of the Forges of Hell* completed Panh's trilogy on S-21.

Vann Nath, who survived S-21 because he was able to paint approved portraits of Pol Pot, became the central figure in Panh's S-21 trilogy and Panh's friend. Kaing Guek Eav, a.k.a. Comrade Duch, became Panh's nemesis. *Bophana, a Cambodian Tragedy* was the first Khmer-language film about the Cambodian genocide.[9] *S-21: The Khmer Rouge Killing Machine* provided an essential introduction to Khmer Rouge ideology and brutality. And *Duch: Master of the Forges of Hell* is arguably the most disturbing work of the three, a thinking person's film about a thinking man who committed heinous acts at the behest of the state. Taken together, the trilogy lays bare the abuses committed at the infamous prison that has come to symbolize the Khmer Rouge genocide.

Bophana, a Cambodian Tragedy (Bophana, une tragédie cambodgienne) (1996)

Rithy Panh returned to Cambodia in 1990 after eleven years living in exile in France. One year later, after the Paris Peace Accords were signed formally ending the war between Cambodia and Vietnam, the idea of making a film on the mechanisms of extermination seized him. The accords had reinstated the monarchy, decided on elections under the control of the United Nations, and called for the return of refugees, but inclusion of the most critical term—*genocide*—was absent from the text. Panh took this as a refusal to allow survivors to remember and as an insult to the dignity of the victims.[10] He decided to demonstrate through his films that genocide had happened.

For his first film about S-21, Panh focused on the largest file in the archive, devoted to one woman, Hout Bophana. It housed over one thousand pages that included numerous drafts of her forced "confessions" along with her love letters to her husband, which constituted the "evidence" of her alleged spying activities. Panh recognized that Bophana was a real-life heroine: her youth, beauty, fidelity, and long suffering made her an icon of resistance to the Khmer Rouge's injustice and cruelty.

The *Washington Post* journalist Elizabeth Becker first recounted Bophana's story in her book *When the War Was Over: Cambodia and the Khmer Rouge Revolution*. Before Panh contacted Becker for permission to draw on her account, he spent months tracking down and interviewing people who were part of Bophana's life during the civil war and the Khmer Rouge regime. Critical to Panh's research was his discovery of two S-21 survivors—Chum Mey and Vann Nath—as well as two perpetrators, Him Huoy, deputy security chief, and Prak Khan, former interrogator and torturer. Him Huoy is forthcoming in his accounting of how executions were carried out at Choeung Ek, S-21's killing fields. He remembered Bophana during the five months she was interrogated, tortured, and finally executed at age twenty-five.

Bophana's story is the through line that allows Panh to weave around it the story of what happened in Cambodia during the Khmer Rouge regime as told by male and female narrators and witnesses who interject their own perspective on the tragedy. A Baray villager tells of a young woman executed for singing a pop song from the sixties. A monk speaks about the two thousand people who came to live in his pagoda. A former deportee relates how people were taken away in oxcarts at night to be killed. Chief among these witnesses is Vann Nath, painter and survivor of S-21.

The film opens with a close-up on a file folder as an archivist explains that the pages are Bophana's hand-written "confessions." Panh moves next to one of the classrooms in S-21 where the famous identity shots of prisoners are displayed. There Bophana's uncle, Mr. Toeuth, searches for her photo and,

FIGURE 4.1 Vann paints Bophana in *Bophana, a Cambodian Tragedy* © RPanh / droits réservés

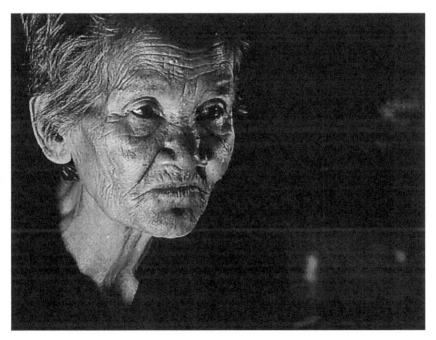

FIGURE 4.2 Bophana's mother-in-law in *Bophana, a Cambodian Tragedy* © RPanh / droits réservés

finding it, describes his last meeting with her, concluding with emotion: "I can no longer speak." Panh cuts to sunlight streaming through a window and pans to Vann Nath, who stands before a canvas on which he is painting Bophana's portrait. Actually, he is painting parallel portraits—one is a classic pose of a lovely young woman with long hair and a pearl necklace. Next to this is Bophana the prisoner, gaunt, with hair chopped short and a confrontational gaze directed at the photographer and viewer. They are so different as to be almost unrecognizable as the same person. "Bophana lived in a country where love was an outrage to the revolutionary party," the narrator says, where the mere act of writing love letters was forbidden and any mention of love could be punishable by death.

Bophana's early history is told largely by her mother-in-law, who is nearly seventy and worn by the sun, by time, and by grief. Close-ups of her dark, lined face and hands, beautifully lit, command the viewer's sympathy and attention. She shows photos of Bophana and Ly Sitha, her husband, and speaks of their childhood growing up together in Kompong Thom City, north of Phnom Penh. Panh returns to her throughout the film, alternating her stories with archival footage of Cambodia at war accompanied by sounds of gunfire and explosions in the background. Marc Marder's music—the haunting flute, the drumming softly heard in the background like a beating heart, and the lover's theme of loneliness and longing—offers needed counterpoint to the wartime background and the shrill Khmer Rouge anthems sung in the propaganda films. His sonorous composition is an elegant retort to the soundtrack of authoritarian rule.

Using her red and white checkered *kramar* (scarf) to wipe away her tears, the elderly woman presses on with her stories. Panh illustrates them metaphorically, inserting scenes, for example, of a young girl dressed in a white shirt and flowing black skirt riding a bicycle along a waterway. The simplicity of this slender figure peacefully riding suggests the young Bophana before she was swept up in the violence of war and totalitarian madness. And when the narrator speaks about her first tragedy, rape, Panh poetically visualizes this violent aggression with the silhouetted figure of a woman barely glimpsed behind a barred window, a delicate and unsensational image of the trauma she was forced to hide.

Panh incorporates archival scenes of Phnom Penh before and after the Khmer Rouge victory as well as East Baray, where Bophana was sent when she was evacuated from the capital in April 1975. He adds contemporary shots of Baray that feature farmers in close-ups trading in the marketplace and, in panoramic shots, working in the fields. The life captured in these color scenes stands in sharp contrast to the horrors of the black-and-white archival images, an effective contrast between past and present that owes something to the structural approach taken by Alain Resnais in *Night and Fog*. Adding gunfire and sounds of explosions brings archival footage of civil war to life.

Panh includes Khmer Rouge propaganda films in many of his films, but here he personalizes them, selecting scenes of black-clad workers engaged in the same back-breaking labor that Bophana performed to satisfy village elders who regarded her with contempt. She was young, beautiful, and, worst of all, fair, all of which inspired jealousy and raised suspicions about her morals.

Elizabeth Becker's rendition of Bophana's short life is full of the stark details that made her life tragic. After she was raped by a Lon Nol soldier in 1970, she attempted suicide but was rushed to a hospital and survived. She gave birth to a son, doing what work she could find to provide food and shelter for her family. Eventually she found a position in Phnom Penh at an American charity that helped widows. There she accidentally rediscovered Ly Sitha at a cremation ceremony: he was now a monk who soon vanished in search of safety.

When the Khmer Rouge drove all city people into the countryside, Bophana's son was with her younger sister, and she never saw either of them again.[11] When she returned to Baray with her grandmother, she fell afoul of village leaders who initially starved her. What saved her was her relationship with Ly Sitha, her childhood friend, who by then had taken the name of Comrade Deth and had survived by becoming a Khmer Rouge cadre. His status kept Bophana fed and safe for a time, but they were separated for months with few opportunities to see each other. Worked mercilessly by the village cooperative, Bophana miscarried Deth's child after ill health and "folk medicine" administered by untrained doctors nearly killed her. What sealed her fate was Deth's link to his once-powerful commander Koy Thuon, who was accused of being a saboteur during one of Pol Pot's purges. Scapegoats were held responsible for the failures of Khmer Rouge policies: enemies could be blamed, never policies.

Because of her education and administrative position with an American NGO, Bophana was deemed a greater criminal than her husband and identified by Comrade Duch as a traitor to Angkar, the name given to the Communist Party of Democratic Kampuchea. In the curious misogyny of the

Khmer Rouge, she allegedly used her seductive wiles to corrupt Deth and lure him into her CIA cell. Becker grimly speculates on the kind of sadistic tortures reserved for women that Bophana would have endured over the months she was forced to rewrite her "confessions."[12] Panh believes the intention behind all coerced false confessions was to erase actual memories so that false memories could be implanted, effectively robbing individuals of a true past, restructuring their memory to supplant their dignity and sense of self. Combined with debilitating physical tortures, this form of brainwashing was an assault on one's very humanity, not just a tactic used to justify the execution of so-called enemies.[13]

Becker tells Bophana's story at length and with considerable detail and journalistic rigor. It is very different from Panh's poetic approach. Panh avoids the sordid details of her ordeal as documented in Becker's account and carefully considers her efforts at resistance, her courage, and her deep love and longing for her husband. Most importantly, he focuses on her identification with the heroine of the Hindu epic the *Ramayama*, which was translated into Khmer in the seventeenth century and known as the *Reamker*. This is a devotional story that teaches the ideal virtues of duty and love in the face of separation and adversity. In it, Prince Rama (Ream) is separated from his beloved wife Sita (Séda) by a lustful villain who abducts her. She suffers greatly but never ceases to be true to her husband. Freed when the villain is vanquished by Ream, Séda must then prove her purity by enduring a trial by fire. She succeeds but then asks Mother Earth to swallow her up because she has undergone too many humiliations.

This epic poem has captivated Cambodians for generations with its primal conflict between good and evil and the contrast between what is wild (*prei*) and what is civilized (*sruk*).[14] Bophana's identification with Séda allowed her to ally herself through classical Cambodian art with traditional values far removed from the revolutionary ideals of the Khmer Rouge. During the five months she was tortured in S-21, Bophana signed her confessions with the name "Sédadeth"—the Séda of Deth. Panh draws attention to the way she endured by identifying with her poetic alter ego until her humiliations, like Séda's, finally came to an end. Broken, she surrendered to the absurd details of forced confessions, but she held fast to her heroic identity. Rather than label her behavior as "escapism," as some commentators have suggested, Panh presents this as an act of rebellion afforded to her through art. She clung to the power of art to sustain her humanity throughout her terrible suffering. It is on her signature as "Sédadeth" that Panh's camera deliberately and frequently rests.

Bophana's letters to Deth are among the most poignant elements of the film. Their words to each other are beautifully spoken in French by actors who have been directed not to exaggerate emotion.

Feelings for my husband,

After ten years of separation, I saw my husband again when Cambodia moved on and started a revolution. We were cousins, then we became husband and wife. . . .

After the sad events I went through in 1970 and other bitterness I experienced later, I felt much pain in my heart, and I said to myself, "Physically and mentally I'm already dead." Each day that went by, Sita shed thousands of tears. . . . And as another day went by, Sita's pains got worse.

Darling, you know that ever since Sita touched the soil of Baray, friends warned her that people said that you were not really her husband. And that Sita clung to you only because she learned that you were a Party cadre. They also said that Sita had been a whore in Phnom Penh and that was the reason she caused trouble in Baray, making up the story that you were her husband.

Oh, darling! There were so many slanders that made Sita cry, that made her suffer so terribly. My friends told me that the Old People sent me to work at the dykes because they did not want to see my skin remain white. They forced me to work. My friends said the other women were jealous of me because they have been members of the revolution for five years and yet none of them had a husband like Sita's. But what has Sita got that they haven't?

Dear husband! Please tell Sita frankly: why have you disappeared for so long? Why haven't you come to look for Sita? Sita understands that you are very busy working for Angkar. But each day living in Baray Sita loses one year of her life.[15]

Deth wrote to her about his concerns for her and his fears for their future:

To Sita, my unhappy wife . . .

I want to have news from you all the time. I'm so worried about your health. Why have you taken so much medicine? Will all this medicine make it impossible for us to have children? Are you going mad! If only I could become a ghost so that you could do what you wanted! I know the sea of your tears as well as you know the mountain of fire of my life.

My adorable Sita! Trust my heart, my darling.[16]

Bophana, a Cambodian Tragedy brings to life one victim of S-21 who has come to represent the 17,000 people who perished there. Her story speaks on behalf of all those innocents who died without a trial, without any defense or verdict delivered, violently, and without proper burial and mourning. By representing Bophana's story, Panh presents her life as a victory over the Khmer Rouge's effort at *kamtèch*—"to reduce to dust," to destroy and erase all traces of human life, to erase even death. He cannot accept that so many of the genocide's dead remain anonymous in unmarked graves. To do nothing about this is, in his eyes, to become complicit in their erasure. By putting a name to the face of one of the many who died at S-21, he disrupts the collective anonymity of victims by rendering one as an individual. Those identically clad workers stooped and hurrying to fulfill insane work goals—their labor equal to the effort of building the pyramids of Egypt[17]—were human beings who could speak for themselves like Bophana. The Khmer Rouge failed because Bophana lives on in books and films, not as an animal without a soul, not something erased and forgotten.[18]

Vicente Sánchez-Biosca, in his insightful essay on the role of Hout Bophana in Panh's films, rightly proclaims her to be "the instigating voice that drives Rithy Panh."[19] But he stops short of acknowledging how this is also true in his fiction films. Panh names the beautiful protagonist in *Que la barque se brise* Mme. Hout Bopha. And the drawing of A'Koy's missing mother in *Farm Catch* is based on Hout Bophana. In *One Evening after the War*, the child born to Srei Poeuv and Savannah is named Bophana. Panh admits that he has inserted her presence in nearly every one of his films. She is like a sister, he admits. One might speculate that Panh has merged Bophana with his older sister, who introduced him to Angkorean art. Panh relied on them both for courage and strength during his darkest times interviewing Duch. Panh has rendered Bophana an icon for Cambodia and a source of solace and strength for him as well as a refuge from his perpetual grief.

S-21: The Khmer Rouge Killing Machine (S-21: La machine de mort Khmère Rouge) (2002)

Although Panh's early films established his credentials as an accomplished artist, it was *S-21: The Khmer Rouge Killing Machine* that brought him to global attention. In it he recuperated the memory of perpetrators and survivors, shattering the silence that had surrounded the Cambodian genocide. With its unsettling reenactments, *S-21* demonstrated how memory and time may collapse to render the past as present and, by doing so, powerfully reveal the truth.

FIGURE 4.3 Panh and Vann discuss scene for *S-21: The Khmer Rouge Killing Machine* © John Vink / MAPSimages

Of the few remaining survivors of S-21 at the time the film was made, two agreed to participate in its making. Vann Nath functions in the film as its inquisitor and the filmmaker's alter ego, "calmly holding up a mirror to each of his ex-captors' acts of inhumanity. . . . He seems the only man in full possession of his path," as one critic noted. The other survivor is Chum Mey, an engineer, who plays a lesser but no less important role in the film's interrogation of the interrogators.

The seeds for the film were sewn when Panh met Vann Nath when he was shooting *Cambodia, beyond War and Peace*. A few years later when Panh was shooting *Bophana, a Cambodian Tragedy*, Vann inadvertently encountered Him Houy,[20] deputy head of S-21's prison security. Panh noticed Vann Nath smoking cigarettes and trembling while he was interviewing Houy. He had not planned for the two men to meet, because he did not think it right to impose on survivors the difficulty of meeting their former guards and torturers. There was tension on the scene, and some younger technicians wanted to punch Houy in the mouth. Vann Nath came out of a state of reverie because he thought he was the only person who could take Houy on. What happened next became the matrix for what would become the film *S-21*.[21] "I saw him rise, take Houy by the shoulder to see one of his canvases," Panh recalled. "He kept asking, 'Is this true or not?' And Houy replied, 'Yes, it's true, you haven't exaggerated.'"

VANN NATH   Come over here. This picture [of a child being torn from his mother's arms by guards in black], it's something that I imagined. I didn't actually witness this scene. But this is how I imagined it when I heard the cries of infants and their mothers. The sounds came from upstairs. Is this picture accurate?

HIM HOUY   Yes, it is....

VANN NATH   ... I'm not forcing you to agree with me.

HIM HOUY   If you tried to force me and if it was not true, I wouldn't say anything. It was like that, otherwise you wouldn't have heard them killing children.

...

VANN NATH   I painted the life of prisoners as human beings who once lived here. That was my only wish. This painting shows a prisoner in a cell. That certainly is accurate. I painted these pictures in 1980, fifteen years ago, after the fall of the Khmer Rouge. The desire to paint them came to me while I was a prisoner. I said to myself that when the country finds peace again, I want people to know how others died here. These are not lies, are they?

HIM HOUY   No, it's the truth.[22]

Like Primo Levi, who feared nobody would believe what had happened to him in Auschwitz, Vann feared no one would believe the nightmare he experienced in S-21. His meeting with Houy gave him the confirmation he needed that what he was painting was true. "Unfortunately," Panh later noted, "we victims also need the words of the perpetrators to tell their side of the story."[23] Panh suggested to Vann that they make a film about S-21, and he agreed.

Panh knew he was ready to begin work on the film after making *The Land of Wandering Souls* with an all-Cambodian crew that he had trained over four years. They had faced challenges and even dangers together and were themselves genocide survivors who knew what had happened during Pol Pot time. Panh believed he had acquired the maturity to take on this project. He claims he had no plan for the film and no funding until he went to the Yamagata International Documentary Festival and received some prize money for *The*

FIGURE 4.4 Vann Nath addresses perpetrators in *S-21: The Khmer Rouge Killing Machine*
© RPanh / droits réservés

Land of Wandering Souls. He used this to buy a camera and microphone. He paid his crew $80 a month, and because they wanted to do the film, they worked for what Panh knew was not enough money. Someone gave him a room; he used some money for a car rental, and he bought the food they ate for breakfast each morning sitting together on the floor. "It's a very, very interesting friendship," he remembers, laughing. "We were all united in our project. We had no money, but we went on like that."[24]

He went to the Documentation Center of Cambodia (DC-Cam), which provided him with the biography of the soldiers assigned to S-21 and their villages. He then traveled around Cambodia to where former S-21 staff lived; he talked with them and tried to persuade them to tell their stories. "I told them that I was not a public prosecutor, and the film was not a courtroom. If they came in peace, they would leave in peace. Talking could help them feel better about themselves. But that said, where the victims and their families are concerned, my work would not cleanse criminals of crimes committed."[25] His mission was to have them compare their eyewitness accounts. It was not easy, and they met with intimidation in some villages where people assembled with machetes to get him to stop. "If you show your fear, you will lose control. Never show them that."[26] It took time to convince eleven people to participate because to bear witness is to take responsibility for one's acts.

At first, Panh let the men tell their stories, full of lies, and then, he presented them with the evidence he had assembled that disproved them; he held them accountable. For example, when Prak Khan denied being a member of the "rabid" group of interrogators—the most violent of the three groups at S-21—Panh told him to start again and tell the truth or he would include the documents that confirmed his actual membership. Panh explained to him what the film would look like, the mise-en-scène and montage, and Khan caved in. He repeated his story, grudgingly telling the truth.[27]

Panh brought the perpetrators together with the survivors at S-21, where they could try to create a kind of collective memory. He felt he needed to shoot in the buildings where memories resided. There were no images of mass executions in the S-21 archive, but there were thousands of portraits of people taken on their arrival at the prison, images that marked them guilty and headed for execution, and numerous documents—registration logs, coerced confessions, execution orders—produced by the killing machine. "If you take away the identity of that human being, if you de-humanize him, it's much easier for the genocide machine to work effectively."[28] Panh wanted to discover what remained human when the prison staff carried out their actions. "What were they thinking of when they raised their hands to kill? . . . What kind of conditioning enabled hatred to triumph and hold back all compassion?" He wanted the film to be a space for dialogue in which each individual accepts his responsibilities in relation to history. He believed that when they were gathered together face-to-face, it would be more difficult for the men to lie. But when they all met, it was a battle. And when the perpetrators tried to lie, Panh shouted a lot.

William Guynn identifies Panh's approach in the film as theatrical and cinematic rather than narrative. The art of staging, framing, and editing acted against the perpetrators' efforts at denial. As director, Panh remained outside the frame—a moral rigor he imposed on himself—keeping his distance from the witnesses and keeping them from deviating from their agreed upon goal of telling the truth. Panh, who was trained as a director of both fiction and documentary films, drew readily from that training when configuring the style needed for each of his films. Guynn writes:

> [Panh] assembles his "cast" of actors, places them in settings, blocks their
> positions, suggests their movements or allows them to improvise, and provides
> them with "props"—all with the intention of evoking a certain kind of
> "performance." The difference from staged theater is that there is no theatrical
> text, no prescribed narrative development, no written dialogue. And the

actors do not play roles in the ordinary sense; they play themselves . . . and the settings are not theatrically constructed spaces but the real space of the Khmer Rouge prison. . . .

. . . His choice of shooting in long takes guarantees a certain freedom for the witnesses. However, he chooses the setting and the nature of the encounters he wants to film, and selects camera angles and shot scales that apply the degree of pressure that the kind of testimony and the witnesses' characters demand.[29]

Much as this is true; Panh also captures life "sur le vif" as the Lumières might say. When Vann Nath and Chum Mey reunited for the first time in ten years, they were in the courtyard of S-21 with Panh, and Chum began to weep. Vann reached out and gently put his arm around his shoulder, softly speaking comforting words to his fellow survivor. When Chum started to cry, Panh "just switched on the camera."

S-21: The Khmer Rouge Killing Machine opens with a prologue that briefly summarizes the history of the Khmer Rouge regime, illustrated with propaganda films produced to document the false reality of Khmer Rouge success. Panh then introduces Him Houy, one of the most notorious staff members

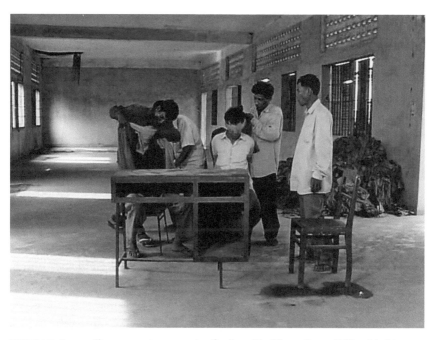

FIGURE 4.5 S-21 staff reenact an interrogation for *S-21: The Khmer Rouge Killing Machine*
© RPanh / droits réservés

at S-21. He is seen planting in his rice field; then he is in his house, seated cross-legged on the floor and holding his infant son. His parents and wife are gathered around him, listening as he complains about his headaches. Panh's decision to begin in the rice fields and with an intimate family scene is deliberate. He introduces the role of the family and community when perpetrators struggle to deal with acts they committed during Pol Pot time. Houy was the only staff member whose family was included in the film because his family knew what he had done. Houy's mother urges her son to find some kind of exorcism to banish his nightmares. Looking straight into the camera, she says she thinks it does not matter if it were one hundred or two thousand people he killed, because he killed. She says she feels pity for the dead and pity for her son. Houy then offers the proverbial excuse that he was afraid of dying himself and had to obey orders; he had no free will. Houy's flat affect—what Peter Maguire once described as his feral innocence and hard eyes, which were not so much mean as lifeless[30]—was mirrored in the faces of other perpetrators in the film. Like Houy, they performed the gestures of their work at S-21—typing confessions, patrolling the corridors, peering into individual cells where high-level prisoners were kept, or slitting the throats of prisoners at night in the killing field.[31]

The film acknowledges that many of the perpetrators were teenaged recruits abducted from their families and deprived of human contact, trained first to raise pigs, then kill the enemy. "I had power over the enemy—I never thought of his life," one guard says in a monotone. The film quickly raises the difficult question of whether they too were victims. Vann Nath asks them, "If you are victims, then what are we?" The film scholar Dominick LaCapra, in writing about the Holocaust, suggests that perpetrators can also be traumatized by their deeds, but this does not entail thinking of them as victims.[32] "For Nath, the effort required in making the film was painful and violent, physically and psychologically, before each meeting and even afterwards," Panh recalls. "His presence, facing his torturers, made it possible to specify who was the victim, who was responsible, who executed the orders. . . . The former jailors could not lie in front of Nath. Even when silent he acted as a 'developer,' revealing the secrets of their souls."[33]

Panh demanded the perpetrators speak the truth, and until they did, he would reshoot their scenes until they finally admitted what they had done. This struggle remained on the cutting room floor, but viewers may sense the perpetrators' resignation after a battle over truth was finally won by Panh. There is nothing ethically wrong about repeating shots, as some have claimed. For Panh, "in documentary, a second take is also a unique take."[34] And so the film includes Prak Khan confessing his brutal treatment of women and reading aloud the methods he used from a prison torture manual. Vann Nath reads about the exsanguination of prisoners whose breathing sounded like "crickets" before they died. Staff unroll on the floor a large panoramic photograph of Choeung Ek, the killings fields where S-21 prisoners were taken for execution and burial. This image leaves a long-lasting impression of the horror awaiting prisoners who were told by Him Houy, as he ushered them into a wooden shack to await their deaths, "Don't be afraid, you are going to your new home."

One of the most effective forms of witnessing in the film is visual and delivered in the large-scale canvases painted by Vann Nath and commissioned by the Vietnamese for S-21. For a genocide without proscription against images, there is no need for the *bilderverbot* that has long been the norm for representations of the Nazi genocide. Not every culture rejects visible evidence; not all cultures value the spoken word above all other means of witnessing. Vann Nath survived because of his ability to paint portraits of Pol Pot. His images after he was freed documented the brutality inflicted on innocent people—a baby ripped from a mother's arms or a line of prisoners shackled, blindfolded, and led at night into the prison. Nath's canvases represented his adaptive action, his way of telling a story that transformed his feelings of helplessness into witnessing.

Midway through the film, one of the guards, Khieu Ches, a.k.a. "Poeuv," who began working as a guard at the age of twelve or thirteen, slips out of the present into the past. He embodies the boy he once was, *as he still is in memory*, a figure of terror and power and abuse, shackling and unshackling inmates, beating and humiliating them. In this electrifying scene, reenactment in the documentary takes on new significance and legitimacy.

When Panh met Poeuv in his native village, he was eager to explain what he had done at S-21 but could not find the words. All he was able to speak were Khmer Rouge slogans. Panh brought him a map of the prison, and Poeuv pointed out where he had worked and showed how he closed the door of the room he guarded. Looking at the rushes later, Panh realized that his gestures were prolonging his words. Panh realized gestures would enable him to recall his memories in precise order, finding words to narrate the specific routine he executed every day, again and again, when beating and terrorizing prisoners. "His gestures, the memory of his body, came flooding back," Panh observed, "because someone trained him to do this. And the memory of the body never lies."[35]

"The idea of putting victims and executioners together is very seductive, but it's also very tricky," Panh has said. "You don't want to be a voyeur. You

FIGURE 4.6 Poeuv relives his daily routine in *S-21: The Khmer Rouge Killing Machine*
© RPanh / droits réservés

have to develop a kind of ethic of the image."[36] How Panh shot this critical scene with Poeuv illustrates what he means by an "ethic of the image." Panh took Poeuv to the prison at night. He lit the corridor as it would have been illuminated with fluorescent lighting, and he played for him revolutionary music that Poeuv would have listened to at the time. Panh guided the cinematographer Prum Mésar to follow Poeuv at arm's length—Panh's ideal distance for shooting—but when Poeuv came to the threshold about to step into the classroom to rebuke revenants shackled to the floor, Panh halted Mésar, intuitively realizing that to follow Poeuv into the room would have made them complicit in his acts. The camera stayed outside, surveying Poeuv's actions in a sweeping motion as he came and went in the classroom, threatening prisoners and addressing them individually. It is an eerie and heart-stopping moment as Poeuv crosses that threshold and steps into his past.

Once Poeuv finished shooting that scene, he returned to his village and fell ill with a very high fever for several days, according to Panh. His reenactment had triggered a healing crisis from which he eventually recovered. Paul Ricoeur once observed that "a patient does not access his repressed memories by himself; he needs something like the authorization of another person in order to remember."[37] Panh served that role for Poeuv.

Some viewers are puzzled by what they see in that scene, and some critics strongly object to it: "While the re-enactment is a useful window into the past, it encourages an *ill-informed judgment* against this man based on how he acts today rather than what he did then. . . . It's hard to tell whether the behavior on display is natural or a response to the off-screen prompting from the director."[38] Poeuv's behavior clearly conforms to traumatic memory. There is nothing new about this: the origins of modern psychiatry at the end of the nineteenth century arose from the study of consciousness and the disruptive impact of traumatic experiences. Jean Martin Charcot and Pierre Janet in France and William James in the United States devoted enormous attention to how the mind processes memories, noting why certain memories become obstacles that keep people from going on with their lives. Janet believed that lack of proper integration of intense, emotionally arousing experiences into the memory system results in dissociation and the formation of traumatic memory. Unfortunately, the legacy of Janet was crowded out by psychoanalysis, with its emphasis on the repression of unacceptable desires, until the 1970s when Janet's ideas were revived to account for the traumatic memories of Vietnam War veterans. Janet's ideas are particularly helpful when considering how the dissociation of traumatic memories may render them virtually inaccessible until they can be reenacted and translated for linguistic retrieval.

The psychiatrist and trauma researcher Bessel van der Kolk differentiates between "traumatic memory" and ordinary or "narrative memory." Narrative memory takes only a few minutes to recount and is an aspect of ordinary life integrated with other experiences. Traumatic memory takes too long—in fact it demands reenactment for its recall. Traumatic memories may return as physical sensations, horrific images or nightmares, behavioral reenactments, or a combination of these. When seen not merely on an individual basis but as a pattern of dealing with a traumatic past, one can see how unacknowledged subconscious memories can take control of one's behavior.[39] For example, Panh tells of a Cambodian survivor of Pol Pot living in France who was a model mother until she cut off her son's head just as her father had been decapitated before her by the Khmer Rouge. "If you can't grieve, the violence continues," he notes.[40] Janet would agree: if a person does not remember, he is likely to "act out"—that is, to repeat the trauma. Repeating is the traumatized person's way of remembering.[41]

Some scholars object to the emphasis placed on "healing" trauma following the Western psychological model.[42] Boreth Ly, a Cambodian genocide survivor and visual culture scholar, argues for cultural understanding that focuses on baksbat[43]—"broken body" or "broken courage," a permanent break that cannot be repaired. Memories of traumatic events are evoked by body language, images, words, sounds, and silence. For Cambodians, "trauma is first and foremost inscribed on the body, and it is the broken body that causes mental breakdown."[44] Ly believes that trauma for Cambodians needs to be understood in an interconnected, communal, collective, and holistic way.[45] But he also endorses Susan Brison's analysis of trauma, memory, and the importance of narration, which leads us back to the ideas of Janet: "Memories of traumatic events can be themselves traumatic: uncontrollable, intrusive, not chosen—as flashbacks to the events themselves. In contrast, narrating memories to others (who are strong enough and empathetic enough to be able to listen) empowers survivors to gain more control over the traces left by trauma: Narrative memory is not passively endured; rather, it is an act on the part of the narrator, a speech act that defuses traumatic memory, giving shape and temporal order to the events recalled, establishing more control over their recalling; and helping the survivor to remake a self."[46] Panh, no fan of psychotherapy, nevertheless has supported the work of the psychiatrist Richard Rechtman, who developed culturally sensitive therapy for Cambodian genocide survivors exiled in France.[47] It is significant that *S-21* begins with a perpetrator searching for relief from the headaches that keep him awake. Houy and his family want him to be released from his suffering over the deaths he has caused. Panh's films contain many survivors who are struggling with emotional scars, including, perhaps, the executioner Houy. Mediums, monks, medications—these are only some of the remedies they turn to for help. *Rice People*, *The Burnt Theater*, *Que la barque se brise, que la jonque s'entrouvre*, *The Missing Picture*, and *Graves without a Name* all revolve around individuals—including Panh himself—who are searching to find peace for the dead and for themselves. Panh's personal experience of baksbat, which is discussed briefly here and in chapter 7, illustrates the importance of connecting Cambodian cultural concepts with Western psychological theories to serve the needs of survivors.

S-21: The Khmer Rouge Killing Machine does not seek vengeance but rather asks what future there is for a country that has denied its past. When Panh released it in 2003, he told journalists that he was convinced his country could not recover its identity unless it put the past on trial, but he doubted it would happen. But after years of denying, ignoring, or selectively forgetting this history,[48] Cambodia convened a UN-sponsored special tribunal to investigate crimes against humanity. Khieu Samphan, successor to Pol Pot and the intellectual head of the Khmer Rouge, had consistently denied responsibility for any crimes,[49] but in 2003, he gave an interview to the Associated Press admitting there was no doubt left that his regime had committed genocide. He insisted he never ordered any killings but admitted he learned about them from Rithy Panh's film.[50] *S-21: The Khmer Rouge Killing Machine* made it impossible for him to further deny this had happened.[51] "He lies! He knew!" was Panh's angry response. There were many ways that nearly two million people were executed, such as starvation and overwork. It was Angkar that demanded villagers impose inhuman living conditions on the "new" people that led to their deaths.

Panh's film was not admitted in evidence at Duch's trial, but the Extraordinary Chambers of the Courts of Cambodia (ECCC) brought Duch to S-21 during the pretrial stage to meet with other survivors and members of the court. Some believe this unprecedented decision was inspired by Panh's film. The ECCC, however flawed, has enabled Cambodia to begin to confront its silence about the past and pay a debt owed to the dead and obligations to their children. Panh's perspective has remained consistent and clear: "We shan't be able to get rid of this . . . culture of violence, cast out the monster that is fear, and put behind us the collective guilt we feel as survivors unless we manage to understand our history."[52] Hun Sen had urged Cambodia to "dig a hole and bury the past," but Rithy Panh knew that testifying about the past was what was really needed. Vann Nath used paintings to witness what he experienced, Bophana embraced an epic character to resist Khmer Rouge values and defend her identity, and Panh used cinema to provoke a much-needed national discussion about the Khmer Rouge genocide. Panh believes that Cambodians must come to terms with their collective history.

S-21 ends with a powerful image, the last shot Panh made after years of preparing this film. It calls to mind something the poet René Char wrote: "An image when it has transcended being and time shimmers with eternity."[53] Panh set his camera down on the floor of the large classroom that once housed prisoners awaiting torture and death. Now vacant, only dust remained in small piles scattered in the corners of the room. He turned on the camera. The low camera angle allowed for a dramatic image as a gust of wind raised an eddy of dust like ashes of the dead. It is the quintessential embodiment of the absent presence of Cambodia's dead. This haunting image addresses the future much as the final lines of Jean Cayrol's narration at the conclusion of *Night and Fog* addresses generations to come. Documentaries like *S-21* make

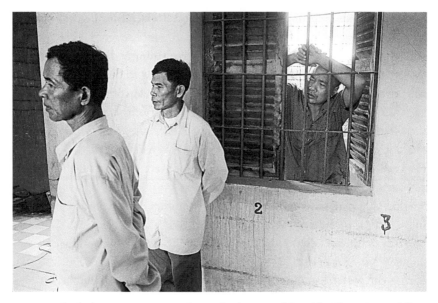

FIGURE 4.7 Panh observes perpetrators during the shooting of *S-21: The Khmer Rouge Killing Machine* © John Vink / MAPSimages

palpable why memory—particularly traumatic memory—is essential to what makes us moral beings.

Duch, Master of the Forges of Hell (Duch, Le maître des forges de l'enfer) (2012)

A mountain never has two tigers.
—Traditional Cambodian saying

Hannah Arendt theorized that the greatest evils of history were committed not by fanatics or sociopaths but by individuals who unthinkingly accepted the premises of a state where their actions, however heinous and degrading, were normalized. Arendt's ideas about the "banality of evil" were inspired by her observations at the trial of Adolf Eichmann, who was one of the major organizers of the Holocaust, responsible for the mass deportation of the Jewish people to extermination camps. She proposed that Eichmann's actions were neither monstrous nor sadistic. They arose not out of a malevolent will to do evil but were the acts of a bureaucrat who lacked thought and judgment.[54] Had Arendt lived to witness Pol Pot's regime in Cambodia, she would have been confronted with another example of a totalitarian state that dominated and terrorized individuals from within, where genocide was central to the control of the human person and the very basis of the regime. She would have encountered new trials designed to educate the masses about genocide. And she would have had to ponder once more the moral problem of evil.

Like Hannah Arendt, Rithy Panh studied a mass murderer during his trial, Kaing Guek Eav, better known as Duch, director of S-21 prison.[55] He was the first person tried for crimes against humanity by the special UN-Cambodian tribunal, the Extraordinary Chambers of the Courts of Cambodia (ECCC) for the Prosecution of Crimes Committed during the Period of Democratic Kampuchea. Panh politely dismissed Arendt's ideas about the "banality of evil":

> I don't deny that some executioners and torturers can be ordinary people. . . . But I believe in the uniqueness of the individual. I'm interested in his past, in his emotional, familial, intellectual trajectory, and in the society in which he developed. And so Duch conceived torture methods, refined them, taught them. He annotated files. Recruited torturers. Trained his teams. Spurred them on. . . . He was continually in control of his actions. . . . Duch isn't a monster or a fascinating torturer. Duch isn't an ordinary criminal. He's a *thinking man*. He's one of the people responsible for the extermination.[56]

Duch was more than a functionary, and Panh set out to situate his actions within the context of personal and collective history. In so doing, Panh revealed "the banality and hypocrisy beneath the surface of Duch's performed intellectualism."[57]

It took a quarter century after the Pol Pot regime was ousted for its leaders to answer for their crimes. It was only after the Khmer Rouge ceased to pose a political or military threat that the United Nations, in 1997, condemned their crimes. In 2001 a law was passed to set up a special court to judge the Khmer Rouge, and in 2009 the joint UN-Cambodian court (the ECCC) began to examine men and women responsible for crimes against humanity. Pol Pot, who belonged within the ranks of Hitler, Stalin, Milošević, and leaders responsible for Latin America's "disappeared," should have been tried by that court, but he died before it began. Comrade Duch, director of S-21, was the first to be charged with crimes against humanity in 2007.

There were many reasons why it took so long for an international court to be convened.[58] Suffice to say that major opposition to a tribunal came from the ruling government, led by Prime Minister Hun Sen, a former Khmer

Rouge soldier who defected to the Vietnamese in 1977.[59] Most people doubted that a court, if one were convened, would be able to deliver justice to survivors.[60] But the criminal cases heard by the ECCC made headline news, acknowledging that atrocities in Cambodia were committed, denied, forgotten, and dismissed by leaders eager to minimize their own role by redirecting attention to the rebuilding of Cambodian society after decades of colonialism, war, poverty, and human devastation. Panh attended nearly every session of Duch's trial, sitting always in the same front row seat in the auditorium so that he could observe Duch before the court and the civil parties.

Duch was assigned two lawyers, one French, one Cambodian. He was guided by his French lawyer François Roux, who counseled him to admit his guilt, express remorse, and apologize for the crimes he had committed while defending himself as a prisoner of Khmer Rouge ideology. He was Duch's best chance. "Roux provided the trial with high standards, credibility, dignity, and competence but became its biggest loser," according to Thierry Cruvellier, a consultant to the International Center for Transitional Justice. During the trial, Duch took over the court and imposed his version of history, but by the end, prosecution lawyers had succeeded in undermining him. Then, in a stunning upset, Duch turned to his Cambodian lawyer, Kar Savuth, and reversed his position, retracting his guilty plea and requesting an acquittal. Savuth claimed Duch was a scapegoat and not one of the fourteen Khmer Rouge leaders, effectively denouncing the legitimacy of the court and demanding all charges against him be dropped. Two years of Roux's painstaking work was overturned by Duch's last-minute betrayal. Six months of Duch's pleas for forgiveness from the civil parties participating in the trial proved to be mere showmanship. The judge found the two defense lawyers' conflicting requests—to mitigate his sentence versus to acquit him—incoherent. Duch was found guilty of crimes against humanity and effectively sentenced to nineteen additional years of imprisonment in 2010. This lenient sentence provoked outrage and an outcry over interference with and corruption of the court. The sentence was appealed, and in 2012, it was overturned. Duch was given the maximum sentence, life imprisonment. He died in prison of lung cancer in 2020.

Interviewing the Devil

Duch was conspicuously absent in Panh's film *S-21: The Khmer Rouge Killing Machine*. All Panh's requests for permission to interview him for that film while he was in custody were turned down by the ECCC. He had not planned to make a film about Duch, but when his request was suddenly approved by the court, he jumped at the chance. He wanted to understand what had made Duch become a mass murder and hoped to persuade him to "take a step on the road to humanity."[61]

The ECCC allowed four teams of filmmakers permission to cover the trials, providing they agreed not to release their films until after a verdict was rendered. Panh was the only Cambodian selected. He wanted to understand how the once powerful man explained his actions and what his rationale had been for acts now labeled crimes against humanity. He wanted to give him the chance to explain, in detail, the death process of which he was the organizer in chief. Panh wanted Duch to respond to his film *S-21*, which Duch had seen. They signed a written contract before filming began. Duch could protest the result of the film, which Panh would listen to, but Panh had no obligation to follow it up. "We had to agree morally and intellectually on the one who would decide if there was a disagreement, and we knew we disagreed. I told him who I was—a victim of genocide—and that we were not on the same side." If he had refused these conditions, Panh said he would have made another film.[62]

Panh interviewed Duch for over three hundred hours shot over two years. He came to realize he was face-to-face with someone performing for the camera, rehearsing his defense for the trial that would decide his future as subsequent moments in that trial made abundantly clear. During the shooting, Panh came close to a breaking point, suffering from depression and near mental collapse after prolonged exposure to the machinations of the master interrogator. What helped him endure was writing about his childhood memories, which came flooding back during the ordeal of interrogating Duch. Panh realized that words were essential if he was to find his way out of the darkness that his meetings with Duch subjected him to.[63]

Panh regained ground when he realized that Duch "doesn't know cinema. He doesn't believe in the play of repetitions, of intersections, of echoes. He doesn't know that montage is a politics and a morality unto itself. And in time there's only one truth."[64] Panh used cinematic strategies to uncover the truth about this soft-spoken, avuncular, arrogant, and complacent master of dehumanization and death. He "filmed his oversights and his lies, his hands, wandering over the photographs. His forceful, sudden respiration, as if the exaltation of former days were still there, in his lungs."[65] In the end, Panh had the last word, and the result was *Duch, Master of the Forges of Hell*.

Performing Truth

When it comes to judging the truth of a character in a documentary, the theory that seems most relevant comes from cinema verité. Jean Rouch and Edgar Morin famously demonstrated in their classic film *Chronicle of a Summer (Chronique d'un Été*, 1960) that we are never more authentically ourselves than when we are performing for the camera. Rouch and Morin cast their subjects as actors, deliberately provoked them, reminded them of the film being made, and staged their encounters with each other to draw out their thoughts and feelings for the camera. Panh's approach to filmmaking reveals traces of cinema verité influences,[66] as well as the influence of Holocaust film innovators like Alain Resnais, Marcel Ophüls, and Claude Lanzmann. Some also see in his work the impact of changes in French documentary filmmaking in the mid-1980s. Panh believed that the viewer could recognize that truth can be revealed even—and possibly best—when someone is deliberately constructing it for the camera.

Unlike Claude Lanzmann, who rejected the inclusion of archival footage of the Holocaust so as not to revictimize the victims, Panh used all that was available to pursue his goal. Existing newsreel footage, propaganda films, mugshots, victim "testimonies," staff confessions, paintings, and other internal documents from the Khmer Rouge archival record were deployed strategically and effectively in all his S-21 films but never more critically than in his duel with Duch. He used evidence to provoke Duch's memories, to serve as a counterargument to his lies and evasions, and often to put Duch "in the frame" with his victims, shooting him touching their photographic images, pointing to his signature on a bureaucratic form authorizing an execution, or watching his staff on a laptop accuse him of conducting torture sessions and attending executions, which he contemptuously denied. Even more than serving as rebuttal, the evidence Panh assembled ultimately destabilized Duch's control over Panh, who, as a survivor himself, felt his vulnerability increase during the marathon sessions he held with Duch. And though Duch claimed he did not recognize Bophana, by the end of filming, he admitted he knew everything about her.

Space and Inner Space

The film begins and ends in the prison cell where Duch has been waiting for his ECCC case to be heard. At the start, he is preparing a cup of tea with the voice of Pol Pot delivering a famous speech heard in the background. At the

FIGURE 4.8 Duch displays photo of S-21 prisoner in *Duch, Master of the Forges of Hell*
© RPanh / droits réservés

end, Duch is alone in his cell, performing calisthenics and reading the Bible. With these bookended shots, Panh captures the arc of Duch's life, from communist ideologue and bureaucrat to evangelical Christian supplicant. Compared with S-21's crude cells of brick or rough-hewn wood, Duch's bright and modern cell with a view and three square meals a day is luxurious. But Panh is less concerned with physical space than the inner space of Duch's mind and memories; he is revealed to be a perplexing yet intelligent man, a schoolmaster and mathematician proud both of his penmanship and the efficient way he ran a killing machine. He possesses an incredible memory and a fearsome laugh. In this cell, everything seems clean and proper, including the redoubtable Duch.

To be a prisoner at S-21 was to be guilty: "confessions" extracted through torture fed escalating paranoia. The files kept on each prisoner were often lengthy and suitable as evidence in a criminal trial, only there was never any trial because there was no system of justice in Democratic Kampuchea. No one but Angkar read the "confessions" people were forced to make that had as their real goal not "information" but the denunciation of more people accused of crimes against the state. This conformed to the genre of Stalinist self-criticism in which the deviant person rewrote his or her life story from a "correct" class position, "to flush out their imperialistic habits."[67] This form of reeducation did not necessarily result in death; but in Cambodia, death, not reeducation and reintegration into society, was the only outcome. There is a yawning chasm between Duch and the thousands of prisoners he once "solved," one of the many Khmer Rouge euphemisms for killing. Roughly thirty years later, Duch was accorded the dignity and justice he denied his prisoners. And thanks to his neglect—or possibly his pride in not wanting to destroy the meticulous records he kept at S-21—thousands of records remained to convict him. They were used by the prosecution and the defense lawyers. And they were used by Panh to relentlessly challenge him.

Panh shot in two rooms at the ECCC: One was a bare room—it had a white wall, a table, and a chair where Duch sat opposite Panh, who remained off camera throughout. The other was an antechamber to the court. Panh preferred the former room. Prum Mésar, his long-standing cinematographer, used a stationary camera on a tripod, making wide shots for cutting in the assembly, and Panh wielded a handheld camera to frame Duch in close-ups. As Panh recorded Duch, his words took center stage. "I question Duch tirelessly," Panh writes in *The Elimination*. "Although he looks at the tribunal prosecutors, judges, and attorneys in the eye—he has a monitor in front of him and knows when he is being filmed—he never gazes into my camera. Or hardly ever. Is he afraid it will see inside him?" Panh observes sarcastically that "Duch talks to heaven, which in this case is a white ceiling. He explains his position to me. He makes phrases. I catch him lying. I offer precise information. He hesitates. When in a difficult situation, Duch rubs his face with his damaged hand. He breathes loudly. He massages his forehead and his eyelids, and then he examines the neon lighting."[68] Duch tended to focus on an indeterminate spot up to his left, what Panh called his "blind spot," which Panh believed helped him to concentrate and stay in control.[69]

At the start of the film, Panh presented Duch with fifty large cards covered with different Khmer Rouge slogans to choose from to read aloud. "Killing an innocent prisoner by mistake is better than leaving an enemy alive." "The language of the slogans is beautiful, rhymed, rhythmic. Suddenly there is no need to think. It is a language that is forged to make you obey," Panh recalls. "It defines the ideological paths to follow. And the things to destroy ... Just like the expression 'kamtèch,' which means to reduce to dust, destroy and erase all traces of human life."[70]

Duch introduces himself by saying he was head of the state's security forces, Santebal.[71] He explains that Democratic Kampuchea had nearly two hundred prisons,[72] which were responsible for far more deaths than S-21, but S-21 was special: it was a secret prison where top figures in the government were "smashed" as traitors. He reported directly to Son Sen, minister of defense, who oversaw the operations of all prisons, and later to Nuon Chea, Brother Number Two. He is eager to point up the chain of command to Son Sen's ultimate responsibility for the operation of prisons. He does not deny his role enforcing work discipline at S-21, training staff in torture methods, making numerous decisions regarding the types of torture used to extract confessions, or designating who would die and when. In fact, he seems to take pride in his accomplishments. Nevertheless, Duch claims he is innocent because he asserts that he was held hostage by Khmer Rouge ideology. He wants us to believe he is not responsible for what happened, that it is the leadership above him who should be held accountable. Near the end of the film, Panh films him in his cell reading the Holocaust survivor Stéphane Hessel's poetry, and one wonders if he has also read Hannah Arendt's *Eichmann in Jerusalem* while preparing for his trial.[73]

Duch identifies himself as "a pure instrument of the party" and a Chinese Cambodian, hence an outlier to Pol Pot's inner circle. He claims that he was doing a job in the party's interest to survive and that he feared betrayal and being killed himself. He casually quotes from his intellectual sources, such Sun Tze, Balzac, and Mao. He takes pride in having perfected interrogation methods and discouraged excessive use of torture, which only occurred when staff took it upon themselves to be overzealous, he assures us. He expresses regret at the savage rape of his former schoolteacher, whom he explained he could not help because it would have shown favoritism and jeopardized him within the hierarchy. He describes the codes he devised to differentiate the stage a prisoner had arrived at on their inevitable path to execution, boasting about his use of colored inks. He is a stoic, not a sadist, he insists.

He quotes for Panh and the camera a stanza from a favorite poem by Alfred de Vigny,[74] "The Hour of the Wolf." He claims its stoic philosophy helped him during his judicial ordeal:

To groan, to weep, to pray are cowardly alike.
Perform with energy your long and heavy task
Upon the path that fate has chosen for you.
Then afterward, like me, suffer and die in silence.

Duch claims stoic philosophy—a philosophy of personal ethics informed by logic—is what governed his life. Françoise Sironi,[75] one of two court-appointed psychologists who conducted assessments of him, accepted this.[76] But the film scholar Vicente Sánchez-Biosca objects to Duch's appropriation of stoicism and disputes Sironi's view. For him, Duch represents "the most cynical perversion of the moral principles which are the basis of stoicism seen as a school of philosophy."[77]

Duch shuts out all personal feelings that did not match the communist ideal, relying on denial, compartmentalization, and rationalization as his major coping strategies. His diagnosis, according to Sironi and the Cambodian psychiatrist Chimm Soetheara, was an inability to feel emotions and articulate them (alexithymia) and a psychological lack of identification with or vicarious experience of the feelings, thoughts, or attitudes of another (disempathy).[78] Duch tried to persuade Panh that he had abandoned his Marxist views when he became an evangelical Christian, an aid worker, and a schoolteacher once again. But Panh carefully demonstrates through Duch's body and his gestures—his changes in vocal tone, his sharp intake of breath when recounting stories of his Khmer Rouge past, and his clenched fist salute when speaking about taking his communist oath—that he was still faithful to the ideology that placed him in charge of a killing machine.

Duch told Sironi that he converted to Christianity in 1996, not for religious reasons but "because the Christians were the winners over communism at that time." (Pastor Lapel, the genocide survivor who baptized Duch, testified to the sincerity of Duch's belief in the Lord at his trial. He was apparently unaware of the more pragmatic reasons for his changing loyalties.) Duch's case was distinguished from all the other cases pending before the ECCC because he was the only one to express remorse for what he did. But Duch felt no guilt because he could not accept individual responsibility for his acts, only collective responsibility. He tried to use his religious conversion as one of the lynchpins for his defense but failed to answer the question Arendt put to Eichmann: What happened to your conscience? Duch had no idea what this meant. If the goal of an international trial like this before the ECCC was to rehumanize perpetrators as well as their victims, Duch was far from realizing that dream.

When shooting Duch, Panh used only two kinds of shots: head-on and from a slight angle.[79] Panh frequently cuts away from extended close-ups and medium shots of Duch to the S-21 identity photos—Hout Bophana is conspicuously present in these shots—and to the video testimonies he had recorded there with Duch's staff. One day Duch yelled at Panh, demanding to know why he kept putting these photos of dead people in front of him. "People are dead, but they are listening to you," Panh responded. Duch soon

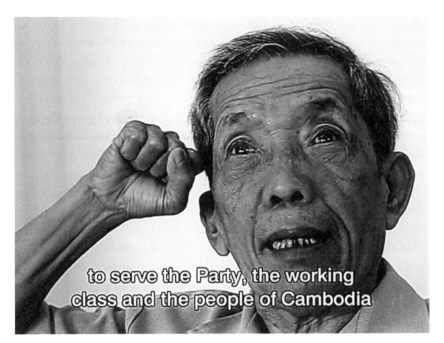

FIGURE 4.9 Duch recites Khmer Rouge oath in *Duch, Master of the Forges of Hell* © RPanh / droits réservés

after asked Panh if he could come with his Bible to their sessions, and there-after, he placed it on the table, a defense against the reproach of the dead.

On seeing photos from S-21 prison, Susan Sontag in *Regarding the Pain of Others* compared them to Titian's *The Flaying of Marsyas*, "where Apollo's knife is eternally about to descend—forever looking at death, forever about to be murdered, forever wronged. And the viewer is in the same position as the lackey behind the camera; the experience is sickening."[80] Is this why Duch became testy with Panh, irritated by being confronted by all the photos Panh had assembled for him? It was not just that the dead were present listening to him, as Panh told him, it was because the images were a reminder of what was about to happen to the prisoners at Duch's command and sickening even for him to contemplate.

Panh includes excerpts from propaganda films made by the Khmer Rouge as well as evidence he gathered during the shooting of *S-21*. Presenting such evidence to Duch was Panh's way of telling him: "Watch out. I know more than you think. Don't lie to me."[81] Often Panh focuses on Duch's face while he is viewing testimonies on a laptop computer, then cuts to a full-screen image of the testimony, and then back again to Duch, observing his often-dismissive facial responses. Over time, the viewer begins to experience a peculiar intimacy with Duch, who mistakenly believes he is creating a persona that will elicit our compassion and trust, one he can use effectively in court. But Panh undercuts Duch with what Sánchez-Biosca terms his "lethal scenography."[82] One watches for his lies, condescension, contempt, and flares of temper. Panh's montage, often off kilter, cuts shots a shade too quickly, keeping viewers off balance, unable to settle into a relationship with Duch as designed by him. The images are so fleeting that they often seem to fly off the screen; it is like ripping a Band-Aid from a wound. Panh's physically assertive editing style checks Duch's efforts at inspiring belief in his "remorse." For Panh, "thanks to cinema, the truth comes out—montage versus mendacity."[83]

Panh believes Duch needed to talk to him. To win him over. And to rehearse his performance for the court. "He's no monster. . . . He's a man who searches out and seizes upon the weaknesses of others. A man who stalks his humanity. A disturbing man. I don't remember that he ever left me without a laugh or a smile."[84] Henri Bergson, in analyzing the comic, noted that laughter conveys indifference, a detachment from sensibility and emotion, which aptly fits Duch's calculated use of it. He used it to buy time when considering his answers to difficult questions or when he hoped it would ingratiate himself with "Mr. Rithy." His laughter had a social meaning, which is why it haunted both S-21 staff members and prisoners alike. When he felt trapped by Panh, he resorted to what Panh termed full-throated laughter. At one point the court admonished him not to laugh because his explosive outbursts were "inappropriate." They did not understand what Panh had grasped: Duch's laughter was a "tell" that allowed him to appear to lose control over his body in order to regain it over his opponent; it was one of the most striking ways he revealed his mastery of interrogation tactics.

Panh countered with his own mastery of cinema—for example, by strategically adding propaganda clips and voices singing the Khmer version of "The Internationale"—which communicated Duch's unceasing fidelity to Khmer Rouge ideology despite his claims to be a changed man. Using image, sound, montage, and an array of witnesses living and dead, Panh mounted his own case against Duch.

Near the end of the film, back in his cell, Duch gives himself the Communion host. He says rhetorically in the only voice-over in the film: "How did I lose myself in the Marxist proletarian dictatorship? How could I go against my people and consider them my enemy? . . . When I am forgiven, I

FIGURE 4.10 Duch's menacing laugh in *Duch, Master of the Forges of Hell* © RPanh / droits réservés

will prostrate myself to give thanks. If I'm not forgiven, that will be that until the end of my days." Duch claimed his conversion to Christianity was a major turning point in his life following the death of his wife, not just an expedient shift of allegiance. Cynics viewed his religious conversion as a way to avoid the karmic debts he incurred for all his evil deeds, as if the devil had not only found forgiveness in this life but had beaten the laws of karma in the next. The court-appointed psychiatrists acknowledged that he had changed his group affiliation to one that allowed for the individual. According to Sironi, in communism, the individual disappears, but in Christianity, the individual exists in union with God.[85] Apparently Jesus seemed a better choice for Duch than Son Sen, Nuon Chea, or Pol Pot.[86]

Duch, Master of the Forges of Hell is a film about ideas and their perversions, about words and their power to blind us to amorality. There is nothing to entertain or distract us, no narrative story with suspense, rising action, or satisfying resolution; no alternate universe in which to escape; no clever visual elements to divert us from the subject at hand. The reviewer who likened Panh's film to Errol Morris's *The Fog of War: Eleven Lessons from the Life of Robert S. McNamara* was both right and wrong. Each artist interrogates men whose actions altered the course of history and whose conscience should have suffered for their acts. But Panh's design is unlike Morris's with its dazzling visual ambush of McNamara with Interrotron and lipstick cameras deployed like so many flies around a tough but wounded prey. Morris dramatically circles McNamara, whereas Panh holds Duch at his ideal distance, arm's length, exerting restraint in calling attention to his key statements, relevant inconsistencies, and the facial "tells" and physical gestures that reveal Duch's attitude toward his victims. Panh creates the circumstance for viewers to see Duch "in the frame" with his victims and perpetrators, his hands touching their images, his signature on their testimonies. Panh propels us to see Duch for who he was and, in so doing, gives Duch enough rope to hang himself.

Panh ends with a black-and-white archival film clip of Khmer Rouge propaganda, an emblematic and fleeting single pan of hundreds of Cambodian laborers hurrying along a bridge, a memory fragment accompanied by one of Marc Marder's simple string laments. He follows this with text on a black screen dedicating the film to his father "for his integrity, courage and dignity." Finally he offers these lines from a poem by René Char, who was among many things a French Resistance fighter in World War II: "Don't bow your head, except to love / If you die, still you love." More stoic than Duch, Panh employs these simple but elegant elements juxtaposed at the conclusion of the film to acknowledge numberless deaths and to speak about his father and, by extension, all the innocents who died. Remarkably, he leaves viewers at the very end thinking about love, not hatred and revenge. This assertion of Buddhist values is both an affront to Khmer Rouge ideology and Panh's final point scored against Duch, his outmaneuvered adversary.

Panh simultaneously released *Duch, Master of the Forges of Hell* and his memoir *The Elimination* in France on February 3, 2013, the day the ECCC delivered a life sentence to Duch. Panh had never planned to make another film about S-21, but when the possibility of a trial became a reality, Panh was afraid the Khmer Rouge would use the tribunal as a platform for its own revisionism. He felt it was important to address Duch, the first to be tried by the ECCC, because he had not had his say in the earlier film. Panh wanted to confront him, not about the question of good and evil but to understand how the killing mechanism worked.[87] Duch's trial proved to be, in Panh's view, "a trial without images for a genocide without images."[88] For many, viewing *Duch, Master of the Forges of Hell* would be the closest one could come to seeing Comrade Duch for who he was and what he had done and not as he had reinvented himself for the court.

Writing *The Elimination* proved to be more than Panh's therapeutic method of dealing with his near breakdown after prolonged exposure to Duch's lies, manipulation, and rhetorical traps. As the scholars Y-Dang Troeung and Madeleine Thien argue, *The Elimination* served as an important counternarrative to the ECCC, staging an alternative historical investigation of Cambodia's past beyond the limits of the tribunal's boundaries.[89] *The Elimination* was also one of the first memoirs to question the "intellectuals of the West" who supported the Western Marxist influence on Khmer Rouge ideology while denying the genocide inflicted by the Khmer Rouge on Cambodia.

The Poisonous Tree[90]

Duch, Master of the Forges of Hell has not attracted mass audiences and has had limited screenings beyond Cambodia and France. It demands the audience's full attention, which today is not a given even in a darkened movie theater. It does not fulfill the expectations of modern audiences looking for shock and awe in a documentary about genocide. It demands that we think.[91] One does not need to be a film specialist to understand the effect of the film. The psychiatrist and anthropologist Richard Rechtman wrote, "Never has a documentary film, the essence of which is based on a monologue, made us feel death so closely. And it is precisely at the moment when the spectator feels himself irremediably immersed in the world of the dead, when he finally understands, in order to experience it intimately, how the executioners proceed, that Rithy Panh frees us" from the heroization of cruelty into which Duch wants to lead viewers. "Slowly, the camera [in *Duch*] takes the field. The man who until then occupied the whole frame, shrinks and is cramped between the four walls of his prison, a sadly ordinary man."[92]

From the moment we see Duch, we are confronted with a man wearing a mask, the soft-spoken elder who seems more scholarly than sinister. Panh peels away that mask to reveal the cadre still dedicated to Khmer Rouge ideology, contemptuous of his underlings and victims, and fully aware of what he has done despite all his efforts to persuade us otherwise. Duch's calculated defense strategy ultimately fails to exonerate him before Pahn's discerning eyes. The persona he carefully constructed for himself throughout his interviews with Panh and during the trial is proven false. *Duch, Master of the Forges of Hell* may not send critics swooning—it lacks bravura cinematography, three-act staging, emotional climaxes, overwhelming dramatic music, and

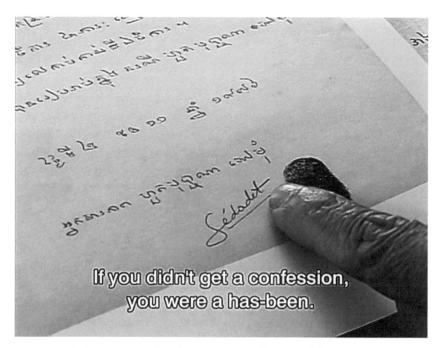

If you didn't get a confession, you were a has-been.

FIGURE 4.11 Duch points to Bophana's signature in *Duch, Master of the Forges of Hell*
© RPanh / droits réservés

satisfying resolution at its end. The drama occurs off camera. But in its restraint and slow reveals, its cerebral focus on the machinations of a mathematician turned torturer, its use of various cinematic strategies that effectively and repeatedly challenge Duch's lies, it is one of the most riveting films ever made about a mass murderer.

When Duch died of lung cancer in 2020, Panh was asked by journalists about his thoughts on his passing. "With his death, you might think that a page is turning—and it's precisely against that that we have to fight. . . . The Khmer Rouge, who are still alive, continue to inject venom into Cambodian society by publishing untruths. We must not give them a free hand." He added: "It is essential to put the history of the Khmer Rouge in its context. Without that work of remembrance, we will never be able to get over this history, which still haunts Cambodian society."[93]

When Vann Nath died in 2011, Panh delivered the eulogy at his funeral.[94] He remembered Vann's dignity, his artistry, his care for others, and his ability to maintain calm and resist anger when confronting perpetrators who had tortured him and so many others at S-21 prison. Vann was the first survivor to give evidence at Duch's trial. He lived for thirty years in the hope of seeing justice prevail and was deeply disappointed when the court initially diminished Duch's sentence to only nineteen years. Sadly he died before the final decision was made rejecting Duch's appeal and consigning him to life in prison.

Final Thoughts

What value is there in making—and watching—documentaries about genocide? For survivors, there is a clear need to ensure that such history be acknowledged, allowing repressed memories to surface, fears to recede, wounds to heal, the guilty to confess, and a nation to move on. Without truth, there can be no reconciliation. In 2003, Khieu Samphan admitted for the first time that the Khmer Rouge carried out "systematic killings." He was head of state during most of the period of Democratic Kampuchea and Pol Pot's prime minister in the exiled regime after 1979, so he had to know all this. But he attributed his awakening to the systematic repression to his viewing of Panh's film *S-21: The Khmer Rouge Killing Machine*.[95] Who knows whether it was the film or the prospect of his imminent trial that prompted this admission. Like Duch, Khieu Samphan reversed himself in his final testimony in his second trial (Case 002/02) for genocide, asserting the Khmer Rouge were not responsible for the deaths of its citizens; it was due to the Vietnamese and the U.S. bombing raids during the secret war it waged against Cambodia in the late sixties and early seventies. Guilt and remorse proved evanescent for all ECCC defendants, who accepted no responsibility for genocide during their rule in Democratic Kampuchea.

Do different cultures demand different cinematic approaches when representing traumatic events? Should norms established for representing the Holocaust necessarily be applied to other genocides? Are there other cultural forms better suited to recuperating collective memory and representing the past?[96] Cultural context should be a factor in determining what is and is not appropriate when remembering the past and documenting it. But at the same time, certain considerations apply to all genocides. The historian Hayden White, in writing about the Holocaust, warns against certain dangers in narrativizing traumatic events. White believes a narrative that "enfables" a traumatic event and turns it into a complete and satisfying story risks undoing the event and its need for mourning by turning it into something that allows us to master the anxiety that memory of the event provokes. Nonnarrative nonstories offer the best prospect for adequate representations of "unnatural" events, according to White: "Modernist techniques of representation provide the possibility of de-fetishizing both events and the fantasy accounts of them which deny the threat they pose, in the very process of pretending to represent them realistically. This de-fetishizing can then clear the way for that process of mourning which alone can relieve the 'burden of history' and make a more, if not totally, realistic perception of current problems possible."[97] What Panh accomplishes with his S-21 films exceeds the achievements of other filmmakers who have turned to drama and sensationalism to grab attention for the sins of the Cambodian genocide.

An intellectual, a teacher, an obsessive workaholic—Duch looks and sounds like us, a point of view shared by scholars like David Chandler and A. L. Hinton, and very likely Hannah Arendt would agree. This is something to consider if we are to examine our capacity to commit evil and rationalize it. In the wake of Abu Ghraib, Guantanamo, and the policy of separating children from parents seeking asylum at the border, rejected by countries that see them as "migrants," not human beings fleeing oppression, we do well to ask ourselves such questions and take seriously what we may not want to learn about ourselves.

Richard Rechtman, in *Living in Death: Genocide and Its Functionaries*, suggests that it is not ideology that creates *genocidaires*.[98] Likewise sociodemographic and psychological factors are weak predictors of who will become a perpetrator of genocide. It is ethical positions that radically distinguish between those who refuse to kill and those who choose to do so when a genocidal administration of death produces indifference to it. This is what fosters the availability to kill among those who focus not on their victims but on themselves and their community where ordinary life is centered on quotidian activities that coalesce around death. This is what is common when we look at the ordinary people who murdered millions, from those responsible for the Nazi Holocaust to the Khmer Rouge's *kamtèch* to today's Islamic State jihadists.[99]

What would Arendt say about the trials conducted in Cambodia? Would the testimony of Duch prompt different conclusions from her about "the banality of evil"? One thing she probably would agree with is that Rithy Panh demonstrates the thinking that for Arendt constituted the exercise of political responsibility, that relentless activity of questioning all that we encounter including ourselves.

Interlude

_____

Dark Tourism

The first book I read after viewing _S-21: The Khmer Rouge Killing Machine_ was David Chandler's _Voices of S-21: Terror and History in Pol Pot's Secret Prison_. I was reluctant to make S-21 my first stop on dark tourism's checklist of things to do in Cambodia.[1] But my trip to Cambodia would not be complete without a visit to the Tuol Sleng Genocide Museum—the name given today to S-21—and to Choeung Ek, the killing fields located on the outskirts of the city. My tuk-tuk driver Mr. Lucky was, as always, accommodating, patiently waiting for me at each location but invariably puzzled that I would want to spend so much time at each. When I entered Tuol Sleng, I was surprised at how run-down the buildings were and the poor condition of the infamous wall-sized panels of identity photos. There was little to suggest the care originally taken by the Vietnamese who deliberately modeled their propaganda museum on European Holocaust sites. But the ramshackle quality of Tuol Sleng somehow seemed fitting given the terrible history contained within its walls. What I remember most vividly was my inability to climb the stairs to the third floor. I began having difficulty breathing as I ascended to the second floor. My heart beat faster, and my breath came in gasps as I attempted to mount the steps to the top floor. I imagined the revenants Poeuv engaged with in Panh's film; they were here, awaiting me too. I tried to dismiss my physical response as the product of an overactive imagination. I gingerly walked down the stairs and out into the courtyard. I failed to find the place where Panh's films screen for tourists. In a covered corridor, I saw Chum Mey and Bou Meng selling copies of their memoirs. It struck me as terribly sad that prison survivors remained tied to it still, dependent on money from people who would hire them as a guide or buy a copy of their story. It seemed as if they had never been set free.

Five years later, I read that the Tuol Sleng Genocide Museum now featured a gift shop and rooms remodeled to better display instruments of torture. Like so many temples of history, it had been co-opted by those intent on profiting from its tragedies. I knew S-21 had changed since I had visited. Apparently political graffiti had been scrawled on the walls, and some Khmer Rouge photos had been vandalized. I know things change. There had been no gallows in the courtyard and no map of Cambodia made from three hundred skulls of victims of the killing fields when I was there in 2015. What does remain constant is the horror that lurks everywhere. Panh tells the story of how birds would invariably arrive when he was shooting and assemble on a wire strung outside a window. When a perpetrator lied, they cried out, which annoyed the sound engineer later on because no one realized the birds were speaking until editing began.[2] When the shooting on the film ended, the birds flew away. Panh felt they were the souls of the dead come to observe what was happening. I found something similar when I went to ESMA (Escuela de Mécanica de la Armada) in Buenos Aires, where leftist protesters branded as "domestic terrorists" were held, awaiting interrogation and torture before being executed during Argentina's Dirty War. The first thing I noticed as I walked onto that beautiful campus were the birds singing in the trees, loudly calling to visitors like me, as if testifying to the horrors committed there.

Mr. Lucky was waiting for me, and we set off for Choeung Ek. He took a back road to avoid congested traffic along the paved highway. For the first time since arriving in Cambodia, I saw the poor, their dwellings cobbled together from pieces of wood and fabric, shanties set beside a murky run-off from some god-forsaken water source. The route was extremely bumpy and long as we traveled outside the city proper. Later I would watch short films made by the young people trained at the Bophana Audiovisual Resource Center for the Dollar-a-Day project. They captured the desperate situation of people like those I saw on the back road to the killing fields.

Choeung Ek had been turned into a for-profit tourist center, with a collection of street vendors selling food and water near the parking lot. Visitors paid a fee to stroll through fields where thousands of S-21 prisoners had been slaughtered and dumped into mass graves. In 2005 the site was privatized, acquired by JC Royal, a Japanese firm granted a thirty-year lease with plans to increase the entry fee by 600 percent. It claimed to be committed to increasing the revenue for the state to "renovate the beauty of the Choeung Ek killing fields."[3] All profits go to the Sun Fund, a philanthropic organization with no known office, apparently founded by Hun Sen. A chorus of newspapers condemned the deal back in the day when independent newspapers were still published in Phnom Penh, but the deal went ahead anyway. I rented an audio tour and set out to see the final destination of S-21 prisoners. I learned that nine thousand bodies had been excavated here. Along the paths, bone fragments and bits of cloth still worked their way up to the surface. Signs were placed at intervals warning visitors not to step onto these remains or claim them as souvenirs. The fields were pockmarked with many shallow depressions around a lake that also once held bodies. Near the entrance was an impressively tall (thirty-meter) glass stupa in which skulls had been laid on top of each other. There were two locations that caught my eye and heart. One was a tree with memorial threads wrapped around its trunk. A sign explained that this was the tree used to "smash" infants to death. Nearby was a covered area where women and children had been buried. In *S-21* Prak Khân demonstrated how prisoners were trucked from S-21 to Choeung Ek. At midnight, only a light powered by an electric generator allowed the driver and executioner to see where to bring those about to die, positioning them to make their death and burial efficient. They were first hit on the back of the head, and then their throats were cut before they were pushed into a mass grave. If the victim's clothing was not soiled with blood, they were stripped, and their clothes collected for reuse. In the daylight, this killing area lacked the horror of the reenactments in Panh's film. I cannot say why, but I found myself numb. Unlike my experience at S-21, where I felt sickened and surrounded by the spirits of the dead, here I felt nothing. Was it because the bodies were gone? Had I become insensitive to evidence of the terror laid out before me? Or was it because genocide was being used for profit? This was not the killing field depicted in Roland Joffé's eponymous film. It was bleak and empty, without a meaningful trace of the lives that expired there.

The ride back to my hotel was long and silent. I was grateful Mr. Lucky decided we could take the main road back now that traffic had subsided. I searched for words that could express my feelings about what I had seen and felt that day. I found myself agreeing with Nick Paterniti that "a visit to S-21 leaves an inconsolable feeling. It rides with you in the taxi back to the unreality of the hotel, through the streets of Phnom Penh buzzing with markets and families. . . . Behind the normalcy of today, even the veneer of progress, lurks that desolation."[3] Panh is well acquainted with such desolation. In *The Elimination*, he writes: "I don't like the overused word 'trauma.' Today, every individual, every family has its trauma, whether large or small. In my case it manifests itself as unending desolation; as ineradicable images, gestures no longer possible, silences that pursue me."[4] Unending, inconsolable desolation.

Several days before flying home, I attended a session of the ECCC. It was the first of four days focused on an appeal initiated by the defendants in Case 002, Nuon Chea (Brother Number Two) and Khieu Samphan, former acting prime minister of Cambodia and chairman of the State Presidium of Democratic Kampuchea. I reached out to my neighbor Gail Collins for help securing a press pass to the ECCC. It would mean I had a guaranteed seat in the auditorium and the opportunity to speak with journalists in the press room during the lunch break. She contacted Seth Mydans, longtime *New York Times* correspondent covering Cambodia, whose writing I had followed for years. He kindly made some calls, and I received an email with a form to complete for my pass. That morning, Mr. Lucky arrived early, and we set off past the airport to the large and imposing building that housed the ECCC. Three things struck me as we traveled.

Along the route, men in military uniforms were stationed at intervals on both sides of the road. I did not know if they were policemen or soldiers, but it was terrifying to see them posted along the route. My overactive imagination, left unchecked, would not allow me to focus on the experience ahead of me. I finally stopped counting them. I was told later that they were a security detail for some dignitary headed into town to meet with members of the government.

Mr. Lucky made good time, and as traffic thinned, I became aware of an entire section along the road devoted to shops selling spirit houses. Some were modest; others were McMansions designed for upper-class spirits. As the tuk-tuk picked up speed, the many spirit houses mounted high on poles began to pass by in a blur. No matter how many were displayed, I knew there were not enough for the two million wandering souls lost during Pol Pot's time.

As we drove past the airport, I realized the tribunal was still far away, and I began to worry that we would not arrive in time for me to join the press queue before the doors closed. The ever-reliable Mr. Lucky got me there in good time and promised to return at four to take me back to my hotel.

There were very few members of the press present. The names of major news services and international newspapers were taped on the tops of desks, but their occupants were absent. The only people in the press room were young writers like George—a staff member for the *Cambodia Daily*—and interns working for the Asian International Justice Initiative that had been monitoring the trials since they began. They were the age of my students, all of them excellent English speakers hailing from different countries. They gave me tips on how to use the headset that I would need to translate the proceedings from French or Khmer. Most of the people queuing outside were Khmer with only a few foreigners evident. One of my young colleagues from the Netherlands explained that one could choose to remain in the press room, where the proceedings were streamed on a widescreen monitor that afforded much better audio and video coverage than one had in the auditorium. I considered the advantages, but I opted to sit in the auditorium. I wanted to be with the school groups and villagers who had been bused to attend the session, and I wanted to see where Panh had sat day after day watching Duch before the court. I had to leave my belongings behind in the press room: one was only allowed to bring a pen and paper into the auditorium. There was a hushed silence in the wide room as we waited for the court to come to order. I had my headset on, and the sound was, as I had been warned, far from satisfactory. While we waited, I remembered the time Panh was outraged by the judge who asked a survivor how he was able to defecate with his feet tied and by the lawyer who asked another survivor, "Did you and the others have mosquito nets?" Panh wrote in his memoir that these questions embodied everything hideous, especially the court's ignorance. Panh quit the courtroom, slamming his earphones on a table, and got a friendly warning that international criminal justice should not be mocked.[5]

Nuon Chea and Khieu Samphan were seated with their lawyers also waiting for the session to start. As members of the Khmer Rouge Central Committee, they had been tried and found guilty of crimes against humanity and sentenced to life imprisonment. But on this hot July day in 2015, Nuon Chea's lawyer was incompetently appealing the results of that trial. In 2017, when their second trial was ending, Samphan would angrily deny genocide had been committed by the Communist Party of Kampuchea. He had fire in his belly at the conclusion of that trial. His last words categorically rejected the term *murderer* and denied any knowledge of forced marriages, discrimination between "base" and "new" people, or the slaughter of minority groups during their regime. What I saw in the courtroom in 2015 was two tired old men who looked like all the elderly men sitting in the auditorium with me. They would not win this appeal. And they would not succeed in passing the blame along to the Vietnamese or Hun Sen's Vietnamese-backed government for genocide in Democratic Kampuchea.[6]

It had been difficult to follow what the witnesses were saying, with their backs to the auditorium, their voices low, and the translations often difficult to understand. A few days later I read a summary of the second day's session for the *KRT Monitor*, reporting that one witness proved "unhelpful." He testified that the Khmer Rouge had rounded up Lon Nol soldiers and killed them after the liberation of April 17, 1975. I told myself I should count myself fortunate to have been inside the court to see the two remaining leaders responsible for crafting the Khmer Rouge ideology and its cruel application well into the 1990s. But I could not help feeling like a voyeur. Much later I would read in James Moyer's essay on film and public memory that "the historical voyeur does not want to be there so much as relish—morosely, even morbidly, perhaps—his *not* being there. This . . . historical luck, as it were, moves us not because it suggests our exemption from history, but precisely because it reminds us of our being in it. Appreciating historical luck is historical consciousness."[7]

The hour-long tuk-tuk ride back into town added to my fatigue. Panh had said it was good that I was going to the ECCC, but I need not spend an entire day there. He was right. And it was especially true if you rode in a tuk-tuk and not an air-conditioned car. I was exhausted and felt I had accomplished almost nothing. When I fell into bed, I could not sleep. Around midnight, the air conditioner quit, and the lights went out. I listened to the shuffle of footsteps running up and down the stairs. No one knocked on my door. I decided to go down to investigate since notifying guests that there might be a problem was not on anyone's agenda. Grabbing my cell phone for illumination, I felt my way down the stairs and out onto the street. A small crowd had gathered, speaking Khmer, French, and English all at once, everyone an expert on how to fix the problem. Apparently, there was a short in the overhead wiring connecting electricity to the hotel. Fortunately, someone stopped the man about to shoot water at the power box. Was this another sign from the spirits who willed me to come to Cambodia, a reminder that death and destruction lurk everywhere in Cambodia, even at midnight in my bed?

5

After the Wars

Fiction and Nonfiction

If exile pains you and does not kill you, it will take you back to the cradle of imagination. It will strengthen you and make you equal to those who stay up late to tame the obscure. Exile, a misunderstanding between existence and borders, is a fragile bridge between images.

MAHMOUD DARWISH, *In the Presence of Absence*[1]

Although many viewers are familiar with Panh's documentaries about the Khmer Rouge genocide, far fewer are acquainted with the films that address the challenges survivors of the Pol Pot years have faced when trying to build a new life after five years of civil war, four years of Khmer Rouge brutality, and ten years of occupation by the Vietnamese. Panh's first documentary film,

Site 2 (1989), focused on the difficulties endured by survivors like Yim Om, who for decades had lived in one refugee camp after another, somehow managing to preserve dignity and hope in a better future for her children. His first narrative film, *Rice People* (1994), represented the life Yim Om dreamed of reclaiming, one where people could live, anchored in an agrarian cycle that preserved core Cambodian values of home and family. These two films contained the seeds of how Panh would employ both genres to explore the lives of Cambodians after the Year Zero.[2]

In Panh's next two dramatic films, he took on the political, economic, gender, and social upheavals that dominated post–Khmer Rouge rule. He looked at the problems posed for those returning in search of family, honest work, and peace, who had no other option than to eke out a living in a devastated homeland or else escape, as he had, leaving behind their language, history, and identity but never the memories of the traumas they had faced.

One Evening after the War (Un soir après la guerre) (1997)

Panh began his career making documentaries that gave him a way to approach people and discover characters. He then approached writing the scripts for his fiction films by building on what he had learned making his documentaries. He noted that the script for *One Evening after the War* was made possible after "the sum total of all the images I have encountered."[3] The film begins on the eve of the return of King Norodom Sihanouk to Cambodia as the film's protagonist Savannah, a twenty-eight-year-old penniless ex-soldier, returns to Phnom Penh after ten years at war. He soon meets and falls in love with Srei Poeuv, but they are compelled by forces beyond their control to pursue ever more desperate measures to try to make a life together, which eventually renders them powerless to escape their tragic destiny. Their love story is told in retrospect by Poeuv, a survivor of more than genocide, who is raising their daughter, Bophana, and wondering where to go to find peace. This original love story is a complex one written by Panh with the scenarist Ève Deboise, who worked with him on their award-winning script for *Rice People*. Panh's use of traditional Cambodian literature and dance contextualizes the conflicts experienced by the lovers and is essential to an understanding of the film.

The film begins with a spectacular opening shot, an aerial view of a railroad train traveling across country. Savannah and his comrades are riding on the flat car at the head of this "death train" where the poor who cannot afford

FIGURE 5.1 Soldiers return home in *One Evening after the War* © RPanh / droits réservés

a ticket can ride: they know that if the rails are mined, they will be blown up, but they have no other choice. Like Savannah, his soldier friends have lost so much. Phal stepped on a landmine and lost one leg. Maly lost his land, his wife, and his children. Each is seeking a way to live in a world that no longer has a place for them.

Savannah appears to be an honest man caught by what Boreth Ly argues is the crisis of "monetary masculinity" in contemporary Cambodia. Early in the film, Savannah goes to the cinema and discovers he cannot afford a ticket. A beautiful girl, Srei Poeuv, offers to buy one for the ex-soldier. His masculinity offended, he initially refuses but finally relents, and then he avidly watches a Cambodian porn film in which a wealthy man, surrounded by prostitutes and two admiring male friends, explains, "In Cambodia, money is power!" This film within a film sets up the opposition between traditional ideals of masculinity, which historically linked sexual prowess to military power, and a modern notion born of transnational and global investments that made wealth the symbol of virility and power. Savannah embodies traditional male values—he is strong, tough, hardworking, handsome, and dominant in a sexual relationship—but he cannot compete for the affection of the beautiful girl he desires because he has no money. Ly goes on to argue that the destabilization of traditional notions of masculinity became the underlying cause of violence against women in postwar Cambodian society, where they paid the greater price for gender and sexual inadequacy among Cambodian men.[4]

Savannah meets his benefactress at the Tonle Sap café, where his friend Maly is a bouncer. He discovers that she is a "bar girl," a high-priced prostitute. When he tries to court her and is rebuffed, he pursues her and finally compels her to dance with him in the *ramvong*, literally "dance in a circle" in Khmer, a traditional dance that is a prelude to seduction for young and old alike. Dancers join a circle to perform the simple step and rolling walk of this elegant traditional dance placing value on the spiral curl traced by their hands. Their supple fingers, curved like petals, imitate the planting of grain, the belief in the growth of the root, the blossoming of the flower, and then the appearance of the fruit. Their gestures repeat, and the circle turns in homage to the perpetual cycle of nature. The dance between Savannah and Poeuv may be the most sensuous and elegant ramvong ever captured on film. Savannah's supple hand gestures and Poeuv's graceful and curvaceous moves bring them into harmony around each other, "like rotations of the moon around the sun." Poeuv gazes into Savannah's eyes twice during this dance as her resistance melts.[5]

Savannah takes Poeuv to his uncle's painting studio, where he disappears and emerges bare chested and puts on the mask of Hanuman. Panh draws upon the *Reamker* and its quintessential Cambodian hero, Hanuman, the monkey god, in shaping the story of Savannah and Poeuv. In this epic story, Hanuman is a powerful commander who helps Prince Rama (Ream) rescue his wife Sita (Séda) from the lustful villain who has abducted her. Hanuman, when performed by the classical court ballet, is the only male role actually danced by a man. Hanuman is a wild, sexually potent figure closely identified with the military.

Savannah entertains Poeuv with his performance as Hanuman, and she laughs delightedly, but when he removes the mask, desire overwhelming him, he forces himself on her, a man who no longer knows how to behave given the new definition of masculinity. She cries and protests, her face registering pain, anger, and disgust with the man who betrayed her and her growing affection for him. She runs away and spits on the money Savannah tries to offer her. In the confusion of their uncertain relationship roles, both are bereft.

The conflict stirred in the viewer is how to respond to Savannah's behavior as desire. It is hard to read Savannah—is he so clueless as to believe his behavior was acceptable or so mad that he thinks money will remedy the situation, a gesture that only prompts more fury from Poeuv? Have they misunderstood each other? Savannah begs her forgiveness, spellbound by her and profoundly confused about how to be a man. Poeuv eventually decides that, despite the rape, Savannah is the only man who really loves her, unlike her wealthy clients. She forgives him, and they become lovers.

FIGURE 5.2 Lovers in *One Evening after the War* © RPanh / droits réservés

Savannah is determined to earn the money needed to buy Poeuv out of her debt to the bar owner. He goes into the ring as a kickboxer, and in a mesmerizing scene, he performs a ritual exercise before the fight that is more an evocation of the elegant grace of the militant Hanuman than a prefight warmup. His attacks on his opponent are beautiful to watch. With his winnings, he takes Poeuv for a river cruise and offers her a lavish meal, a gesture of his triumph and desire to please her. Again, Hanuman reappears from another chapter of the *Reamker*. Savannah swims to Poeuv, who is seated on a raft "like a mermaid," a pose that evokes the story of Hanuman and Savanmacha, the mermaid daughter of Prince Ream's enemy who has been sent to destroy Hanuman but instead falls in love with him.[6] Using such themes from classical literature is one of the ways Panh renders the lovers' story mythic and contemporary, drawing on cultural figures banished by the Khmer Rouge, who were determined to strip society of all its traditional arts and spiritual values.

When Poeuv is evicted from her rooms in the White Building, a powerful architectural symbol of Cambodian modernism and respect for artists that was already in decline, she has nowhere to go, and Savannah takes her to the railroad car where he is squatting. Their happy if ramshackle life there together is short-lived when her madam's enforcer threatens to kill her if she refuses to pay back her debt, a message he delivers in the cemetery where he has dragged her. This is one of several key scenes in the film where Poeuv sheds tears. She feels compelled to return to her "clients" but hesitant because of the child she is carrying. Savannah, meanwhile, is shaken by the cynicism

FIGURE 5.3 Srei Poeuv returns to work © RPanh / droits réservés

of Maly and his drinking buddies, who cast doubts about Poeuv's faithful-
ness, much as Sita's fidelity was doubted by her husband, Rama. Poeuv is
shocked by Savannah's jealousy and his violent blow, a gesture out of character
for him. Unable to bear Poeuv's return to her "work," he follows her one
night and pulls his gun on her client, who reaches for his gun too, only
Savannah kills him first. He has crossed the line and joined Maly: he has
become a gangster and a killer. He agrees to commit a robbery to get the
money needed to free himself and Poeuv from a future without freedom.

Panh strategically allows us to see glimmers of the people they once were.
Together Poeuv and Savannah collect the songbirds they have filled their little
home with, and they release them into the air, hoping like them to be released
from their caged existence. When a bird appears in the fangs of a cobra soon
after, it is an omen that Savannah and Poeuv will not escape their life-and-
death struggle to survive in contemporary Cambodia. In a botched attempted
robbery, Savannah is betrayed by Maly, who acts only to protect himself. Their
male camaraderie, celebrated early in the film, has been replaced by cruelty,
inhumanity, and violence. Poeuv, who narrates the story, asks where she can
find peace.

Woven in the film are lingering traces of colonialism, most apparent in
the various forms of transportation. The opening scene, one of Panh's most
brilliantly cinematic, features an aerial shot of the "death wagons." This

evocation of the literal and figurative power of the railroad engine, longtime symbol of colonial dominance, is shown in its ironic decline. Panh's camera settles in close-up behind the figures of the three friends—Savannah, Phal, and Maly—a visual position Panh frequently takes in his films as a train or boat ferries his protagonist into the unknown. The railroad returns later in the film, but now the railroad car is no longer functional. It is in a state of collapse and sidelined as a shack where Savannah and Poeuv find shelter. It is from this dilapidated shelter that Poeuv watches children play on another flat-car, their future like that of her unborn child, constrained in a landscape of decay. The colonial past—the railroad—is in tatters. A classically overcrowded third-world bus conveys Poeuv and Savanna between the urban and the rural when they go to visit Poeuv's mother in her village, dropping them off on the edge of a deceptively bucolic field.

Panh introduces another recurrent figure in his films—the madwoman—in this next scene. He cast Peng Phan, the lead actress in *Rice People*, as Poeuv's mother. Like the mother in *Rice People*, she too is shackled in a bamboo cage, having lost her mind following the execution of her husband by the Khmer Rouge, a scene presented in a brief flashback. Deprived of her husband, incapacitated by her loss and the burden of maintaining the family, she relinquishes her responsibility to her two daughters, Sokha and Poeuv. Sokha remains at home to tend the farm and care for the family; Poeuv goes to the city, where she sells her body to provide for them. When Poeuv and Savannah ride back to the city on the bus, she is tearful in her retreat from her dysfunctional family—from her mad mother and her insensitive sister, who ignores the physical and emotional price she pays to be able to provide for them. The bus headed to the big bad city now includes a young girl and the "madam" who has bought her for $300 and is noisily voicing concern that she will not get a good return on her investment. Poeuv's tears are shed for a host of reasons, but Panh's placement of this scene suggests the young girl is on the same journey Poeuv once took from rice fields to bar. When they arrive in Phnom Penh, the innocent girl stands tall at the doorway of the bus to survey the landscape of her new life, and then she is rudely pulled down and thrust into the crowd. Without words and with brief juxtapositions like this, Panh shows how many women support their families in a new era of prosperity for some but not all.

If the railroad's dilapidation heralds the last traces of colonialism, the shiny motorcycle taxis—*motodops*—suggest the new engine of transnational capitalism taking Poeuv to her nighttime clients. She sits astride one dressed in a skin-tight silver dress, hurrying to her destiny in the nighttime city. The motodop with Poeuv astride it is the final image of the film, an ambivalent image since it is unclear whether this is an image of the past, present, or future for Poeuv and her daughter. Has Poeuv escaped from her sex work or not? The female body has long been portrayed as an allegory of the geopolity of the Cambodian nation. The "taxi girl," like the "bar girl," is the prostitute who fulfills the demands of NGOs, wealthy foreigners, and corrupt officials with money to indulge all their desires. Transportation is essential in the movement of bodies as commodities in the new era of *mondialisation*. The apparent progress heralded by such modern technologies of transportation is misleading and hides the price Cambodians pay to enjoy such "progress."

One of the most significant if underestimated characters in this film is the mute boy who manages to "speak" for those who have lost their voices. When he first appears, he is hiding in a tree, an observer who watches Savannah bury his gun and with it his violent past as a soldier. The boy is a keen witness, who appears at critical junctures in the film. He alerts Poeuv to Savannah's despair and self-destructive behavior, and he joins their celebration over their misguided plan to escape their financial woes. The mute boy lives on the margins, making his way with no one to rely on. Savannah's kindness to him, giving him his army cap and providing some food in the film's opening scenes, shows that Savannah is at root a good man. The boy is like a Shakespearean fool; his seeming disability actually hides the depth of his understanding and his caretaking role. Voiceless, he nonetheless speaks to those who can listen and heed what he has to say. He is a quintessential Panh character. In the film's final scenes, he is present but now transformed, cleanly dressed and shod with his hair neatly combed, looking fondly over Poeuv's daughter, Bophana, as they play together. He has become the next generation's masculine figure, who continues to look out for the family's well-being. He is a symbol of Cambodia's disabled masculinity, a disability born out of past traumas, and he suggests the possibility of a gentler masculinity at a remove from violence where the capacity for love matters more than power, money, and might.

Geoffrey Cheshire, writing for *Variety*, admired the classically proportioned tragedy about the aftermath of Cambodia's two decades of war and acknowledged the handsome French production values to a Southeast Asian milieu of poverty and social turmoil. Despite praise for the screen presence of the actors Chea Lyda Chan and Narith Roeun and the "lush lensing" of the cinematographer Christophe Pollock, Panh's assured handling was not sufficient to warrant an audience beyond "upscale European arthouses and Asia-oriented fests." This was one of many times when Panh, ahead of the curve, produced a film that it would take audiences years to recognize for all its worth and not to relegate it to "special audiences" in arthouses.[7]

Let the Boat Break, Let the Junk Crack Open (Que la barque se brise, que la jonque s'entrouvre) (2001)

Panh's next fiction film was made in Paris. *Que la barque se brise, que la jonque s'entrouvre* (2001) was a made-for-TV film that offers an intimate glimpse of Southeast Asian immigrants haunted by their pasts. The protagonists are Bopha, a Cambodian refugee from the Khmer Rouge and the owner of a small restaurant on the Avenue de Choisy in Paris. She is played by the beautiful singer and actress Vantha Talisman. Minh, played by the actor Eric Nguyen, is a Vietnamese boat person who is a delivery driver for his grocer uncle by day and a taxi driver by night. Minh's arrival in France, like Bopha's, was a desperate escape from a homeland in the midst of war and chaos. They meet one night when Minh is called to drive Bopha to a private casino. He follows her inside and is fascinated by her and by the gaming world she inhabits with casual ease. She asks him to play for her to bring her luck. He does not know what to do but manages to win. She asks if he will work for her, and so begins their relationship and his introduction to the world of gambling. As each of them seeks to lose themselves and their pasts in games of chance, Minh's luck quickly runs out.

Bopha has a teenaged daughter, Lacksmey (A'Molica Kheng), who is curious about the past and about her dead father, but her mother will never talk about him. Despite her serene appearance and seeming calm, Bopha is suffering, and the physical manifestation of it is experienced in her phantom leg pains, remnants of torture under the Khmer Rouge. Although Bopha is surrounded by a supportive community of Cambodian women who work for her, Bopha only finds relief when gambling keeps her nightmares at bay. Eventually, she consults a French doctor who advises her that she must talk about her past if she wants to heal herself. When Lacksmey tells her she wants to go to Cambodia to search for her father, Bopha is beside herself with anxiety, unable to tell her why her father died.

Bopha and Minh come from warring nations, and their respective diasporic communities hate each other. Fostering peace between these communities is one of the reasons Panh made the film. The title uses the metaphor of the boat as a vehicle that unites Minh and Bopha in their shared quest for

FIGURE 5.4 Bopha gambles in *Let the Boat Break, Let the Junk Crack Open* © RPanh / droits réservés

openness and love after their devastating pasts. Although the lovers share common ground in their suffering, their families cling to racial and ethnic animosity. Both sides are unhappy over their affair and try to split them apart. Minh's family thinks Bopha is too old for him and sees her leading him astray from his hardworking, traditional values. When his uncle repeatedly reminds him of his mother's sacrifices to get him to France, Minh revolts, angrily proclaiming he wishes he had never made the journey. As his gambling debts mount, Minh fails to show up to help his uncle and gets drawn further into the shady world of debt collectors and thugs. Desperate, his uncle visits Bopha to ask for her help. He brings the drawings Minh made when he arrived, violent images of death and drowning at the hands of pirates, scenes Minh witnessed as a child smuggled aboard the boats transporting Vietnamese fleeing war.

Bopha tries to persuade Minh to give up his gambling to no avail. In the climactic scene, Bopha and Minh are seated opposite each other in a shady game on which everything depends. Bopha places on the table the gold necklace with the jade pendant Minh gave her, declaring it is worth five or six million francs. Minh lays down his chips. She starts to fold when he tells her to wait and adds, the camera tight on his face, "Like that, the money will stay between you and me." He uncovers a card, and the others gasp. He has won the hand. Bopha gets up from the table with her jade pendant in hand. In the final scene, Bopha is home, opening an envelope from Lacksmey in

Cambodia, and smiles at her note, written on the back of a photo of the lovers: "It is for want of loving that we think of the distance. Let the boat break, let the junk crack open. . . . One arrives in Ceylon in those wrecks if the desire to get there dominates you."[8]

This is the only fiction film that Panh has written without a collaborator. It seems clearly drawn from his own experiences as a refugee in Paris trying to deal with his own nightmares. In his memoir, *The Elimination*, he writes movingly about his difficulty dealing with his success at Cannes in 1994. It was a suicidal time. When he made some money with *Rice People*, the terrible thought struck him that he could not share his good fortune with his dead parents. Alarmed, he felt all the money had to be given away. He writes:

> After dark I'd walk down the *Grands Boulevards*, surrounded by prostitutes, petty crooks, tourists, and Parisians adrift in the night. I played various table games—poker, baccarat, *chemin de fer*—in all the Clichy and République and Bastille casinos and gambling halls. I won fortunes. I remember walking through the streets of Paris with a fortune in my pocket. I lived for those miraculous fifteen minutes—and for this lie: I was rich; I had the world on a string. Then I'd become poor again, thank God. Gamblers lose. I laughed and drank a lot with Arabs, Jews, Armenians, Chinese. We were on the skids. We all knew we were going to lose. Besides that was why we were there. The important thing was to flame out so brightly that nothing was left: no chips, no banknotes, no seven-faced dice, no joyful roulette wheels, no casinos, no gamblers. Nothing. No one. . . . After some weeks I abandoned the night. Like a good boy I returned to my screenplays, to my films, but sleep wouldn't come back.[9]

Making films may be the ultimate high-stakes risk-taking act. Panh understood how gambling could serve as an escape for wounded people like Bopha and Minh. And he knew how phantom pains can return when least expected. When the film was televised in 2001, Panh spoke with Christine Chartier for *Arte* about its making, noting that the gambling that Bopha and Vinh are drawn to is at the same time a jump into the void, Russian roulette, and a solo adventure to escape everyday life. Once Bopha communicates her passion for gambling to Minh, he throws himself into it like someone who would jump into the water with a stone around his neck. Their happiness is short-lived, according to Panh, because "they learned to fight to survive, but not to be happy." Bopha succeeds in finding some happiness by rescuing Minh from his plunge into debt and despair. He recovers enough money to save himself and shares it with her: their rescue is mutual and far more about emotional healing than money.[10]

This *cinéma pudique*—a modest love story of two lost souls—is simply constructed in marked contrast to the complex plotting and multileveled meanings of *One Evening after the War*. The mise-en-scène of tight close-ups and emphasis on interiors, especially the claustrophobic dark interiors of the seedier gambling dives, seems a better choice for a televised film made in Paris, where production costs are greater than in Cambodia. Raising money to make films is always a challenge for Panh, and it took him one and a half years to be able to make this film.

Panh downplays the erotic attraction between the protagonists. One reason for this modesty is to allow Panh to focus on their traumatic experiences and their difficulty in reaching out for help. Twenty years after finding refuge and the ability to achieve some order and stability in one's life is when survivors often find their memories resurfacing. Panh had been working with the Parisian psychiatrist Richard Rechtman, who treated many refugees suffering from the long-term effects of posttraumatic stress disorder. Panh wanted his film to reach Indochinese refugees whose past threatened their well-being. The brief but compelling exchange between Bopha and the sympathetic doctor she visits gently encouraged survivors to seek professional help in dealing with their pain.

There is little information available on how this film was received either by critics or by television viewers in France. It is a spare, low-keyed story that is well acted by artists marginalized and rarely given a chance to perform in French cinema except in minor roles. Both Vantha Talisman and Eric Nguyen had never been cast in leading roles in film before. They and Chin Thang-Long were the only professional actors in the film; all others were nonprofessionals selected by Panh. *Let the Boat Break* is a deeply affecting story told by an artist who chooses carefully how best to serve the needs of his primary audience.

The Cambodian genocide informs nearly every film Rithy Panh has made. He has wryly observed that he has made only one film. But there are other, important, and recurring themes in his work. To begin, there is his subtle yet biting critique of globalization. Then there is his focus on women and children. This may surprise those who only know the documentaries where men figure as the principal characters. But women are more often than not the subjects of his films. This is arguably because Cambodian women have embodied the worst abuses wrought by totalitarianism, colonialism, genocide, and globalization. In *The Land of Wandering Souls* (about migrant laborers digging trenches to lay optical cables for Cambodia's new communication infra-structure) and in *Paper Cannot Wrap Up Embers* (about Cambodian sex workers), Panh gives voice to ordinary people, many of them women, who are struggling to survive in modern-day Cambodia. They continue Panh's inquiry into the toll exacted by denial of the past and submission to the economic and political forces driving Cambodia to "prostitute itself" to please new "colonial masters" of global capital.

The Land of Wandering Souls (La terre des âmes errantes) (1999)

The Land of Wandering Souls marked an important new beginning for Panh; it was the first film he made with an all-Cambodian production crew. Ever since he returned to Asia to make his first film, he knew he needed a crew that spoke Khmer and understood the land and its culture. With the help of Atelier Varan, he began training a new generation of Cambodian film technicians in Phnom Penh. He conducted this training on his film sites, shooting all day and then looking at dailies and analyzing their results well into the night with his Cambodian crew. After a few hours of sleep, they were up early for another long day of shooting. Until he had covered training for all skills needed for a professional shoot, he relied on the expertise of French crew members who agreed to pass on their knowledge to their Cambodian apprentices. *The Land of Wandering Souls* was the first film made with a Khmer team who under-stood the world he was depicting, a team that would spend eight months on the road shooting what Panh still considers to be his strongest film.

The film opens with images straight out of a corporate ad for modern tech-nology and its benefits for the developing world. But this is Rithy Panh, and the viewer quickly detects the irony of Western hegemony and the way the global economy mercilessly exploits its workers. The film follows a group of impoverished villagers forced to become migrant laborers digging trenches for the fiber optic cables that will connect Cambodia to the wider world. Of course, such infrastructural advances will benefit the few, not the many. Panh's camera observes the workers close-up as they dig from dawn to dusk, earning barely enough to feed themselves and always foraging for food. We see the children catching frogs in rice paddies and one mother "harvesting" red ants that serve as the sole source of protein for their daily meal. They sleep outside, bathe in the streams, and work day and night. The people we come to know will return to their villages after eight months of work penniless,

FIGURE 5.5 Panh, Prum Mésar, and Sear Vissal follow laborers in *The Land of Wandering Souls* © John Vink / MAPSimages

their final pay stolen by a corrupt foreman. These laborers—men, women, and children—uncannily resemble workers in the time of the Khmer Rouge who toiled to clear land and dig irrigation ditches for their overseers. The similarity Panh draws between the people of these two eras is unmistakable: with the swing of a pickax and the parallel movement of his camera, a strong vertical movement from sky above to rocky trench below, Panh etches with his camera a gash in the earth that resembles a wound, connecting Khmer Rouge brutality with the exploitation of migrant laborers by global capital. The camera does not permit us any distance. And as this new labor force breaks the earth, they also uncover traces of Cambodia's traumatic past, which has not ceased to grind them to dust.[11]

This is what Panh says about his shots, which I have translated from his notes for the film:

In *La terre des âmes errantes*, there is a sequence where the young boys are hollowing out the trench. One of them lets the pickax fall and goes to sprinkle it with water. The camera fixes on his face. A long close-up shot. This face holds a secret, one reads anguish and exhaustion on it. If the shot did not last, he would only be one child like another. One senses that he wants to say something, but he does not say it. Finally, he returns to dig in place of his sister. The mood of this scene made me think of the poems of Prévert. Often, when shooting, a line of poetry comes to me and will not leave me, it serves as my compass. One can get lost so easily in the sadness or in the chaotic sounds of the world. As René Char said, "the essential is always threatened by the insignificant" (l'essentiel est toujours menacé par l'insignificant).[12]

The film consists of twenty-six scenes that follow the lives of several recurring characters. Chief among them is a family of nine children, a father who is an amputee, and his resourceful wife. She is pregnant, and by the end of the film, she has given birth and is back home with little to show for their hard work but another tiny mouth to feed. There is a couple who show affectionate flirtatiousness despite their circumstances. And there is a woman whose husband has left her. And always we see the children—from nursing infants to adolescents already part of the labor force.

The sequences alternate between labor, moments of rest, trips to seek medical help or basic necessities, food scavenging, and ruminations on working conditions. Each night, camp is made, dinner is eaten in the open, and families sleep on mats, which are packed up the next day as the work continues in another location. Panh's camera records not only the workers but many others who inhabit the same space, including monks walking along the route with other commuters. In one striking scene, the trench is dug directly underneath an open-air market, located off the side of the road. As men snake a cable under tables and chairs, patrons continue eating their meals. As the film scholar Chi-hui Yang points out, the road is a zone of labor, commerce, transport, and, now, communications flow. Each of these spaces occupies the same location but serves very different functions.[13]

The work crews dig along country roadways and into the city with its paved highways and congested public spaces. The dangers along the path shift according to location and time. In the countryside, shovels and axes strike unexploded bombs from the "American war" and uncover the bones of the Khmer Rouge dead. The film's title is a thinly veiled reference to those "wandering souls" who never were commemorated with funeral rites, and so their peace remains disturbed in the afterlife. Of course, the present-day wandering souls are clearly these workers who migrate along the route for months, earning some income so that they can maintain their lands and way of life back in their villages. The "land" of wandering souls is literally the land we see being uprooted in the name of a progress reserved only for the few.

The film frequently slips through present to past. At the beginning, the amputee's wife approaches an elderly woman to beg for rice. The old woman kindly offers her several scoops and then talks of her own experience. Panh's camera lingers on her lined face, and as she speaks, she becomes increasingly emotional, dividing her glance between the mother and Panh:

> We have to share what little there is if we're to live together. She has nothing, I have nothing. I'll be glad to see an end to all this. I lived through three wars in three different periods. The first was back in the days of Lon Nol. They shot each other, bombed each other. I jumped into a well, carrying my mother on my back. Then there was Pol Pot. We were oppressed and beaten. I had to dig irrigation canals. The memory is unbearable. I still have the scars on my breasts. I had to carry baskets full of earth. I lost the feeling in my hands and feet. I had to beg too. But I feel sorry for her. She has nothing to eat. I help her so she can eat like me.

Panh includes no archival material, but such testimony establishes the connections between past and present. And the unrelenting physical labor that threads throughout the film constantly calls to mind Khmer Rouge propaganda films of workers clearing rocks and carrying them in futile schemes to irrigate a land without water—the "great leap forward" engineered by Pol Pot's despotic rule. Panh counts on viewers to see through the present to Cambodia's traumatic past.

A powerful sequence near the end of the film poignantly illustrates how the past continues to haunt the present. Two men sit in a field with a piece of fiber optic cable, examining it and speculating about how it works. The talkative man is the group leader, his interlocutor one of the diggers. They examine the wires that make up the cable and consider theories about how it works. The cable is a foreign object removed from their frame of reference, and they do not understand how it works. What begins as curiosity turns into frustration and finally sadness. Panh focuses on the face of the quieter man, wearing the traditional kramar, who laments:

> The Khmer Rouge didn't only kill people. They turned men like me into ignorant people, who don't know where they're going, where they are. We had no schooling, we don't know anything. If I could find them, I would condemn them to death and execute them myself. They turned my generation into ignorant masses, into animals. We can't find jobs, we can only be workers. An ignorant man can use his strength, but not his head. What can he do, being ignorant? There are jobs, but an ignorant man has no skills. He can dig the earth, carry it on his back, that's it. He can't be a builder. The Khmer Rouge drove us mad.

Without editorializing or propagandizing, by using the cinematic means of repetitions and the couplings of imagery, Panh defines the fiber optic cable route as anything but opportunity and potential. These migrant workers are just as enslaved as the Khmer Rouge's forced laborers futilely digging irrigation systems that would never deliver water to arid land or build a fantastical society based on notions of Angkor's past glory. Today Cambodian peasants remain slaves of utopia, just a different brand. Panh presents globalization as the modern iteration of colonialism and totalitarianism with roots in the annihilation of a subjugated and dehumanized people.

So often in his films, Panh includes children who crystalize meaning and provide some comic relief. Here, child's play suggests how children draw connections between the technology of war and of communication. Panh observes several children playing in an open field using two paper cups and a string to talk to each other. Close-ups on the faces of the two boys, largely hidden by the cups they keep switching between ear and mouth, provide us with an intimate if anonymous connection to them, dependent mainly on their voices thrown across the string. Their telephone is a crude but apt imitation of the technology their families have been laboring to make possible, which will usher Cambodia into a global future, a future poised between bombs and commerce, dependent on migrant labor from people too poor to enjoy what they have labored to produce.

Not all characters in this film are heroes. Panh takes pains to portray the corrupt foreman, showing his bombast and swagger, a character clearly at odds with his humble work crew. We see him bragging, dancing in a drunken state, and nervously answering questions about the windup of the project. When we learn he has absconded with everyone's money, we are not surprised. We have observed his weakness, and his behavior is predictable. Panh does not turn him into a cardboard villain but allows us to see him as a flawed man tempted by easy access to a little power and other people's money. His immorality exists within a matrix of impunity.

As the historian David Chandler explains, in the nineties, Cambodia was thrust into the world of Southeast Asia from which it had been isolated since the eighteenth century. No longer a protectorate or a component of Indochina, Cambodia became part of a region about which its people knew little and for whose modernity they were largely unprepared. Today Cambodia is a small, modernizing country, what Chandler deems a mix of continuities and refusals rather than calculated or prudent responses to the rapid and often destructive influences of modern times. Whether its newfound economic independence will ever benefit ordinary Khmer more than those in power remains to be seen; however, the Cambodian people's resilience, talents, and desires suggest that the future is not a foregone conclusion.[14] Rithy Panh's filmmaking is working for that future.

Paper Cannot Wrap Up Embers (Papier ne peux pas envelopper la braise) (2006)

This title comes from a Khmer proverb about the inevitability of truth revealing itself: just as a piece of paper cannot wrap smoldering embers, Cambodia's collective trauma cannot be denied by a desire to forget. As Leslie Barnes also notes, the title evokes the fragility of narrative when faced with the task of "enveloping" traumatic pain. Panh told Barnes that one of the women in the film used the proverb as a means of expressing her doubts about his project: that telling her story would provide her little or no emotional or material comfort.[15]

Paper Cannot Wrap Up Embers has thrown some viewers off balance and even drawn attacks. Over many months, Panh listened to the women in the film tell in their own words what it feels like to be trapped in a dead-end life with no escape apart from drug-induced fantasies or daydreams of rescue by marriage to a rich man. There is nothing sensational or particularly erotic about his representation of these women. And because some of the women are philosophical and articulate in analyzing their predicament, sceptics have charged that the film must be scripted and staged and that, by denying this, Panh is dishonest as a filmmaker.

The scholars Leslie Barnes and Sylvia Blum-Reid believe such criticism comes from viewers who expect a different kind of documentary where the filmmaker stands as the authoritative voice of the film. Panh's method here is closer to direct cinema than the made-for-TV documentary many audiences know, where they expect to be told what to think. Panh rejects such expectations. He believes in his subjects' ability to speak for themselves. He builds rapport with them much as he did with the prison guards in his film *S-21: The Khmer Rouge Killing Machine*, who eventually speak about their crimes—but with one significant difference. In the former film, Panh asked the guards to repeat their testimony and their gestures over and over again until he felt they had finally spoken the truth. But with *Paper*, there were no directions given, no rehearsals or demands for retakes. Instead Panh observed the women over eighteen months in their sparsely furnished rooms on the boulevard Sothearos in Phnom Penh. Panh's approach was a far cry from documentaries that parachute into a situation, confirming viewers' facile assumptions about prostitutes as poor, ignorant victims incapable of providing insight into their lives or changing them. Panh allowed the women to say what they had to say and demonstrate an intelligence the documentary as spectacle often ignores or denies. He edited three hundred hours of material, well aware that there was much more to their lives than a two-hour film could "wrap up." He worked with Louise Lorentz on a book of the same title, based on outtakes, that traced a parallel path in telling the stories of these women's lives. It was published in France when the film was released. The book was part of a process begun more than fifteen years earlier when Panh made his first film about a family in Site 2, a displaced persons' camp on the Thai border. Da, the principal character in *Paper*, grew up in that camp.

We meet thirteen women in *Paper* who range in age from nineteen to twenty-three. They live in the derelict modernist property called the White Building, which was located in the heart of Phnom Penh. We also meet their madame (*la maquerelle*), their pimp (*le rabatteur*), one woman's boyfriend, and their drug connection. Very little happens. It is shot in the daytime when the women sleep, prepare meals, and distract themselves by cutting out photos from magazines. We watch them paint their nails, graffiti the walls, wash each other's hair, and put on makeup before going out to seek their clients. Panh also observes them prepare "mâ," a drug they cook and then inhale through a straw in a bubbling water bottle. Mostly Panh's camera observes the monotony, insecurity, and futility of their days. Many scenes are shot at floor level with an occasional overhead shot that reveals the array of drug paraphernalia scattered around one desperate woman or the incredible tracking that slowly moves from one woman in silhouette to another as both gaze out over a rooftop observing the gathering storm clouds that are always on the horizon of their lives. Patiently, over time, Panh and his spare crew earn the trust of these young women who gradually open up and speak about their fears of being beaten, maimed, or killed by their clients, of contracting AIDS, and of never being able to return home. The film unfolds slowly, with talking sessions alternating with close-ups on telling details—a finger tracing a pattern in the ashes of a cigarette, a child peering through a window grid, and always, the faces of the women straight on or in profile. Sometimes they are silent; sometimes they muse aloud about what they are feeling or thinking. Notable among them is Da, the only one who will succeed in getting out of the sex trade and reclaim her child to pursue another life.

This is not a classically structured narrative driven by characters or events, although it observes an Aristotelian unity of place. In its seemingly aimless

FIGURE 5.6 Da in makeup in *Paper Cannot Wrap Up Embers* © RPanh / droits réservés

FIGURE 5.7 Da lost in shadows in *Paper Cannot Wrap Up Embers* © RPanh / droits réservés

structure, the film mirrors the circularity of lives trapped within the vacant rooms they inhabit by day and the long nights they spend with multiple clients followed by another day of sleeping before it all starts over again. There are the occasional visitors, such as an "old" woman in her thirties who is already past her prime and so able to earn only a few dollars turning tricks out of doors. Most poignant are the visits from family members—the child who will not go to his mother's open arms, clinging to his grandmother, who has brought the toddler to her daughter along with her contempt and demands for more money to pay the rent, water, and electricity bills. In the ordinariness of these incidents, and in the women's comments to each other, we discover the awful weight of their duty, fatigue, fear, and anomie.

Panh never reduces the women to the class of "sex workers." They are individuals with histories that define them. They discuss with each other the dangers of going off with clients, the physical violence they routinely experience, and the constant emotional abuse that comes at them from all quarters. We see one woman badly beaten about the face, being nursed by another who listens to her story. Another confesses angrily that because she was beaten by a white man, she is afraid of all whites. Whether they are addicted to drugs or alcohol or, worse, suffering with AIDS, the women support and encourage each other, sharing their meals, their stories, and their tears. Each is presented as a person with a dignity that defies her daily life. They are unable to escape the demands of male desire and capitalist consumption, according to the film scholar Pavinong Norindr, who believes they are "resigned to their fate." On the contrary, Panh's camera suggests the tears shed, drugs inhaled, and faces bruised make resignation an unlikely response to these women's tragic lives.[16]

There is a scene in the film that begs further exploration. One of the women is tossing on her mat in pain. The viewer may assume she is recovering from an abortion, and Panh does not uncover the cause of her distress in the film. But in *Uncle Rithy*, Panh's Cambodian crew members discuss the making of *Paper*. Doeun explains that she was actually suffering from appendicitis and her maquerelle would do nothing to help her. So Panh took her to a hospital and paid for her surgery. The crew visited her there and supported her during her recovery. Panh does not disclose his role in saving her life in the film or in the book.

Prostitutes in Phnom Penh represent a second generation of genocide survivors, women who have been sold or who opt to sell their bodies to support impoverished families that have never recovered from the harsh years of Khmer Rouge control and Vietnamese occupation. Many of the women in *Paper* grew up in refugee camps after Pol Pot was driven out by the Vietnamese. Without land or charitable support from NGOs, these women's families need someone to earn a living, and the young are often forced to take desperate measures to do so. Panh has written: "Behind this social sorrow is the history of Cambodia, the open wounds of years of the Khmer Rouge. . . . The obvious sign of the social fracture appears in the economic and political exploitation of the body and the spirit. The father-soldiers dead in combat leave child-workers or, worse, prostitutes."[17] This documentary compliments his earlier fiction film *An Evening after the War*, offering a more intimate view of what it means to be a "bar girl" in Cambodia.

Panh wanted viewers to listen to those who are spoken of more often in terms of statistics, erased behind the vast and necessary politics of the fight against AIDS and against human trafficking. Panh wanted viewers to see them with other eyes and hear them. A face, a voice, a name. To *be with them*.[18]

Without editorializing or propagandizing, using the cinematic means of repetition, juxtaposition, and coupling of imagery, Panh presents migrant workers and prostitutes as just as enslaved and dehumanized as the Khmer Rouge's forced laborers. Cambodia's poor remain slaves of utopia, just an updated "brand" driven by a new ideology. Films like *Paper Cannot Wrap Up Embers* and *The Land of Wandering Souls* voice the concerns of individuals relegated to the margins and rarely heard from. Panh does not speak for these others but rather allows them, women and children, peasants and prostitutes, survivors of the Khmer Rouge and their descendants, to enter the discussion about what Cambodia needs to do to ensure a future for all its people.[19]

The People of Angkor (Les gens d'Angkor) (2003)

What a refreshing change of pace *The People of Angkor* must have been for Panh after completing *S-21: The Khmer Rouge Killing Machine* a year before. It was the first of two films in which he focused on "ordinary" Cambodians today. With it and *The Burnt Theater*, he experimented with hybrid forms, mixing fiction and nonfiction and using photos to embody memories of the past. Both were made primarily for Cambodian audiences—they celebrate the creativity of Cambodians and offer advice to young and old facing diverse obstacles in a postrevolutionary society. For cultural outsiders, they provide revealing insights into the art, culture, and resilient heart of the Cambodian people.

The People of Angkor opens with a quartet of men walking through a forest with sunbeams streaming down on them. They are wending their way to a collection of carved stones lying on the forest floor. Their voices are overheard as they work on cleaning and reassembling them, and their voices become part of the vivid soundscape of birds, insects, cello, and contrabass that make us feel as though we are there too. One man is interpreting the story on the frieze they are reassembling, lovingly pointing to the figures as he narrates an incident in the life of Séda, wife of Prince Ream, in the *Reamker*. Here, she is despondent because her husband has rejected her. In this stone, she is giving birth with a midwife helping her. Because her baby is at risk, she gives it to a hermit to keep. But the hermit is not trustworthy. He uses magic to create a double for the baby, whom he plans to kill. He goes to give Séda the impostor but finds her suckling her own infant son. She rescues both boys. Meanwhile, her husband, who ordered that Séda be killed, is filled with remorse. With this account of the stones, we are immediately drawn into the world of classical Cambodian literature and art as interpreted not by scholars but by workmen at Baphuon, one of the temples of Angkor Wat. Panh makes clear from this wonderful opening scene what the subject of this film is. It is not about the UNESCO World Heritage Site and tourist mecca, the oriental temple of global fascination. It is about ordinary Cambodian people who know a great deal about their culture and history and have respect for it.

Thanks to the beautiful cinematography of Prum Mésar, we see the Khmer world as splendid in its veiled mysteries. And thanks goes as well to Panh's sound man Sear Vissal, who captures the vivid sounds of the forest and makes us feel as though we are actually there. Quickly we discover the difference between this magical realm, dappled in sunlight and shade, where these men live and work and the overbright, overcrowded public areas at Angkor Wat where foreign tourists mill about and behave rather stupidly, having their photos taken in front of one of the indulgently smiling stone Buddhas.

There is one principal character in this film, the only one we get to know by name, A'koy, the boy who sells knickknacks, musical instruments, and books about Angkor to the tourists who swarm the temple sites each day. He confides to his "uncles" that his mother abandoned him because she had to escape from the beatings she received from his father. He is angry with both his parents, but he also misses them, especially his mother. A'koy finds an alternate family among these kindly men, these uncles, and with this setup, Panh reorients us to a different experience of Angkor Wat and Cambodia with a boy as our guide. Panh was once a boy who saved his own life by telling stories in a labor camp. He knows what it is like to pin one's hopes on the power of a story to touch a listener. This is a film of stories and their power to touch us.

Panivong Norindr writes insightfully about Panh's strategy in this film:

When these heretofore silent, subaltern figures rarely noticed by the cultural tourists are given the opportunity to speak, they reveal that they possess extraordinary insights into the history of Angkor and Cambodia. They are no longer simply the victims of the Vietnam War and the American bombing campaigns in Cambodia, the victims of the violence and torture meted out by the Khmer Rouge, the beneficiaries of international aid and non-governmental assistance; they become fascinating subjects of knowledge whose intimate intelligence of Angkor transforms these archeological sites into animated spaces, places re-humanized because they are inhabited by people who work and worship, dream and fantasize in Angkor.[20]

Panh contrasts different ways of thinking about the past by contrasting one of the uncle's stories about the subject of a well-known bas-relief, a story that mirrors the life and hardship that farmers experience to this day, with the version A'koy hears being told by guides regaling foreign tourists. The uncle offers his description of the carving:

UNCLE "Peasants spend their lives ploughing, planting. . . . They have to fight, build dikes, harvest, thresh, then cross the forest to sell it to the merchant to buy *prahok* and salt. But the merchant gives very little money. How can they buy *prahok* and salt? He grips the sack and weeps into his hands. It's like today."

A'KOY "According to what the guides say, these people are carrying rice to go and sell it when one of their friends is devoured by a tiger. They are scared and start running. They reach the pagoda. He grips the sack and weeps because his friend has been killed by the tiger."

Somewhat puzzled, the uncle concludes, "I don't know now. They all have different versions."

Here are two stories based on the same images, one from the viewpoint of a farmer whose life is rooted in his rice paddy, the other an adventure for foreign visitors expecting danger, violence, death, and the defeat of peasants carrying rice. It is a story of colonialism, really—so simple, so seemingly unrehearsed, so powerful. The final word comes from one of the uncles, who simply says, "No one notices poor people." Countering this state of invisibility is a central aim of *The People of Angkor*.

By reframing the sites of Khmer cultural production and decentering our vision away from the ancient monumental architecture, Panh invites viewers to really see these "invisible" Cambodians. And by introducing viewers to the magical and sacred realms, giving voice to the desires and ambitions of the Khmer people, he makes it difficult for viewers to merely consume Angkor Wat aesthetically. His film offers an antidote to the desire to petrify Cambodia and its architectural grandeur and fix its cultural traits in a few emblematic signs and figures, according to Norindr, who thinks that Panh guides us "to focus on the invisible, the marginal, and the subaltern."[21]

Khmer heritage is a living memory that dwells in the daily practice of rice cultivation. Rice is more than a staple of the Cambodian diet; it is a practical art that anchors Cambodian identity in the land and in a spirituality whose faith in the impermanence of the material world—a central tenet in Theravada Buddhism—is recognized. Throughout the film, Panh mixes mythological and animistic beliefs with Hinduism and Buddhism, which are all part of a complex system of Cambodian beliefs. This is the first time Panh shows a monk looking into the past on behalf of the forlorn A'koy, a trope that will surface several years later in Panh's autobiographical trilogy where photos and psychic mediums play a critical role.

The People of Angkor is a film about men—or rather four father surrogates who take a boy under their care. Panh, well schooled in documentary history, profits from what Robert Flaherty discovered when making his films: a father, a son, and a dog are sure to win the hearts of viewers, only here, it is four father substitutes and a rooster who amply fill these rolls. Each uncle has something to share with the boy. The proud owner of the cockfighter named Lemon Soup tells A'koy about the spirits of the forest, recounting a story while seated at the base of a great tree.

Another man shows him where his favorite *apsaras*[22] are hidden on the bas reliefs at Baphuon. Yet another guides him to his favorite place in a coursing river where underwater stone carvings of reclining apsaras are visible to those who know to look. He also points out the lingam and yoni stones, embodiments of male and female Hindu gods, also buried there and over which the river flows, carrying fertility to the crops that nourish the people. Finally, an uncle explains the meaning of the four monkeys A'koy sells to tourists; it is a cautionary tale for the boy, who risks losing everything he dreams of if he fails to get an education. Collectively, the men support and encourage the boy, sharing their love for their culture, the natural world, and him.

Lurking in the margins throughout the film is the allure of the Buddhist apsara. A'koy addresses a carving of one of these female divinities in supplication at the beginning and end of the film. He is bereft without his mother and searches for maternal answers from the beautiful feminine divinities carved on the temple walls. He carries a photo of a woman who looks like his mother and wants to know if he can find her. Sadly, he learns from the monk that the woman in the photo is dead, shot when she was trying to escape the Khmer Rouge in 1979 while crossing a river. The river is a symbol of birth and is also considered a pathway to freedom. A woman giving birth is said to be crossing the river. Panh, who ceaselessly mourns his own mother, weaves into the film the importance of women even in their absence.

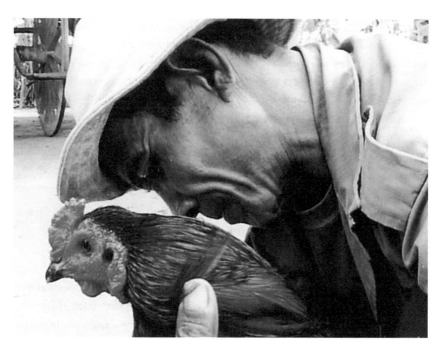

FIGURE 5.8 Lemon Soup in *The People of Angkor* © RPanh / droits réservés

Throughout the film, A'koy is seen looking at a series of eight-by-eleven-inch, black-and-white archival images of Angkor Wat, many dating to the days when it was first being renovated by the French, and this memory prompt becomes a device to structure the film. Photographs, which freeze evanescent moments of the past and mirror the fragility of memory itself, offer Panh a delicate way of reclaiming that past. It is an interesting gesture, perhaps not fully realized here, but his use of the photos is a rehearsal for the ways he will use them in later films.

Throughout the film, there is an undercurrent of longing for education—movingly expressed by one man who regrets taking his gifted son out of school: he had no money to spare for his education because he spent it on food. A'koy wants to become a temple guide but knows it is unlikely to ever happen because he would need to learn how to read and be able to learn other languages. Attending school is difficult when all he can do to make his way in the world is sell souvenirs. He has no idea what his future will be, and he asks the monk for help as he does the apsara.

Panh relies on these people with their real-world problems to encourage Cambodians to consider the importance of education as well as the value of asking for help when dealing with difficult problems. For a nation still suffering from trauma and equipped with few health care practitioners who can help, this is a daunting task, one Panh has tried to facilitate in various ways for Cambodians both at home and in the diaspora. The cockfight is a story as old as the temple walls and still part of life today. It plays a key role in the film and surprisingly serves as a way of addressing men about the importance of healing. The uncle's beloved rooster, the fierce Lemon Soup, apparently wins his fight against his adversary Sour Cabbage, but the bird is badly wounded, and his doting owner—who confesses the bird is like a woman to him—attempts to heal him with ointments and folk remedies. The cock is surprisingly docile in the hands of his caretaker, but his future is uncertain. Who would have thought Lemon Soup could serve a larger role for traditional people in need of healing help?

The film is a hybrid, part fiction, part documentary. The terminology *docudrama* is distinctly inappropriate. The boy's story feels true, as do the stories told by the men who are his companions, yet their grouping together seems too artfully choreographed for it to be spontaneous discovery on Panh's part. His directorial skills have always been keenest when he is working with ordinary people, and if the viewer is uncertain about whether they are actors or not, this is testimony to Panh's ability to leave one happy with this ambiguity.

The Burnt Theater (*Les artistes du théâtre brûlé*) (2005)

The Burnt Theater artfully illustrates Panh's penchant for beginning in medias res. "I love films where there is no event at the start: the film begins and is already in the midst of its story," he writes. "To describe the structure of my films, I like to think of the image of a wheel: it turns on itself and advances all the same."[23] *The Burnt Theater* opens with percussive sounds and then a wide shot revealing a scene of chaos as people run to and fro, trying to escape from imminent danger. A woman flees, hysterical, hugging her baby; a man lies dead; and another woman begins an angry lament about the Khmer Rouge. Where are we? What is happening? Suddenly the scene cuts to a cluster of men whose leader steps forward and angrily criticizes the speech being given by the woman. It turns out that they are on the overgrown stage of the "burnt theater," the once splendid Suramarit National Theater, designed and built by Cambodia's great modernist architect Vann Molyvann in 1968 as part of postindependence nation building. The theater was retitled the Tonle Bassac National Theater after Lon Nol came to power. It was then neglected for twenty years but used by Pol Pot for his own propaganda rallies. In 1994, during a renovation project, fire led to the National Theater's near destruction, leaving its 250-person troupe homeless and depressed. Endless delays kept support to restore the theater from being realized, and it then became a symbol of the failure of the nationalist project.[24] In 2005, when Panh made this film, the future looked very bleak.[25] He believed in these artists, who were among the 10 percent of dancers, actors, and shadow puppeteers who survived the Khmer Rouge and were now living on ten or fifteen dollars a month. They were not only victims of governmental indifference to traditional culture but of Cambodia's neoliberal policies, which reached their zenith as property speculation.[26]

All during the film, we hear the obnoxious sounds of pile drivers and concrete mixers preparing for the construction of a casino and shopping mall. This is, among other things, an aggressive manifestation of globalization. In making this film, Panh was engaged in a last-ditch effort to stay the wrecking ball and advocate for the transmission of traditional Cambodian culture to a new generation. Most of the people on the outdoor stage are members of the renaissance in Cambodian arts that flourished during the eighties. The war being enacted on the jury-rigged stage is actually the war of capital versus culture, and sadly capital is winning. The blasts heard are not bullets being fired, but they are just as deadly for the future of the artists of the burnt theater.

Four people have principal roles in the film: Peng Phan, the angry actress on stage; Doeun, the resilient actor who reminisces about playing Cyrano de Bergerac; Hoeun, the puppeteer, musician, and actor who misses his distant family; and Bopha, a younger-generation journalist who is writing about the desperate measures of a new generation ill equipped to survive today. Peng and Doeun are part of Panh's extended family of collaborators who function in various roles in his films. Doeun played M. King in *The Sea Wall* and was part of the crew for the documentary *Paper Cannot Wrap Up Embers*; Peng played the mother in both *Rice People* and *One Evening after the War* and helped with costumes for *The Sea Wall*. They do what they can, not just for a paycheck but because they belong to a community that needs them.

It is not clear at the start of *The Burnt Theater* whether these actors are in a documentary where they speak about their own lives and occasionally perform theatrical roles or whether they are acting throughout, following a script cleverly devised by Panh and his longtime creative partner Agnès Sénémaud. Spoiler alert: there is no script, but this ambiguity is deliberate. We wonder if the actress Peng has really taken up embroidery to get by and ruined her

FIGURE 5.9 Prum Mésar, on camera, Sear Vissal, on sound, and Panh directing *The Burnt Theater* © John Vink / MAPSimages

FIGURE 5.10 Panh films the dwarf actor Loto in *The Burnt Theater* © John Vink / MAPSimages

sight in the process or if this is a part she plays that depicts genocide survivors struggling to cope with trauma, in need of help but unable to find relief from the psychological pains that plague them. Panh plays with the audience's expectations, which allows us to see how fiction and fact combine for people who have experienced all these roles, as survivors, actors, and ordinary people forced to find other ways to make a living in a nation that no longer values them. Panh includes other performers, such as a once celebrated comic actor, the dwarf Loto, and commercial filmmakers from central casting whose idea of on-screen romance is terrible, but at least they pay.

As with many of Panh's films made during this period, the dialogue is spoken in Khmer and addressed largely to Cambodians who will understand what lies within this opening scene. Cultural values of civilization contrast with what is wild; elegance challenges chaos and upheaval. Panh borrows from several traditional forms of Cambodian theater, beginning with *yike*, in which drumming pulses throughout and plotted dialogue is mixed with improvisation.[27] Panh ingeniously incorporates the percussive drilling on the construction site into a kind of yike drumbeat, a detail that may be lost on Western viewers. Panh's experimental use of Cambodian theater forms is far more interesting and complex than docudrama, a term mistakenly applied by some critics of this film, which entirely misses the inventiveness of the film's structure.

Panh borrows some of the varied forms of Cambodian theater but ignores Cambodian classical ballet, although a rehearsal by folk dancers is seen from a distance. Much as he reclaimed Angkor Wat as a site belonging to Cambodians, not tourists, in *The People of Angkor*, here he addresses popular forms of Cambodian theater so different from the court ballet known in the West but rarely viewed by Cambodians. He focuses on the *lakhaoun niyeay*, or "modern spoken drama," a theater of ideas that can introduce risky political thoughts and features translations and adaptations of classical Western plays by writers like Molière, Chekhov, and Shakespeare. This is what Doeun performs in a scene from Edmond Rostand's *Cyrano de Bergerac*. He lends his feathered hat and sword to Hoeun, humorously teaching him how to speak tongue-twisting lines in French because Hoeun would love to play the role himself. Hoeun is a poet, musician, and master of another form of spoken drama—*sbek touch*, or "shadow puppetry"—which consists of improvised stories told with articulated leather puppets that entertain audiences of all ages. He performs a sweet vignette about a mother bird with her babies. Shadow puppets anticipated the arrival of cinema, which may explain why they are dear to Panh.

Without some familiarity with traditional and modern Cambodian theater, most Western viewers will be at a loss to understand the mix of styles here. This may be why the film has been misunderstood by some reviewers and proven more popular in Asia than in the West. Of course, everyone will recognize karaoke performed by Doeun and Hoeun, who give their interpretation of a romantic ballad made famous by the inestimable Cambodian singer Sin Sisamouth.

Is Hoeun really heartbroken living far from his family with little to show for his commitment to his art? Is Peng really suffering from the debilitating effects of trauma like so many others? Their stories are all too common for a generation of survivors forced off their land and into the city to survive. The lively actor Doeun now juggles many jobs—acting in small parts in bad films and dishonest political commercials or driving a motodop taxi around Phnom Penh. He is resilient, but he is forced to take on work far below his abilities. Bopha asks them about their lives, and her curiosity represents the generation born after the genocide that must cope with the hidden histories, painful memories, and lingering ills of their parents and grandparents. One solution to their emotional problems is both whimsical and impractical. Doeun and Hoeun each shout their litany of pain into a ceramic pot and then cover it quickly with a lid before smashing it spectacularly, one way of exorcising the pains within and releasing tension with dramatic satisfaction.

In one sense, very little "happens" in *The Burnt Theater*—dancers rehearse, musicians practice, and our actors duck collapsing ceilings and slide down crumbling staircases in their makeshift professional home. Panh takes us outside the theater when Bopha visits a huge garbage dump where people climb over mountains of decaying produce searching for remnants of food and objects to sell. She interviews some children processing metal cans and clips a boy's fingernails, asking him how he deals with the many injuries to his hands, and he replies he is used to it now. We see Peng in her apartment in the White Building, which soon will be demolished as artists and activists are forced to find other housing in an increasingly gentrified Phnom Penh. Peng goes to the clinic and chats with others dealing with health problems. Hoeun and Doeun ride a motodop through city streets and into the surrounding countryside and talk of what matters most to them. But always the camera returns to the endangered theater, where Hoeun hacks away at the jungle-like overgrowth of weeds in the open pit of the theater in the final scene. The artists cling to each other's company in the National Theater's final days. The constant drumbeat of the pile drivers underscores the inevitable, that time is running out. The final image of two tears rolling down Hoeun's face is not so much sentimental as realistic, a naked moment of mourning for what is slipping away not only for these artists but for Cambodian culture.

The relationship between cultural and economic development in Cambodia is almost nonexistent apart from tourism. Panh believes that if you "forget to develop culture and identity, you remain economically poor and spiritually impoverished. . . . To the world at large, you are just another pool of cheap labor."[28] Making *The Burnt Theater* was Panh's ill-fated attempt to prevent another act of cultural violence not witnessed since the days of the Khmer Rouge.

There is one hidden surprise in *The Burnt Theater* that deserves attention. When Peng is telling Bopha about her experience in the jail where she was sent by the Khmer Rouge, she illustrates her story by moving little houses in a simple diorama of the village. It is a cinematic experiment that leads to another. In Panh's next film, *Paper Cannot Wrap Up Embers*, there is a scene in which Da positions little plastic soldiers on a village layout she has drawn with crayons. Both films included brief but important rehearsals for the solution Panh finally found—clay figurines placed in elaborate dioramas—that would allow him to tell his own story of survival during the Khmer Rouge regime, *The Missing Picture*.

6

Colonialism

France and Cambodia

> Colonies do not cease to be colonies
> because they are independent.
>
> **BENJAMIN DISRAELI** (1863)

As a refugee in France fleeing the Cambodian genocide, Rithy Panh saw Alain Resnais and Jean Cayrol's *Night and Fog* (*Nuit et Brouillard*, 1954) in a film club in Grenoble when he was eighteen. It revealed to the traumatized teenager that what he had experienced under the Khmer Rouge had happened before under the Nazis. The film's ending includes a thinly veiled allusion to France's mistreatment of Algerians then in revolt against the French colonial order. A few years later, as a film student in Paris, Panh discovered *Les Statues meurent aussi* (*Statues also Die*, 1952), an anticolonialist film by Resnais and Chris Marker that praised African art and culture and criticized European imperialism. That film, like *Night and Fog*, was censored in France.[1]

They would have a profound effect on Panh, who discovered through them that filmmaking was a tool of expression he could use to tell his own story.[2]

France's furthermost outpost was Indochina, composed of Vietnam (Tonkin, Annam, and Cochinchina), Laos, and Cambodia.[3] When Cambodia was threatened by enemies at its borders in 1850, King Norodom turned to Emperor Napoleon III and asked him to set up a protectorate over Cambodia. Although France saved Cambodia from absorption by Siam (Thailand) and Vietnam, it reduced the king to a puppet and exploited the country for all its worth. The protectorate lasted ninety years, from 1863 until 1953, long enough to disturb the foundation of Cambodia's traditional society. It ended in the wave of decolonization that swept the globe after World War II. The French left Indochina reluctantly, forced out by their defeat in the First Indochina War, in which Viet Minh forces battled the French Expeditionary Force.[4] The protectorate was formally abolished in 1946, and in 1953 Cambodia's King Sihanouk welcomed the return of full independence.[5]

Rithy Panh's life—shuttling between Cambodia and France—has afforded him a unique perspective to examine the alliance forged by an imperial power and a Southeast Asian country struggling to survive enemies within and without. Although he did not grow up during the French protectorate, his parents and grandparents did, and they told stories of what happened during those years.

As the historian John Tully explains, France's aims in Cambodia were contradictory: the desire for power and glory mingled with the venality of the profit motive. It was defended by a belief in *la mission civilisatrice*—"the self-appointed duty of Europeans to bring the supposed benefits of white civilization to the brown Caliban."[6] *Mise en valeur* was one of the pillars of French colonial ideology. It connotes not only economic development of the kind pursued by other imperial nations but also the moral and cultural improvement to be forged in the colonies. It was a means to measure and display the beneficial impact of the French enterprise abroad, a form of auto-legitimation for imperial France.[7] The French ruled Cambodia as a dictatorship of police and civil servants. Despite abolishing traditional slavery, the French introduced new forms of bondage on plantations and on public work schemes. Dissidents were arbitrarily detained and tortured, and prisoners were routinely ill treated. The French Revolution's Rights of Man and the Citizen were not for export to the colonies.

The French did some worthwhile things during the protectorate. They preserved Cambodian political unity and restored lost northern and northwestern provinces. They restored aspects of Khmer culture—specifically

Angkor Wat, the symbol of its nationhood—and contributed to a Buddhist renaissance, building libraries and publishing classical texts in cheap editions. They gave Cambodia a protracted period of peace and stability. And they built roads, railroads, and other communications systems, enabling Phnom Penh to become a modern metropolis.

As for the negative, France did not leave behind representative government, an independent judiciary, or a guaranteed free press. They left Cambodia an economically backward state with a small Indigenous middle class. They gave administrative positions to Vietnamese, partly from expediency and partly from a policy of divide and rule, further fueling resentments between these long-standing enemies. Colonialism served to strengthen Cambodia's existing tendencies toward autocracy and the exclusion of the general population from decision-making, a legacy that lingers until today.[8]

When the deputies in the French National Assembly passed a law in 2005 stating that France should be proud of its civilizing mission, Panh angrily thought it should have been apologizing for all the evils it had committed under the guise of bringing civilization to its possessions.[9] France should have admitted that colonization was the worst mistake committed by the Western world. His response was to make two very different films—one a compilation documentary drawn from archival films of the colonial era, *France Is Our Mother Country* (*La France est notre Patrie*, 2015) and the other a fiction film he adapted from a roman à clef by Marguerite Duras, *The Sea Wall* (*Barrage contre le Pacifique*, 2008).

France Is Our Mother Country (La France est notre patrie) (2015)

The expansion of exploration and trade during the eighteenth century influenced the Enlightenment's concept of universal human rights, but the industrial and technological expansion that occurred during the nineteenth century converted this idealism into capitalist systems of colonial exploitation around the globe. Exploitation of raw material, cheap labor, and markets for manufactured goods demanded that the imperial doctrine be presented in beneficent terms. *La mission civilisatrice* became the Third Republic's official governmental policy in 1895,[10] the same year the Lumières invented the *cinématographe* and created the first film audiences.[11] In 1912, the governor-general of Indochina established a *mission cinématographique* to make films that represented the country as peaceful and stable but

backward and in need of capital investment from home.[12] Cinema, the early
film scholar Tom Gunning points up, played an important role in the colonies. Cinema circulated widely, dissolving the separation inherent in space
and time and collapsing distance into the new proximity of a global image
culture. Early film companies begun by the Lumière brothers and Pathé-
Frères offered up the world in the form of consumable images.[13] Their travel
films brought the idea of a global home to the average citizen and proved to
be successful propaganda encouraging many to seek their fortune and future
in France's vast overseas empire. Marguerite Duras's parents were among
them.[14] Cinema quickly became instrumentalized as a tool for colonization,
"a pivotal element of the colonial apparatus."[15]

France Is Our Mother Country is drawn almost exclusively from silent,
black-and-white films made by French filmmakers and propagandists.[16] Panh
borrowed the look of early silent films with their decorated intertitles to
create a frame to distance himself and viewers from the colonial perspective. Films chosen were among many well-known firsts in cinema history,
including *actualités*, newsreels, governmental and commercial films, and
military records. Panh began with the working title "Cochinchine," but in
the process of researching, he decided to cast a wider net to include scenes of
"la plus grande France"—from the Maghreb of North Africa to Central and
South Africa as well as Southeast Asia. Taken together they represent a history shared by all subjects of the French colonial system. Panh's assemblage is
filtered through his perspective and infused with irony, sarcasm, and criticism. Reviewers often comment there is no commentary, but through the
barbed intertitles, emotionally evocative soundscape, and dialectical editing
of film fragments, he communicates his own story of French colonialism.

Panh spent two years researching in public and private archives mainly in
France. In the end he focused on films by the Lumière operator Gabriel Veyre,
who was situated in Vietnam between 1899 and 1900; films by Léon Busy,
one of many filmmakers hired between 1908 and 1931 by the philanthropist
Albert Kahn for his ambitious Archives de la Planète;[17] a ten-part BBC television documentary series, *The Wonderful World of Albert Kahn*, broadcast
in 2009, and drawn from Kahn's vast private archive;[18] and *La France est un
Empire*, a feature-length propaganda film conceived and directed by the novelist Jean d'Agraives between 1939 and 1943.[19] In addition to these essential
films, there are numerous film fragments from Pathé, Gaumont, Le Secours
Catholique, and ECPAD (Agence d'Images de la Défense—Fonds Indochine, Fonds Première Guerre Mondiale, Fonds privée). It will come as no
surprise that Panh's treatment of these films differs greatly from the way they

were originally presented in French movie theaters. The thousands of meters of unedited films made for the Kahn archive never reached a general audience; they were shown only to intellectuals and experts with the intention that the archive serve only scientific, ethnographic purposes and be kept at considerable remove from popular audiences' entertainment.

La France est Notre Patrie is not the first documentary to address colonialism in Southeast Asia. *Mother Dao, the Turtlelike* (1995), by the Netherlands archivist Vincent Monnikendam, was made from films shot between 1912 and 1933 by the Dutch East Indies Company. Following a poetic retelling of the West Sumatran origin story about Mother Dao, who created the first man and woman, luminous black-and-white nitrate films unfold the wordless story of the colonial system in Indonesia. *Bontoc Eulogy* (1994), by the Filipino American filmmaker Marlon Fuentes, is a hybrid film mixing archival footage with staged scenes about the filmmaker's grandfather, a Bontoc Igorot, who was exhibited at the 1904 St. Louis World's fair and never returned to his village. *Bontoc Eulogy* stimulated considerable debate about the limits of mixing fiction with fact in a film that was both misunderstood and critically acclaimed for its daring scrutiny of the ethnographic gaze. They are precursors to Panh's film mainly in their desire to call attention to the questionable practices of colonial masters in Southeast Asia. Panh's film strategy, however, has more in common with the work of Péter Forgács, the prolific Hungarian filmmaker and archivist who mines European home movies for his films about the Holocaust, Spanish Civil War, and other twentieth-century tragedies. What archival filmmakers do, regardless of their subjects, is invite viewers to see "cinema," how it controls and constructs meaning. As one anonymous reviewer wrote about Panh's film, "The camera fixes people into place, like a collector might stick an insect with a pin. In taking back this footage, subverting its initial purpose, the filmmaker renders explicit the machinery of oppression."[20]

Panh explained his method to an interviewer: "I navigate the images and try to say something. I don't respect areas or dates. I search for an affinity of images: images that I feel, that shock me, and from there, I try to tell a story that my parents told me or that I read in books. . . . I was never colonized. I just want misunderstandings to disappear."[21]

La France est Notre Patrie begins with one of the most powerful metaphoric images in Panh's imaginary—a decaying colonial building overtaken by the immense, sinuous roots and branches of the *Tetrameles nudiflora*, with limbs like tentacles that wind around whatever stands in its path, overtaking the colonial ruin here and all that it represents. This astonishing opening image conveys the revolt of nature and its triumph over the alien incursion of colonialism. The revolving shot encircles the ruin much like the tree. Dance music seamlessly allows for the transition from the ruin of today to color home movies of yesterday showing families dancing on the balcony of their colonial home, enjoying the last pleasures of colonial privilege. This extraordinary image of the devouring tree is reprised in wide angle at the end, the only scene in this compilation documentary shot by Panh.

Much as he does with his analysis of film fragments of Khmer Rouge propaganda, Panh analyzes the propaganda embedded in colonial-era films to expose the deceptive messages they promoted to naive viewers at the time. His film is a dialogue between intertitles and film fragments. Panh's intertitles function not as information but as a rhetorical tool. Most significant and damning is the first title, written by the medical doctor Legendre, whose mission in Indochina was to furnish scientific justification for colonialism. He is quoted as declaring: "All the great events, all the great revolutions of history have been the work of the white race, the only creative among all races." Panh immediately juxtaposes this with scenes of the temples of Angkor Wat, emphatically rebutting Legendre's assertion without sparing a word to make his point. A series of intertitles written by Panh collaborator Christophe Bataille follows. They express the ideology promoted to French movie audiences over fifty years. "France seeks neither possessions nor glory. Its vision of mankind is fraternal and generous." "All the people of the empire will know equality and progress." "Those who resist enlightenment are justly punished." "Working for the motherland is a joy." These titles are sandwiched between film fragments that challenge the texts with cinematic evidence from the everyday lives of colonized people. As the film approaches its conclusion, the tone of the intertitles shifts and the decorative frame around them disappears as a modern sans serif typeface introduces a critical, darker tone: "An empire that believes it has a mission is a lost empire." "Open your eyes, young sons of France. The empire of sorrow. Forgotten, peace and prosperity, science and literature." "France is our country. It is not an empire, not a dream, not a mother." "France has left. It is a story of pictures and a story in pictures, beautiful and toxic."

Gone is any notion that primitive people, enlightened by colonial benevolence, should be grateful. A torrent of images of native people drafted to fight in wars for the empire, to work in coal mines, rice fields, rubber plantations, and brick kilns, demonstrate the falsehood inherent to colonial rhetoric. Panh's intertitles work closely with his dialectical visual montage to provoke, amuse, and deepen viewer reflections about the colonial past and its relationship to the present.

Added to words and images is the third component, the often haunting, sometimes jarring, unpredictable audio collage of music—now jazzy, now discordant, now hauntingly familiar—and natural sounds of insects buzzing, birds calling, waves lapping, storms thundering. With carefully chosen words, sounds, and images, Panh creates a disturbing portrait of the colonial era for a film he has stitched together with a purpose.

Although viewers may find this approach a complete departure from a director known for his powerful, interview-driven films about the Cambodian genocide, *France Is Our Mother Country* is very much in line with his signature use of cinematic evidence to challenge falsehood and denials of guilt. The film employs his method of interrogating perpetrators and demanding accountability, only in this case, there are no perpetrators present to answer for their crimes. There is a kinship between Legendre's colonial justifications delivered in a decorative intertitle with the Khmer Rouge slogans elegantly written on cards Panh hands to the director of S-21 prison in *Duch, Master of the Forges of Hell*. Ideological slogans are a means of indoctrination that Panh cinematically contests in both eras with evidence of crimes demanding accountability.

Panh's selection of images for *France Is Our Mother Country* is drawn from a large pool of archival films—some were made by filmmaker-salesmen marketing the cinématographe for purchase around the globe; others, by travelers like the philanthropist Albert Kahn in search of knowledge and a better understanding of other cultures; some are home movies made by colonists for their amusement and for family and friends; others were made to promote France's political, economic, and religious interests during a time of occupation, collaboration, and resistance. The challenge of "reading" films made by diverse directors over half a century in varied nations for different purposes is considerable. "I take the images out of their contexts to give to each image a new sense," Panh explains.[22] And in his "indigenous way," as he sardonically states at the very end of the film, Panh arranges these fragments without words acknowledging that they play with us. "They teach us how to look, how to look at them." Whether viewers can tell their own stories from watching these fragments is questionable. It is more likely that Panh's design will lead viewers to see what he has carefully constructed for them to see. But being dependent on the goodwill of his French followers and sponsors, he needs to tread carefully when making a film critical about France. It is probably wiser to claim there is no commentary, no story, than to acknowledge one is there coursing throughout the film.

In making *La France est Notre Patrie*, Panh was working for the first time without his brilliant, now-retired editor Marie-Christine Rougerie. Anna Borie lent an entirely different digital sense of time as assistant editor. Since then, he has taken on the editing job himself. Sometimes the images chosen are humorous—as with shots of lumbering, overfed colonial hunters astride burdened animals. But more often the images are disturbing, like the shot of a child, initially smiling for the camera, whose exaggerated expression quickly changes to one of fear as the reel runs out. With images like this, he juxtaposes contrasting scenes against each other or weaves similar ones throughout the work, images made in different places and times that nonetheless convey the persistence of colonial attitudes and behaviors. For example, numerous film fragments show Indigenous people in various postures of begging, the objects of colonial largesse. Seen as an aggregate, they trumpet the abject poverty of these "enigmatic and simple people" and the unequal power dynamic that "benevolence" asserts over them. The most infamous begging scene is of colonial ladies in Saigon tossing sapeques (coins) to children, what Bertrand Tavernier reports in his voice-over for the *Lumière Brothers' First Films* collection is "a great comment on colonialism in fifty seconds."[23] How women—both native and foreign—were seen and valued emerges as one of the major through lines in the film.

The first sequence of an Indigenous woman—probably in a home movie—presents her with a deer-in-the-headlights look in her eyes, impeccably attired in Western clothing, tentatively taking tottering steps toward the camera, egged on by a couple of Frenchmen who laugh conspiratorially in the shadows behind her. Why is she hesitant? What are they laughing at? Viewers can only guess at the answers given the ambiguous nature of this film, but it is easy to imagine she is uncomfortable, dressed up in clothes native women were not supposed to wear,[24] prodded to do something she did not want to do. Another disturbing sequence, accompanied by an intertitle, features a parade of foreign soldiers and sailors climbing up steps with their arms around their "little spouses"—their native *congaï* or concubines. In another scene, several young women wearing only their underwear pose for the camera amid a group of spectators. An intertitle helpfully differentiates the "sensual" and "submissive" natures of Vietnamese and Cambodian women, and an interior shot of men drinking and embracing them suggests the demimonde of bar or bordello.

Women as objects of desire with little agency abound throughout, but one of the most interesting films, shot by Léon Busy, stands out. Originally titled

Scène de Déshabillage, Tonkin (1921), it depicts a slender Vietnamese woman undressing and then dressing in traditional clothing for the camera. Like another scene by Busy of a girl washing her hair in a river, she stands at full height and looks at the camera, aware that she is being watched. Her self-awareness brings to the fore the pornographic potential of the scientific ethnographic gaze, and it is possible that Busy shot it slightly out of focus to try to undercut that voyeurism. Some film scholars have commented that this out-of-focus image may emphasize the myth of Indochina as a woman who is ultimately unknowable.[25] Perhaps. Still, she has agency. She does not adopt an erotic pose but rather stands upright, looks directly at the cameraman/spectator, and defies being seen as a fantasy object. This rare reciprocal gaze between cameraman and subject upsets the conventional power balance between a white male observer and a colonized female Other.[26] "Powerful people don't watch the camera the same way as weak and poor people," Panh observes.[27] Here is one woman who is not defeated by someone in power.

Angkor Wat often features in these films. Fashion footage of haute couture models posing with the temples and elephants as props hint at how little value the Métropole placed on ancient cultures, Eastern religions, or women's dignity in this glib commercial shoot. Panh contrasts two images of women dancing: girls learning classical Cambodian dance gestures from their teacher on a terrace at Angkor Wat with a trio of native girls in pink tutus *en pointe*, opposing ideas of classical dance in which the Western ballet dancers seem absurdly out of place. Once again Angkor Wat provides incontrovertible evidence that art, religion, and history belong to all and are not the gift of the French to a primitive people without history or culture.

Panh artfully arranges his treasure trove of archival evidence for audiences that may have little or no knowledge of the history of French colonialism or the sources for these films. This creates some confusion, as reviewers' misunderstandings point up. Beyond the broad themes evident here—of forced conversion to Christianity, military conscription during wartime, the objectification, sexual exploitation, and racist treatment of native people, and the pillage of natural resources for the profit of French colonists—ambiguous images can lead to unreliable conclusions. Without historical context, viewers can flounder about trying to understand what it is that they are seeing. One suspects this too is part of Panh's method. But most of the time, contrasting themes argue clearly and unmistakably for accountability and against hypocrisy. No intertitle is needed when Panh cuts from bordello scenes to religious processions in honor of Our Lady of Lourdes. Arguably the most sinister sequence in the film shows a class of little boys bowing to a portly priest in pith helmet who drives off with one little fellow grimly seated beside him in the car, a scene no longer perceived as innocent by viewers today.

These and other themes of exploitation and abuse are essential to the film's voiceless discourse along with the insistence on incessant labor required for processing rubber, harvesting rice, felling trees, laying railroad tracks, building bridges, and working on factory lines. As *La France est Notre Patrie* approaches its end, there is the increasing presence of military at war, scenes of paratroopers descending from planes, infantry entering unfamiliar territory, dead soldiers lying in the mud or being carried away by comrades, villages burning, and peasants being punished or killed. It is colonialism's descent into a spiral of violence as the empire becomes the enemy and ultimately concedes defeat. The ineluctable relationship between the colonial era and the future beyond the protectorate, which gave way to new wars and a genocidal regime, is left to audiences to imagine. The dizzying imagery of overworked colonized laborers is echoed in Khmer Rouge propaganda films of "new people" worked to death, films that will be shot a few years after the demise of the protectorate. "A film cannot change the world," Panh says. "But maybe it can open your eyes and tell you that you have in your hand the possibility of change."[28]

Panh told an interviewer that the inspiration behind *La France est Notre Patrie* was a response to Europe and Australia's refusal to accept refugees. He realized that some populations were fleeing to the West in large part because others had exploited their country's resources. Once again, powerful nations had viewed weaker ones as fair game, much as colonial powers like France did when they were "protecting" the land and people of Indochina. "No one wants to take responsibility, to take care of this," he lamented. "One does not ask to take on another's difficulties but simply to show solidarity, to share responsibility for these populations in difficulty."[29]

The Sea Wall (*Un barrage contre le Pacifique*) (2008)

Alain Resnais's *Hiroshima mon amour*, a dramatic encounter between a French actress and a Japanese man after World War II, began as a documentary, but after months of contemplation, Resnais decided to bring the novelist Marguerite Duras onto the project because he realized he needed a collaborator who could spark his imagination with the music of words. Panh was fascinated by Resnais's idea of constructing a fiction film in which pieces of unaltered reality are caught in a fictional net, and this gave him encouragement for what he wanted to accomplish.[30] Duras's writing for *Hiroshima mon amour* led the young Panh to read her novels, which was not easy because his French was not very good yet. With his Khmer dictionary in hand, he translated her first autobiographical novel, *Un Barrage Contre le Pacifique* (*The Sea Wall*), which is set in Cambodia in 1931. He liked it immensely, especially because of her anticolonial stance,[31] and he kept it "under his pillow" for years.[32] It was just a matter of time before he would translate it to film.[33]

Duras's novel was both documentary and fiction: she had lived the story of *The Sea Wall*,[34] but she relied on the freedom of fiction to recount it. "I wanted to feel as free as she was," Panh told an interviewer. "I really like this way of respecting reality while transcending it. With this adaptation, I wanted to shoot an open film, generous, popular . . . a family drama, a sentimental story, and also an uncompromising description of the colonial system."[35]

Duras's novel was an immediate critical success when it was published in 1950. Americans were struck by the similarities between the *pauvres colons* (poor settlers) and poor whites in the United States during the Great Depression. In France, most readers found *The Sea Wall* an indictment of colonialism and the evils of imperialism.[36]

In searching for a screenwriter to collaborate with him, Panh found Michel Fessler, who had grown up in French Africa. Like Panh, Fessler had read and reread *The Sea Wall*. It was the only novel that allowed him to relive the sensations of his childhood, and it became the foundation of his passion for literature. His father, a military man, told stories about his experiences during the war in Indochina, speaking of monsoons, rice fields, the seashore, and the women, inspiring a curiosity in his son to see this land and meet its people. Fessler and Panh shared similar ideas about Duras's novel and how it should be adapted, with words like "remove, keep, transform, invent" key to their process. Fessler traveled to Cambodia with Panh who wanted him to know the country and discover the places that inspired the novel before any writing began. "The plain with its black buffaloes, the islands of the concession, the mountain overlooking the mangrove, and the South China Sea so close— everything was there before our eyes as in the novel," Fessler told an interviewer. He had written many film scripts, but he found *The Sea Wall* to be the most intimate and rewarding work of his career.[37] Panh felt that Fessler sketched a powerful, accessible, and fluid line of narration that gave him the opportunity to indulge his fantasies reined in by the practical Fessler.

In Panh's literary adaptations, the plot always serves as a point of departure for his own vision. "It is necessary to be situated beyond history, inside and outside at the same time," says Panh.[38] His interpretation of Duras's story went against the grain of then current literary criticism of her work, which minimized the significance of history and place in her novels and promoted the myth of Duras as a politically disengaged author who simply wrote stories.[39] These critics took Duras at her word when she claimed she never mixed political theory with literature: they accepted the notion that her story appealed to values that had a "universal meaning" transcending her Asian world.[40]

Panh's emphasis on *The Sea Wall*'s political context edged out development of the erotic zone of the capital, which takes up much of the second part of the novel and was the focus of interest for many feminist and poststructuralist critics. Julia Kristeva claimed the novel was a "drama of love and madness [that] occurs independently of the political drama; the power of passion surpasses the political events, however atrocious."[41]

Other critics like Nicola Cooper took the political dimensions of the story seriously as a counternarrative to the ideal of *mise-en-valeur*: "This portrait of abject colonial failure functions not only as a *mise-en-scène* of the psychological, individual, sexual, and social impact of the failed colonial dream but also an indictment of the corruption of colonial administration in Indochina."[42] However, Cooper considers the mother guilty because she is unable to recognize how she is implicated in the crime she accuses the colonial authorities of perpetrating and indignant because she has been prevented from gaining her share of the colonial spoils. This is clearly not Panh's view.

For Panh, the characters in *The Sea Wall* are definitely a product of their time and place. All action in the film takes place on the mother's concession and at the nearby colonial watering hole, Café Bart, where colonists come to flaunt their wealth, display their immaculate white clothing, and enjoy their class status. For once, Panh was not interested in the story of a madwoman, which is how colonial women were frequently depicted, unable to escape the narrow confines of daily life in the colonies and so destined for madness, desertion, and death.[43] Panh focuses on the mother's failing physical health as a consequence of her relentless efforts to save the land for her children and for the local people who lived side by side with her and were also threatened by the predatory practices of colonial land agents intent on stealing their property and evicting them. Her desire to have her crops succeed is not about getting her share of the colonial spoils but about finding a way to make a sustainable life for her children and her neighbors. The final scene in the film is the ultimate justification of her utopian vision. A film is never the same as a novel and needs to find its own way: Panh had other ideas and felt free to adapt the story to follow his vision.

FIGURE 6.1 Isabelle Huppert with children in *The Sea Wall* © RPanh / droits réservés

The mother, who is played with characteristic delicacy and remarkable restraint by Isabelle Huppert, pursues a "crazy" scheme to build a sea wall along the South China Sea to protect her rice paddies from tidal inundations that ruin her crops. She has been swindled by corrupt administrators who have taken all her savings to purchase land that was worthless in the face of such flooding. Their deception leaves her at the mercy of cadastral agents and bankers eager to seize her land when she cannot harvest her crops.[44] Sadly she is losing an unequal fight with two powerful adversaries, nature and colonial bureaucrats. Her children—whom she mistreats in alternating fits of anger, obsessive love, and remorse—are also fighting their own battles. Joseph, who is played with muscular intensity by Gaspard Ulliel, wants to escape from the hold the land has on all of them and strikes out in search of adventure, sex, and individual freedom. Like his mother, the twenty-year-old is another victim of colonial propaganda: he too dreams of realizing the fantasy of a successful life overseas. Suzanne, who is played by the quietly provocative Astrid Bergès-Frisbey, is oppressed by their isolation and poverty and by her own sexual longings. She is torn between a confused love for her brother and jealousy over her mother's preference for him. Suzanne, a precocious girl of sixteen, is unsure how to respond to the family's urging her toward marriage with the wealthy Monsieur Jo in order to save the farm.

Panh altered Duras's characterization of Monsieur Jo by strategically casting him as a wealthy Sino-Cambodian played by Randal Douc, who would later become the elegant narrator for many of Panh's films. The slender and attractive M. Jo definitely is not the ugly, effete landowner of the novel but more like the Chinese lover in Duras's later Indochina novels. Duras never identified the nationality or race of M. Jo in the book, but in interviews she referred to him as Chinese. Panh says he imagined him coming from a rich family of traders who was sent to study in France. He speaks French without an accent and is not Western but Westernized. "He is the kind of guy who best exploits his compatriots," says Panh. "He lives in a world where money can buy everything."

Panh retains some of the sexual ambivalence and erotic tension that is in Duras's novel, but only in small measure. Suzanne subverts colonial norms by flirting with M. Jo and riding in a closed car with him. At the time, automobiles in the colonies served as sites of symbolic, physical, and sexual violence. M. Jo's luxury car is an unracialized space. However, its grandeur barely compensates for M. Jo's unsuccessful sexual advances,[45] while Joseph's exhausted Citroen B1 advertises his well-practiced virility, affording him the necessary means of escape to his lover. Both men's vehicles speak volumes about their masculinity and power. By identifying Suzanne's would-be lover as Chinese, Panh briefly acknowledges the colonial taboo of an interracial relationship between a white woman and a "yellow man," just enough attention to allow their encounters to reflect features of Duras's autobiographical novel for viewers expecting erotic charge. Panh's goals lie elsewhere.

Panh is not interested in the triple threat of race, gender, and sexuality.[46] His interest is in the power of a Chinese entrepreneur who will supersede the French in appropriating Cambodia's riches. Suzanne is only one of those desired objects, her body a symbol for all of Cambodia's exploitable resources. She is not attracted to M. Jo and exploits his desire for her, tantalizing him with the prospect of sex for favors like a new phonograph and a flawed diamond ring. Like the ring, M. Jo is not what he seems to be. Although Suzanne ultimately rejects M. Jo, his grand scheme will prevail. Acquisition of land, wealth, and Suzanne are all aspects of the same will to power and wealth that propels M. Jo and his ilk. He is the next face—and race—of the colonizer, with or without Suzanne at his side.

The film opens as yet another flood of seawater invades the rice paddies, and the mother (whose name is never spoken) is confronted with the loss of another

FIGURE 6.2 M. Jo dances with Suzanne in *The Sea Wall* © RPanh / droits réservés

crop. Her son, Joseph, arrives soon after the discovery. He is leading a dying horse—another bad investment that serves as a symbol for the dying hopes of a poor colonial family struggling to survive. Panh swaps the order of these scenes as they appear in the novel to foreground the mother's attachment to the land and her alliance with the villagers, who share her vulnerability to the dishonest manipulations of the colonial system. Her bond with her Cambodian neighbors is essential to his interpretation of the novel and is established most clearly through the figure of the Corporal who works for the mother and also farms his own land. His loyalty to the family continues even when local discord spreads and rebellion stirs, a dangerous movement fostered by her angry advice to the outraged farmers to cut off the land manager's head. Following the discovery of his decapitation, there is a critical scene of wanton brutality filmed at a distance as the militia descend on the village, burning homes, rounding up men, and marching them off in shackles, their land confiscated and their families set adrift. This is the tragic history of villages that rebelled against the cadastre system and were burned in repression.[47] Panh films the militia attack as it sweeps across the horizon. In the foreground, the Corporal quickly grabs water and runs to offer it to the prisoners to drink, but he is beaten back by the militia, who forbid him this gesture of compassion. Sharp lines are quickly drawn by colonial forces summarily ejecting all the villagers off their land.

With this critical scene, Panh makes clear what was at stake not only for a family of "poor colons" but for disenfranchised Cambodians.

Once more the film departs from the novel at its end. After the mother's death, Suzanne does not leave with her brother. She is shown strolling through the rice fields, lovingly stroking the "pregnant stalks" much as her mother did, a slight smile playing on her lips. Panh then cuts to the final scene, one of surprising anticolonial triumph. It is a magnificent aerial view of a lush field of rice growing on the very concession where Duras's mother—Madame Dieudonné—devised her plans to save it. Her seemingly crazy idea actually succeeded: titles reveal that the polder is exceptionally productive today and is known still as "the fields of the white lady." Madame Dieudonné's dikes ultimately protected the paddies and allowed them to flourish, proving that Cambodians were more than able to farm their land if only given the chance. For Panh, the idea of the dam was "a collective utopia. It symbolizes resistance. I like utopia, collective struggle, solidarity," he told an interviewer. "It's what happens when the question of power comes into play that puzzles me. For Duras, even the weakest have the right to dignity and life."[48]

Before embarking on the film, Panh was determined to find the concession where Duras's mother had farmed. Scouting locations led him to Ream National Park in Preah Som, where he not only found the concession but elderly people there who remembered Marguerite as a young girl and Joseph hunting with his double-barreled shotgun. Panh claims that without the discovery of this land, he would not have been able to make his film. It was not just that it meant he could show that the mother's scheme had proved viable but that Cambodian farmers could manage their own land. According to Panh, the denial of the peasants' access to their own land was the worst crime of colonialism.[49]

As with his first narrative film, *Rice People*, Panh's process began months before any shooting began: once he found his site, he built sets, constructing a traditional Cambodian stilt house for the family home, landscaping the surrounding ground himself, planting gardens and adding animals—oxen, chickens, ducks, and dogs—to give it the feeling of actually being lived in. He also began scouting for local people who could play the parts of villagers.

During the making of *The Sea Wall*, the French documentary filmmaker Jean-Marie Barbe—one of Panh's friends—came to shoot *Uncle Rithy*, a charming and insightful portrait of Panh and his creative process during the production of *The Sea Wall*. It offers fascinating moments with Panh directing Huppert, Bergès-Frisbey, and a little boy whose personality tickled his sense of humor. Barbe interviewed Panh at length and, in many behind-the-scenes moments, also interviewed Panh's crew, exploring the esprit de corps Panh has fostered over the years by working with the same actors as well as the technical crew he has trained, many of whom are also genocide survivors. At the start of his film, Barbe includes clips from several of Panh's early works, including *Souleymane Cissé*, Panh's portrait of the Malian director whose cinematic vision and views on colonialism so closely meshed with his own. It is a smart choice because of what Cissé tells Panh about the importance of "damu," a philosophy Panh shares and that is evident in all his work. Cissé says in voice-over:

> In daily life, the Bambara word *damu* is the very positive impression you have after observing a being or a thing that remains for a long time in your heart and in your mind. *Damu* is maybe "grace." There's a damu of the soul, a damu of things, a damu of a man. What is it? When you watch how a human being lives, you can observe everything that he is, everything that surrounds him. To express all that, you can help unveil unexpected aspects and even surprise him. When you look at a human being, when you manage to understand him, you have to show him with his damu. There are wicked beings, however. We shouldn't reject them but try to understand them, to give them what is possible, to try and reveal their own damu to them.[50]

Panh speaks animatedly to Barbe about the "grace" of Isabelle Huppert as well as that of Duong Vanthon, who plays the Corporal. Panh's recognition of a person's quality has nothing to do with their status and everything to do with their "soul." This is how he casts a film and selects his crew. It is perhaps the antithesis of colonialism's predatory, hierarchical, condescending relationship to the Other.

Huppert, in an interview for French television, disclosed the main reason she decided to take on the role of the mother was her desire to work with Panh. She had read Duras's novel before he approached her to play the role and was surprised that he had her in mind for it since the tiny Huppert bears little resemblance to the physically larger-than-life mother of the novel. For Panh, such things did not matter because he knew she had the grace and creative intelligence to understand the mother and how to play her. When Huppert read the script, she was also surprised to see Panh had focused his narrative on the evils of colonialism, but she found the challenge of coming to Cambodia and working with him compelling.[51] The film proved to be one of the most expensive of Panh's cinematic undertakings, and so securing a renowned actress like Isabelle Huppert for the leading role was essential. Her

FIGURE 6.3 Panh, Huppert, and crew view take for *The Sea Wall* © John Vink / MAPSimages

participation may have accounted for some of the myopia of critics who were more distracted by her star turn than by Panh's ideas.

Made in 2008, *The Sea Wall* had nothing to do with the nostalgia for the colonial era that was all the rage in France in the nineties, when films like Régis Wargnier's *Indochine*, Jean-Jacques Annaud's *L'Amant* (*The Lover*), and Pierre Schoendoerffer's *Dien Bien Phu* enjoyed box office successes. Films like these fostered a problematic understanding of France's relationship to Indochina.[52] *The Sea Wall* was radically different and, though politely received, "came and went with surprisingly little attention or press," as Florence Jacobowitz noted in writing about its world premier at the Toronto International Film Festi-val.[53] She provided one of the most detailed and insightful reviews of the film in English, outstripping most popular reviews by French writers who admired one or another of the actors and largely ignored Panh's story. Despite excellent performances by the cast, Panh's "sophisticated attention to *mise-en-scène*, lighting and costumes, color and tone," and his rethinking of melodrama to "emphasize the validity and value of protest," *The Sea Wall* was largely ignored in the Francophone world and had no theatrical release in the United States. One wonders if Panh's unblinking view of the evils of colonialism, challenging Indochina's "phantasmatic assemblage invented by the French," dampened French enthusiasm for the film.[54] Regardless of why Panh's adaptation of Duras's novel failed to captivate critics and audiences, for Panh the effort was not just about making a movie. "Each film you make is like a form of resistance," Panh observes. "It's saying, 'I am presenting to you my point of view of history.'"

Several years later, Panh admitted he felt the film was unfinished, that he had not gone far enough in realizing his idea for the film. For the first time, he received condescending reviews that questioned whether a Cambodian could adapt Marguerite Duras for the screen. Panh felt he had been "too impressed" by Isabelle Huppert, an intelligent and gifted actress, whom he was too shy to direct for the film he had wanted to make.[55] It is difficult to know what that film might have become had Panh been more secure working with A-list actors. But it is also possible that, in tackling the evils of French colonialism head-on, Panh soured the heretofore enthusiastic response of reviewers expecting a film that would deliver on Duras's erotic content but not her critique of colonial oppression. Beautifully realized with superb craftsmanship in art direction, cinematography, musical composition, and performances by professional and amateur actors, *The Sea Wall* should be remembered for its depiction of the colonial system. It is one of the few films made about this era to dispense with exoticism and voyeuristic appeal to reveal instead the harsh realities of life during the protectorate. And in its depiction of the treatment meted out to the Cambodian people, *The Sea Wall* sets the stage for consideration of the "utopian vision" of an agrarian society envisioned by the Khmer Rouge, which can be seen as a continuation of many of the practices and attitudes they inherited from the French. *The Sea Wall* was certainly inspired by Resnais's approach to film in which pieces of unaltered reality are caught in a fictional net. This idea is a useful key to understanding all of Panh's fiction films.

7

Remembering the Past, Mourning the Dead

Cinematic memory is a kind of techno-shadow of history's methods of mass displacement, imprisonment, and killing. . . . Film is the method by which history becomes most acquainted with itself—the "ugly" process by which massive violent and exploitative power takes exquisite stock of itself.

JAMES F. MOYER[1]

The historian Hayden White suggests that only those who have experienced "unbelievable" events can render them believable. As a survivor of Democratic Kampuchea, Panh brings to his autobiographical project something no outside observer possesses, a capacity for empathy and understanding born out of the need to survive atrocity with one's humanity intact. Each of his auto-biographical films is dramatically different in form from the others; each offers a different perspective on time, space, place, memory, and loss. *The Missing Picture* shuttles between the time of childhood spent happily with a loving family before the fall of Phnom Penh and the four years the teenaged Panh was confined in Khmer Rouge labor camps, barely surviving as his family members died one by one of starvation, overwork, sickness, and despair. *Exile* offers a poetic view of Panh's interior life during this time of exile from his family, his culture, and his sense of self. He survives in a private world of fantasies, fears, and losses all contained in a memory theater of his own devising. It ends with Panh's escape to a refugee camp before his flight to France, the start of another stage of exile. *Graves without a Name* is set in the present but concerns the challenges Panh and other genocide survivors face when trying to give a proper burial to victims of the Khmer Rouge. In Buddhism, without a proper burial and ritual mourning, the dead souls must wander, prevented from rebirth. This film revisits the land and the people of north-west Cambodia, where Panh was sent when Phnom Penh was evacuated. It introduces ordinary people—monks, mediums, and the local perpetrators of genocide—who still till the fields where the dead lie hidden.

Farm Catch (*Gibier d'élevage*) (2011)

Before Panh released *The Missing Picture*, he made a fiction film that is, in its own way, a prelude to his trio of autobiographical films. This film is based on "Shiiku," a short story by the Nobel Prize–winning author Kenzaburō Oe, who was twenty-three years old when he wrote it in 1958. Panh read Oe's stories about Hiroshima when he was young and went on to discover his other works, impressed by Oe's pacifism and humanitarian activities. He found in "Shiiku" a vehicle that would allow him to explore the life of a boy entangled in revolution.

Panh again collaborated with Michel Fessler in adapting Oe's story about a bomber pilot during World War II who crash-landed in Japan and was subjected to brutal, inhumane treatment by the Japanese villagers who found him and treated him worse than an animal. The story had already been adapted for the screen by Nagisa Oshima in 1961, but Panh, as is his custom, chose not to view it. Panh took Oe's story as a point of departure, placing the film in Cambodia in 1972 when American pilots were dropping 500,000 tons of bombs on Cambodia in an undeclared war that devastated the land. Panh, who studiously avoids gratuitous images of violence, shifted the focus of his story to a young boy, A'Pang, who was abandoned by his parents and left to fend for himself in a village that despised him because of his parents' apparent disloyalty. A'Pang is contemptuously nicknamed "the bastard" by village elders. The only person who seems to take any interest in him is the Khmer Rouge leader who recognizes in his intelligence and neediness a potential recruit.

Panh shows in the film how villagers in 1972 were already being forced into harsh labor, deprivation, and severe punishments at the hands of the Khmer Rouge. When an American pilot is found by a gang of boys and delivered to the Khmer Rouge leader in charge of the area, A'Pang is given responsibility for guarding the enemy, whom the boys call "Okay." Neither the pilot nor the villagers share a language in common, and many misunderstandings lead to further mistrust and fear on both sides, but over time the villagers become used to their "enemy." A'Pang is the first to show compassion for the pilot with whom he identifies because both were abandoned and left to survive on their own. He provides the pilot with food and water and helps to rescue him from a flooded well after monsoon rains nearly drowned him. But all the while there is a tug-of-war going on inside A'Pang as he is pulled between this vulnerable Black man and the authoritarian Khmer Rouge leader who gives A'Pang responsibility, respect, and a rifle. Over time, the pilot builds a relationship with the boys, showing them how to make paper airplanes and how to fix a broken radio. He playfully shares with them music and dancing, and they begin to learn bits of each other's language. All the while the pilot remains vigilant, looking for a way to escape. He seizes his chance and succeeds, but in a climactic moment, A'Pang and the pilot confront each other. The boy shoots his rifle but hits his friend instead. The pilot carries the wounded boy back to the village, knowing his fate is sealed.

This initiation into the deadly power conferred by the Khmer Rouge on him tips the balance for A'Pang. He had turned against the villagers already, reporting them for hoarding food, for criticizing Angkar, or for bullying his former friends. He saw what became of the couple he denounced, who were not taken off for "reeducation study" but executed and left to rot in a field outside the village. But it was not until he used his rifle that he became one of the Khmer Rouge. In the final scene, when the pilot is being marched off by the army leader, led like an animal with a rope around his neck, A'Pang appears dressed for the first time in the black clothes and red-and-white kramar around his neck that signified his status as a cadre. Clutching his rifle, he says good-bye to Grandmother Yun, who looks at him sadly but does not

FIGURE 7.1 A'Pang surrounded by Khmer Rouge in *Farm Catch* © RPanh / droits réservés

speak a word. His friend has survived. A'Pang tells him he does not know when he will return and then runs off to join the column of soldiers leading the pilot to his fate.

Panh does not dwell on death, torture, or other violent aspects of Oe's story, which focused on racism, sadism, and brutality. This is not Panh's approach. It is interesting to compare his way of depicting the villagers with the way Angelina Jolie treats them in *First They Killed My Father*, her film based on a memoir by Loung Ung, another child separated from her family during the genocide, who was also forced to survive by relying on her wits and inner strength. Panh produced Jolie's film but takes no credit for her artistic choices. In *Farm Catch*, the specter of death hovers throughout the film with recurrent images of archival color footage of American air raids along with voice-over commentary by bombers thrilled with their success at incinerating houses and people. However, Panh does not need to show burned corpses or ravaged fields to suggest the effect such warfare has on helpless people.

Panh invariably introduces a key feminine figure in his films, even in one like this, which is largely about men and boys. The missing mother that A'Pang yearns for is depicted in two pen-and-pencil drawings that he hides in a box, portraits viewers of Panh's films will recognize are based on the image of Hout Bophana. The pilot has his image too, a color snapshot of his wife and child, and the importance of women for both adversaries is significant in this story. A'Pang's mother is called a "whore in Phnom Penh," just as Bophana was branded when she was evacuated from the capital. A'Pang could be Bophana's missing son or even a stand-in for Rithy Panh, who lost his family too and was subjected to compulsory ideology lessons and demeaning public self-criticism.

Panh's interest is examining how children can be indoctrinated in a genocidal ideology and practice. He includes several scenes in which the villagers are lectured by the army chief and expected to cheer and clap in obedience to the strict ideas laid out by him. The chief is a strikingly handsome man and seems friendly toward the boy whom he promotes to a leadership role. We see how the Khmer Rouge could succeed in converting A'Pang to their beliefs. By contrast, the pilot's sense of humor and playfulness with the boys win their hearts. He is not trying to mold their thoughts and behaviors, and his openness is an antidote to the fear that engulfs them. But his kindness is not enough to win over the lonely and angry A'Pang. Lost in a large Khmer Rouge uniform with a cap that engulfs his head, he is on the brink of disappearing, no longer an innocent child, as he announces his decision to follow the Khmer Rouge. This tragedy more than the inevitable death of the pilot overwhelms the last scene.

Panh's cinematographer Prum Mésar follows the events unfolding on the ground from a little above it, a perspective that allows for a smooth transition from the scenes of American bombing raids that open the film. Mésar's next shot in the film is eloquent and a long shot that places the villagers' homes behind large bomb craters in the foreground. As with *The Sea Wall*, Panh's teaming up with Michel Fessler assures a narrative flow and slow reveal of the principal characters. The French actor Cyril Gueï, who plays the pilot, had seen Panh's *S-21: The Khmer Rouge Killing Machine*, which greatly impressed him. When Panh met Gueï to discuss the scenario for this film, Gueï was very interested in participating because he felt Panh's work spoke to humanity; it was not just about the past but about the present age. Although the pilot has little to "say" during the film, he has to express himself by physically demonstrating his thoughts and feelings, communicating with his young guards without a shared language, a challenging task for any actor. Gueï's mobile expressions, his muscular body, and expressive eyes say more than words alone could convey. He confided to an interviewer that he was frightened when the boys were directed to attack him on camera because they were young and had no sense of control. He worried that he might hit one of them if he were inadvertently hurt. Only Gueï and Vutha Yim, who plays the Khmer Rouge leader, were professional actors. All the others were villagers who performed their parts well. Panh knew that city children could not have climbed trees or herded water buffalos as these children could. And their familiarity with each other was another plus. Panh enjoys working with nonactors in his fiction films, and he found the villagers brought to the screen individual talents and a passion to act. Jhem Chuop, who plays A'Pang, proved to be a nice youngster, who grasped what was being asked of him in creating a villain.[2]

As Panh attests, his fiction films build on his earlier documentaries, and here Panh borrows from *The Land of Wandering Souls*, especially for one of the most poignant scenes. The pilot is playing with the children, who have rigged two cups and a string together to create an imaginary communication system between the pilot and his control center. A'Pang, speaking in Khmer, utters sheer poetry about his mission to land on the moon, but later he admits that this is a far cry from the pilot's actual mission to bomb the rice fields and destroy the villages. It is the pilot who is the innocent here, enthusiastically going over his list of things to check before taking off on a raid, the kind of interchange he would have had over his communications system. The boys laugh at one word he keeps repeating that sounds like "banana" in Khmer, and they wonder why he wants to eat bananas. This confusion produces much laughter and smiles all around. Humor, laughter, and death are linked in this scene, which proves to be the prelude to tragedy. Since Panh favors beginning a narrative in medias res, he mirrors this choice by ending the film before the narrative's end, allowing the viewer to imagine the unspeakable events to come.

The Missing Picture (L'image manquante) (2013)

Panh was severely depressed as a result of his lengthy interviews with Duch. What seemed to help him was to begin writing his memories of childhood, which came flooding back to him after hours spent with Duch. Finding words helped him to face his own past and led to two remarkable works released simultaneously: his award-winning book, *The Elimination: A Survivor of the Khmer Rouge Confronts His Past and the Commandant of the Killing Fields*, which was favorably compared by some critics to the memoirs of Primo Levi and Alexander Solzhenitsyn,[3] and his Oscar-nominated film, *The Missing Picture*. His collaborator in both, Christophe Bataille, later said that he had not realized how Panh's extended encounters with Duch had brought on a crisis of anxiety for Rithy. He was in mortal danger, according to Bataille, and the act of writing served as a means of rebuilding his identity.[4]

The manuscript for *The Elimination* was a long time in the making. Panh met Christophe Bataille in 2004 at the French publishing company Grasset. Bataille was there to see his editor, and Panh came with a book, a collaboration with Louise Lorentz based on his film *Paper Cannot Wrap Up Embers*. Bataille had liked Panh's film on S-21, and Panh had liked Bataille's award-winning first novel, *Annam*, a story about eighteenth-century missionaries to Vietnam that demonstrated a poetic writing style and sensibility that suited Panh well. They talked, and, on impulse, Bataille offered his help if Panh ever decided to write his own story. Panh smiled. Time passed. Six years later, Panh emailed Bataille: "Come to Phnom Penh. This time I am ready."

Bataille told an interviewer he spent ten days and nights in Democratic Kampuchea. He worked with Panh, probing his memory, checking dates, reviewing images, and then he returned to Paris to work on the text over the next five months. It took Panh three weeks to be able to read the first draft. He told Bataille to take him out of the book; his notes about his visits with Duch would have to suffice. Bataille said no and wisely advised that if Panh did that, then Duch would be the victor. If he insisted, then Bataille would withdraw from the project. So they fought a "good fight" via email and text over the next two years and 122 drafts.[5] Panh was finally satisfied when they found the form for the book. It was based on montage: cutting between his diary notes about his experiences with Duch and his memories of childhood; it was the way he would edit scenes in one of his films.

Although much of what Panh wrote about his experience during the Pol Pot years made its way into *The Elimination*, it did not fulfill his long-standing need to put his personal story onto film. Ethically, Panh believed he could not ask actors to take on roles and actions that depicted the violence of genocide. He had to find another way. He spent a year and a half interviewing dozens of villagers in Battambang Province, where he and his family had been deported by the Khmer Rouge. When nothing really new emerged as a form, Panh decided he needed a new "cinematographic proposal."

While he was reviewing footage of Khmer Rouge propaganda films and researching files at S-21 for his interviews with Duch, he found a confession written by a cameraman who acknowledged photographing young people working in abysmal conditions. Later this man made a technical mistake in a film about Pol Pot and was summarily executed. Panh had hoped to find some of the films this cameraman shot; he thought the Khmer Rouge might have kept them as proof of his "betrayal." But all Panh found were three other cameramen who worked with him, and so Panh interviewed them. One of them admitted that he had filmed people starving, but he quickly destroyed the negatives under pressure and so saved his life.[6]

"I imagined as the main thread [for this film] someone who would have filmed or photographed an important scene, who would have hidden the reel in a can and buried it somewhere. I would have liked to find it," he told an interviewer. It was appealing because the cinema and the earth both constitute a repository for the past, the geological and technological medium where the dead are buried. "I would have liked to find a picture of the Khmer Rouge executing somebody. But if you have this image, I'm not sure that it can explain the truth of what happened."[7] And, he added, he could never show such an image even if it existed, much like Claude Lanzmann, who also declared, had he found *la pellicule maudite* (the damned film) of Jews being gassed, he too would have destroyed it.

"I don't want anyone telling me I'm a voyeur. I work with facts. Images. Archives. I work with history, even if it makes us uncomfortable. I verify everything. I translate every word. I analyze every sign—what's said, what's written, what's hidden. If I have a doubt, I cut. And I show what was," Panh wrote in *The Elimination*. Such precision and apparent emotional detachment are hard to achieve when dealing with one's own life, but history, memory, and creative imagination finally came together once Panh found his "cinematographic proposal."

When Panh first returned to Cambodia, he had avoided visiting his family home in Phnom Penh after he learned it had become a gambling dive, then a karaoke club, and a brothel. When construction made it unrecognizable, he decided to make a model of his home from memory. He asked one of his crew, whom he spotted one day carving clay figurines, to make a scale model of him as a boy to use with the cardboard replica of his house. When he saw what Sarith Mang was able to do, Panh realized he had found the way to make his film. The figurines allowed for a "certain purity in the artistic approach." "It's scary, frozen characters who do not speak for an hour and a half," Panh thought. "There could have been the temptation to make a cartoon. But the strength of the figurines is precisely their immobility."[8]

Like the sculptor Sarith Mang, Panh had played with clay figurines as a child, and he had used one in a poignant scene in *Rice People*. When Yim Om is being taken away from her rice fields because the villagers cannot cope with her madness, her youngest daughter reaches out and tenderly offers her clay doll to her mother. For those familiar with Panh's work, it is a minor but moving intertextual link between his first fiction film and, twenty years later, his first autobiographical documentary.

FIGURE 7.2 Rusting film cans in *The Missing Picture* © RPanh / droits réservés

Sarith Mang lost family members during the Khmer Rouge regime. When Panh asked him to collaborate with him on the film, he was eager to create reconstructions that would also do justice to his own family's pain and suffering. And as the father of two daughters, he wanted to show the next generation what had happened.[9] He had grown up in Site 2, the refugee camp where Panh shot his first documentary and where Da had also grown up. When his family eventually moved to Phnom Penh, he found different jobs, including helping out a friend's family with their work chipping rocks from a mountainside. They taught him the basics of sculpting using stone and wood. Mang became acquainted with the set director on Panh's films, and Panh gave him a job working as an assistant. Panh's discovery of Mang's hidden talent led to the creation of over five hundred figurines and many dioramas that serve as backdrop for the film. At the start, Panh would often sit next to Mang while he carved, explaining to him what people wore, what they were doing, how they lost weight, and what they said. "Sometimes I'd say to him; 'much more happiness' or 'much more sadness,' like when you direct an actor," Panh noted. "It was very important that their faces be expressive and emotional. I wanted people to see their humanity."[10]

The figurines reminded Panh of Picasso's sculptures and Chagall's drawings because they evoked a kind of childhood innocence. Panh thinks it was his child's unconsciousness that saved him during those four years. There was so much he only understood later, with hindsight and an adult's awareness.[11] Mang created Panh's figurine as a tiny alter ego with hands over his ears and mouth wide open, modeled on Edvard Munch's painting *The Scream*. It is an image of mute protest, anxiety, and even madness. His red polka-dot shirt differentiates him from the anonymous "new people" all dressed in black. Silent as they all are, they communicate volumes about their fragility, malleability, and dehumanization. The figurines maintain just enough artifice to enable viewers to withstand ever more tragic revelations of life under the Khmer Rouge. The dioramas were made from cardboard, bits of wood, plastic, and iron wire. For the paddy fields, the design team worked with real rice-plant cuttings.[12] Panh had used a simple diorama to facilitate Peng Phan's storytelling about her survival in his film *The Burnt Theater*, a scene that foreshadowed what was to come in *The Missing Picture*. But Mang's figurines allowed for the placement of "new people" onto archival films of the deserted city of Phnom Penh. The children flying above footage of U.S. bombing raids over Cambodia allowed Panh the satisfaction of declaring, "You can bomb us, but we can still float and fly as children." Superimposing figurines over archival footage throughout the film showed the human experience that was missing from Khmer Rouge propaganda.[13]

The first scenes of *The Missing Picture* establish the film's dialectic of destruction and creation.[14] Some reviewers have claimed the opening scene pans across rolls of decaying film spilling out of rusting cans and then cuts to hands carving the statue of a man in clay, but there are three critical sequences in between them. The first is of the Apsara Dance performed with serene beauty by Princess Bopha Devi for her father's eponymous film.[15] Before there is any thought of searching for missing pictures of executions, Panh scans the decaying film stock and finds a strip of film with an image of Cambodian art and myth. Apsaras, which were carved into the bas-reliefs on ancient Angkorean temples, were goddesses who emerged from the churning sea of milk where good and evil struggled for power; they danced for the gods and provided humanity with the nectar of immortality. As prima ballerina of the Royal Cambodian Dance Company and daughter of Norodom Sihanouk, Bopha Devi embodied Cambodian culture, religion, and political order, all of which the Khmer Rouge were determined to destroy without leaving a trace.

Hout Bophana has served as Panh's muse in nearly all of his films since 1996. Her S-21 identity photo appears briefly early in *The Missing Picture*, as viewers might expect. But Princess Bopha Devi is Panh's muse here: her exquisite performance is the embodiment of feminine beauty and an acknowledged symbol of Cambodian culture. She silently stands in opposition to the darkest acts of totalitarian oppression committed by the Khmer Rouge.[16] Her

FIGURE 7.3 Apsara viewed by young Rithy in *The Missing Picture* © RPanh / droits réservés

expressive gestures precede the film's title card. What follows next is the first of four scenes of crashing seawater that appear at intervals throughout the film. Viewers feel the existential menace of these waves about to engulf them, the violent sea breaking repeatedly with tremendous, overpowering force. The possible meanings for this elemental image are myriad, and this ambiguity is essential to the film, but plagued by interviewers wanting to know just what the waves mean, Panh has offered various explanations: memories that overwhelm him, disappointments that teach him how to deal with pain, or anxieties that are always with him as a survivor.

Viewers should try to summon their own associations. One could say the waves represent a force over which the filmmaker has no control, a poetic illustration of powerlessness in the face of totalitarianism and death. Panh quotes from a poem by Jacques Prévert that was his father's favorite:[17] "Black hair, black hair, caressed by the waves / black hair, black hair, tousled by the wind." The waves on the screen are not those gentle caresses; they speak of the harsh world unforeseen by Panh Lauv, who mistakenly trusted members of the Khmer Rouge leadership.

Less than four minutes into the film, we have been introduced to some of the poetic ambiguities that will thread through his autobiographical trilogy. What follows these waves is another scene of classical dancers, only here they are blurred in the same fashion that Panh blurs imaginary mourners for his father's funeral-in-words, a dramatic scene that occurs later in the film. Are these shadowy figures real or imaginary, alive or dead? Blurry images communicate dreamy realities that render presence insubstantial and

FIGURE 7.4 Sculpting the father in *The Missing Picture* © RPanh / droits réservés

indeterminate. After presenting these ghostly dancers, Panh arrives at his new "cinematic proposal." From the ruins of the past and the dreamlike, mythical realm where good and evil clash and crash, human hands take up the earth, made from water and sand, and create the image of a man, the filmmaker's father. This figure is more than an object; it is the soul of his father. More than a reference to the biblical creation of Adam or to Prometheus's creation of man out of clay, Panh offers a homely and distinctly Cambodian object of childish creation. Here the son creates the father. And with a knife, a paintbrush, and clay, he creates hundreds of characters who stand for the two million souls eliminated by the Khmer Rouge.

In this short but complex opening, Panh assumes a godlike role that comes with great responsibility: film affords him the means to create the Lazarean return of his beloved father as well as his carefree and happy childhood.[18] But along with this comes the denied history of the genocide that he is determined to bear witness to regardless of the burden such debt to the dead imposes on him.[19] Panh's role is paramount from the outset. He is the constant presence narrating the film, but a ghostly presence since he is silent, speaking only with the voice of an actor[20] and the words of a writer, and when he does appear, he too is blurry and insubstantial.

Like notable survivors of the Nazi concentration camps such as Primo Levi, Jean Cayrol, and Charlotte Delbo, Panh feels he died during the genocide, but no one sees it. He was particularly inspired by Charlotte Delbo, whose writing has meant a lot to his intellectual life, his work, and his personal life. In *The Measure of Our Days*, she writes: "I'm not alive. People believe memories grow vague, are erased by time, since nothing endures against the passage of time. That's the difference; times does not pass over me, over us. It doesn't erase anything, doesn't undo anything. I'm not alive. I died in Auschwitz, but no one knows it."[21]

Delbo found a way to "pierce the skin of memory to expose the naked self divested of its heroic garments . . . the victim of unbearable pain," as Lawrence Langer explains. She forged a unique form—part prose, part poetry—that lured the reader into "the maelstrom of atrocity while simultaneously drowning all intellectual defenses." This is what Panh does in *The Missing Picture*, side-stepping intellectual analysis for a deep dive into a sensory experience of drowning, the powerful metaphor he summons within minutes of the film's start and repeatedly throughout the film. With figurines, dioramas, and archival films, he presents the ordinary, happy memories of childhood suddenly engulfed by the unrepresentable and unforgettable. Delbo called life after the camps "the *afterdeath* of the Holocaust." She invited her readers again and again "to see." *Il faut donner à voir.* They must be made to see.[22] This is Panh's mission.

Vicente Sánchez-Biosca astutely observes the "missing picture" is "a pretext to initiate a desperate and metaphorical search through an intricate web of images of diverse status animated by different intentions, all of which torment the subject or precipitate him towards melancholia. . . . The challenge for a man of images is to give form to what resists being represented."[23] The missing picture is more than a lost film sequence that lays bare the crimes of the Khmer Rouge, more than propaganda films that constituted the pseudo-reality of a Khmer Rouge utopia. Panh suggests early in the film that the missing picture is "us," the "new people," evacuated from cities and destined for "reeducation," which is to say elimination by the Khmer Rouge. Like Delbo, Panh knew that they were not meant to return. The missing picture is an expansive conceit that includes all that is absent and inaccessible for Panh.

Critical to the magic of this film is the music composed for it by Marc Marder. Born and educated in New York, Marder came to Paris in 1978 as bass soloist for Pierre Boulez's Ensemble Intercontemporain and decided to stay. He has composed music for over one hundred films—including all of Panh's films—as well as varied theater and concert works. Marder's contrabass is the underlying voice in Panh's films.

Panh brought Marder to Cambodia early in their collaboration. He wanted him to listen first, to listen to the people talking, the noise of the neighborhood, the sound of the rice field. This led to his unique mix of flute and percussion instruments with sounds of rain, insects, and ambient noises of outdoor life. Panh rarely shares his script with Marker while shooting. Often there is nothing for the composer to rely on until he sees the film in editing. With *Site 2,* Marder viewed the film without any subtitles. He did not know Khmer, but he nevertheless translated Yim Om's words with his contrabass. It was translation into another language. And it was just what Panh wanted.[24] Marder's music is so intertwined with Panh's films that some listeners may take its tonal contributions for granted. In 2013 the score for *The Missing Picture* received the Sacem France Musique Prize for Best Music for Film.

When Panh told Christophe Bataille he wanted him to prepare a film called *The Missing Picture*, Bataille was puzzled. Panh sent him a one-minute silent video "with his little guys." At night Panh sent him pictures over the internet, and by day Bataille sent back words. Panh's responses were like those of a director: "more poetic," "more sober," much like his comments to Mang when carving the figurines. Panh did not want Bataille to use possessives. Panh preferred that he write *the* mother and not *my* mother, "a bit like Duras," Bataille thought. "This was because he wanted a form of universality."[25] Their collaboration on the text would eventually lead to the narration for the film and, ultimately, another book.

The Missing Picture is not an animated film, although there are a few remarkable animated sequences within it. It is a nonlinear performance of Panh's childhood memories, presented through the playthings of childhood, suddenly undermined by the arrival of the Khmer Rouge. Occasional flashbacks to Panh's early family life punctuate the unfolding tragedy and mortal threat posed by endless hours digging ditches day and night, planting rice paddies under sweltering skies, and losing family members who succumbed one by one to overwork, illness, and starvation. After his happy discovery that storytelling could earn him work in the kitchen and more food to eat, he sadly learned that speaking forbidden truths would send him back to the fields. So Panh retreated to silence, burying the storyteller within him to survive brutal totalitarian rule.

In depicting episodes of daily humiliation and dehumanization, Panh highlights moments that haunt him still, like the disappearance of the child dying beside him in a hospital without doctors, medicine, or hope. Using cinematic magic, he transports her to a happier time, projecting her image in a family photograph onto a shroud-like screen for an evanescent moment before children too are gone forever.

Seeking help for his grief, Panh appears—or rather his clay figurine does—beneath a large portrait of Sigmund Freud. Recumbent on a Khmer bed, the

FIGURE 7.5 "New people" roped together in *The Missing Picture* © RPanh / droits réservés

adult dissolves into the boy in the polka-dot shirt. He is speaking to his ana-
lyst as a crowd of family, friends, and neighbors materializes and crowds the
room. It is a clever image that combines Western psychoanalysis with Cambodian collective support.[26] Panh knows how to use subtle humor to prevent
the viewer from succumbing to the pathos of his memories. The one time we
actually see and hear him during the film is on a tiny TV set where he is being
interviewed. His parents are there watching him, talking about his "blah
blah." His mother says to his father, "You would have liked him to be a teacher
like you." Though amusing, this scene is also heartbreaking, the dream of
earning praise from parents who will never again see him or his work.

Panh says with resignation at the film's end: "Of course, I have not found
the missing picture. I searched for it in vain. All that remains is the blood-
drenched earth. And there is never enough earth to bury the dead. But a
political film should unearth what it invented. So I make this image. I look
at it. I cherish it. I hold it in my hand like a beloved face. And this missing
image, now I give it to you so that it will not cease to seek us." With these
final lines, Panh concludes the film with the most disturbing and lasting
image in it—a medium shot of a grave with a male figurine being covered with
dirt, but the dirt cannot bury him. The body keeps resurfacing over and over
again no matter how much dirt is tossed on it, uncanny evidence of the Sisyphean task Panh has tried to fulfill. Charon could only ferry the dead across
the River Styx if they had been properly buried and mourned. Buddhism also

demands that a proper funeral be given the dead before they can be reborn. Unburied and unmourned, the Cambodian dead must wander without peace. Panh is haunted by them, and so he gives us an image of what this haunting feels like. It is almost a relief when thundering waves come pounding down once more. Panh rescues us with Cambodian pop music playing over the credits, which is accompanied by scenes of him shooting his tabletop film set along with tarantulas mischievously crawling over a biography of Pol Pot. He closes with a pan of his multicolored figurines watching us. Panh is kind even as he insists that we try to see right up to the very end: "I put in the film this big wave that can swallow you. You try to stand up and continue because it's something you have to do: to transmit, not the horror, but the dignity and humanity of the people who died. An artist brings more than testimony: he brings imagination, creation, the idea of how to fight against totalitarianism. I made the film because I want this story to belong to everyone."[27]

Panh's meticulous re-creation of the necropolitics of Democratic Kampuchean using handmade toys and literal flights of fantasy transcends the distinctions between fiction and documentary. In 2013 the film won the Cannes Film Festival's coveted Un Certain Regard prize, which Panh dedicated to the Iranian director Jafar Panahi. Panahi had made *This Is Not a Film* a year earlier after being sentenced to six years in prison and twenty years without being allowed to make a film. "I think that Jafar Panahi has struggled a lot for this freedom, just to speak, to make, to create. You can consign someone to their home, prevent them from working, but you can't steal his imagination and his thoughts," Panh said in his acceptance speech. In 2014 *The Missing Picture* received an Academy Award nomination for Best Foreign-Language Film, a first for Cambodia and for Panh. Although the film did not win, the nomination conferred something precious with or without a gold figurine for Panh to place beside his clay ones. He told an interviewer for the *Wall Street Journal* that nominations like this protect people like him. "The world knows who you are. You can work. You can express yourself. You can help other people. It's a symbol of freedom." And in 2016 Panh joined the Chilean documentary filmmaker Patricio Guzmán at the Lumières Awards— France's equivalent to the Golden Globes—to share the documentary award, Panh for *The Missing Picture* and Guzmán for *The Pearl Button*.

Panh's Oscar nomination showed global audiences that documentaries can take bold, creative risks, win audiences for tough subjects, and accomplish all this without sacrificing ethics in the process. Defying categories, *The Missing Picture* made it easier for filmmakers to be recognized for original, genre-bending work. It also attracted widespread attention to Cambodia as an ideal location to make movies now that a new generation of skilled film professionals can offer something special for anyone wanting to make films in Southeast Asia. Because of all this attention, *The Missing Picture* has inspired a rich, diverse, and complex appreciation for Panh's cinema from some of the best international scholars writing in English about his films.[28]

Exile, the Film (2016) and the Installation (2017)

Hannah Arendt's classic essay, "We Refugees" (1943),[29] was inspired by her experience in a detention camp for displaced persons at the end of World War II. She was among the first to point out that the legal limbo into which Jews were thrown by the denial of their German citizenship was a prelude to the extermination camps. For Arendt, the irony was that the "human person" appeared just as human rights were being withdrawn. But Arendt refused to consign the refugee to the position of a pathetic supplicant before the law, insisting that refugees were the avant-garde of their people. Arendt's thoughts about refugees are timelier than ever as more and more refugees today flee oppression in a world increasingly fearful and rejecting of them. Giorgio Agamben revisited Arendt's ideas and applied them to the dire situation that is proliferating in the twenty-first century, sadly discerning a "perfectly real filiation between the refugee, internment, concentration, and death camps."[30]

This situation is no abstract subject for Rithy Panh, who survived the death camp that was Democratic Kampuchea and escaped to the refugee camp where he lived until he located family in France and secured political asylum in late 1979. Then, like Arendt, Panh experienced what it was to be stateless. He had to invent a new identity, learn a new language, embrace a new culture, and forever after grapple with the trauma of his past and the never-ending reality of being in exile. Ten years later, he returned to Southeast Asia to make his first feature film, a documentary about refugees living in the largest Cambodian refugee camp at that time and deemed one of the most densely populated areas in the world.[31] With it he captured the everyday realities of individuals trapped in cramped and dangerous quarters; it marked not only the beginning of Panh's career and unique approach to filmmaking but also his enduring concern for refugees. Today those concerns include the latest victims of state-supported massacres. In a stirring op-ed essay for *Le Monde* in May 2017, he demanded investigation of hidden detention centers in Syria where crimes against humanity were being committed, crimes disturbingly similar to those committed by the Khmer Rouge, which his films have helped to document and prosecute.

Panh's film (2016) and multimedia installation (2017) make clear where his commitments lie. The film *Exile* captures the inner space of resistance and self-protection that Panh retreated to during his years of bare survival. While shooting it, he thought about creating an installation that would connect his experience with the situation of refugees today. Creating a multimedia installation was new for him, but it was something he had been considering doing for a long time, encouraged by friends like the visual artist Christian Boltanski. *Exile* in both forms was presented at the Festival of Film and International Forum on Human Rights (FIFDH) in Geneva in March 2017 and stood as the centerpiece of the festival, which honored Panh's body of work and defense of human rights.

Exile, the Film

The film *Exile* is the more challenging, complex, and personal of these two works and arguably the most enigmatic of his films thus far. Judging from reviews, it was warmly received by Francophone reviewers, who praised it as a "cinematic poem" and called Panh a "memoirist of dead souls, clerk of the court on totalitarianism, archeologist of sorrow."[32] But English-language reviewers have been less enthusiastic, finding it "ravishing" but pragmatically marginal, often misunderstanding it or dismissing it as art house fare of limited interest to the public.[33]

According to Panh, "Exile is an abandonment, a terrifying solitude. In exile, oneself is lost, one suffers, one fades away. But it is possible to find oneself in the land of words, of image, in reverie that is more than childish. It all starts with exile, and nothing is anything without it."[34] Working on a small film set on the roof of the Cambodian Film Commission, he created a theater of memory in the form of *la maison poétique*, the metaphoric home he carries within him. Susan Sontag says it well: "What the mind feels like is still, as the ancients imagine it, an inner space like a theater—in which we picture, and it is these pictures that allows us to remember."[35] The basic scene is the bleak interior of a wooden hut that is constantly morphing to encompass rice fields, forests, lakes, deserts, and distant planets, as well as the Panh family home they had to abandon when the Khmer Rouge evacuated Phnom Penh. This cinematic image is sepia-toned like an old photo. Inhabiting this intimate space is the filmmaker's alter ego, portrayed by the artist Sang Nan. The boy hunts, cooks, harvests rice, picks corn, sews, shelters from storms,

FIGURE 7.6 Dreaming in *Exile* © RPanh / droits réservés

and performs the endless labors demanded of the "new people." Threading throughout the stark reality of survival are surreal scenes where Panh's thoughts, feelings, memories, and dreams take shape before the viewer's eyes.[36]

Panh's silent alter ego appears unemotional, a more introverted and complex figure than the boy in the polka-dot shirt in *The Missing Picture*. He prepares food—grilling rats and insects—and a pot of gruel with a few grains of rice. Midway, he buries his most precious possessions—photographs and books—and returns later to dig them up, finding his own unfamiliar face reflected back to him in a shard of mirror. It is as if Panh is exhuming himself as a boy. The narrator says, "In this night of ignorance, you need to steal fire. Lock your gaze on a face. Cling on to a magic word, to a poem." These were words to live by for the boy who relied on poetry and stories to help him survive.

Often, he lies curled in sleep because "sometimes sleep or dream is the last exile." At times, he levitates as do many objects in the film, whether boulders, planets, or puffy white clouds. Rising above grim reality, he dreams of all he has lost. He contemplates the moon much as the poet Bashō once did. He says in the voice-over narration, "I loved the moon. I sent her wishes. Promises I couldn't keep. But the night lets you down. Nothing ever happens. Except for the return of morning." The moon offers escape from the misery of day and a different measure of time, one of the key subtexts of the film, when dreams hold infinite possibility. With his planetary images superimposed over the meager hut, Panh projects himself into an alternative universe where he can stand on the moon and look back at the earth, detached and distant from the prison of his life. It is as if he has become the Little Prince for a desperate new age.

The disembodied narration is in constant dialogue with the images, sometimes in sync but more often in ironic counterpoint. It is delivered from a time and place remote from the scenes on-screen and in a language different from the Khmer Panh spoke as a boy. Images position the boy in the past; words position the adult filmmaker in the present. It is here in the present that he remembers what he endured and what he lost and where he ruminates about the roots of terror and revolution that perplex him still. As in *The Missing Picture*, the text was written with Christophe Bataille and spoken by the actor Randal Douc. The style of narration is somewhat reminiscent of Chris Marker's film *Sans Soleil* (1983). Like Marker, Panh is an absent presence who teases his audience about who is speaking, and, as in Marker's film, everything seen and heard is based on the filmmaker's past and his elegiac midlife reflections on time. But unlike Marker, Panh allows the viewer little space to process his dense, idea-laden text.

Exile is neither a narrative nor an essay, despite what reviewers claim. One might call it a nonlinear autobiographical narrative, or one might venture further and consider it a transitional form poised between narrative and documentary using the language of poetry and image to achieve a more intimate experience of the artist's inner self. Much as Panh transformed viewer expectations of documentary reenactment with *S-21: The Khmer Rouge Killing Machine* (2002) and *The Missing Picture* (2013), here he challenges documentary norms yet again, demonstrating how visual poetry can document the reality of inner life and resistance. He takes issue implicitly with Adorno's rejection of poetry after Auschwitz: "When one is faced with destruction, one must secretly protect and cultivate . . . one's capacity to create. . . . You need to have this poetic imagination."[37] He writes in *The Elimination*: "My films are oriented toward knowledge; everything is based on reading, reflection, research work. But I also believe in form, in colors, in light, in framing and editing. I believe in poetry. Is that a shocking thought?"[38]

Exile is documentary as poetic metacinema with special effects and themes borrowed from classical filmmakers like Méliès (*A Trip to the Moon*, 1902), Resnais (*Night and Fog*, 1955), and Tarkovsky (*The Mirror*, 1975). It also conjures Malraux's *musée imaginaire*, where archival photos are arranged on the walls as if in a nineteenth-century bourgeois salon filled with fine art. It is the space of nightmares where myths, fears, and echoes of the past combine to haunt the dreamer with monstrous figures, black snakes, and cawing birds

FIGURE 7.7 Memory gallery in *Exile* © RPanh / droits réservés

that disturb his days and nights. One can observe a correspondence with Arendt's plea for a "fearful imagination by which perception is forever shocked out of the familiar apprehension of the real, the present is haunted by the past, the self is haunted by its own otherness, and the visible is haunted by the elsewhere," as Max Silverman notes, adding that what we see is not traumatic memory but rather "concentrationary memory" because the haunting is the invisible but ever-present trace of the concentrationary (or genocidal) universe.[39]

Here too are wishful glimpses of Sisyphean labors magically transformed as heavy boulders float and spin in air and soothing dreams, in which a ghostly hand caresses the boy's face much as he caresses the face of his mother in a photo. If *The Missing Picture* paid respect to Panh's father, *Exile* honors his mother, whose presence is felt throughout the film. Perhaps the most haunting scene is of a family meal, once lovingly prepared and suddenly abandoned with only these traces left of the family that sat down together to eat; revisited later, the meal is decomposing, stripped of all color and covered with dust, dead objects that embody loss with heartbreaking concreteness.

The boy inhabits the intimate space that Gaston Bachelard celebrates when writing about the dialectics of outside and inside in *The Poetics of Space*. Bachelard could have been describing this film when he quotes Maurice Blanchot in *L'arrêt de mort (Stay of Execution)*: "About this room, which was plunged in utter darkness, I knew everything, I had entered into it, I bore it within me, I made it live, with a life that is not life, but which is stronger than life, and which no force in the world can vanquish."[40] This space, which is commensurate with inner life, possesses overwhelming silence, according to Bachelard. It was this silence that allowed Rithy to reclaim his self. This is made clear in his memoir, *The Elimination*, when he explains how he dealt with one obligatory self-criticism session: "On the evening . . . after I told the story of the Apollo 11 mission, I didn't think for a moment of explaining myself. Or defending myself. I said *what it was necessary for me to say*. I conformed myself to the desires of the Khmer Rouge leaders. I spoke in order to be able to return to silence. To be invisible is to be a living being; almost an individual."[41]

Mesmerized by Panh's oneiric images, by composer Marc Marder's contrabass, by the dulcet tones of Douc's voice, the viewer may be only vaguely aware that what is spoken comes from literary works by some of Panh's favorite poets, like René Char and Jacques Prévert, or from political theorists like Mao, Pol Pot, Saint-Just, and Robespierre. Initially, Panh thought he would only quote from the *philosophes* of the French Enlightenment, but he abandoned that idea. Occasionally, he identifies the authors quoted but more often they remain anonymous, their words woven into the monologue, much as the ideas of those who have influenced one can become indistinguishable from one's own thoughts. Why does Panh do this? He hints at one reason early on: "I've known slogans that were so beautiful, so simple, slogans that sounded so pure and beautiful, so powerful, I've repeated them so often . . . I hardly dare repeat the words. They're so clear you might believe them."[42] This warning against the seduction of totalitarian language reflects his experience of being indoctrinated by the Khmer Rouge and his struggle to resist.

Music was a crucial refuge. Stealing into the forest to make up lyrics to sing to half-remembered tunes by the Beatles and the Bee Gees was one way he resisted the earworms of Khmer Rouge ideology. Longtime collaborator Marc Marder allows Panh the freedom to arrange the music he composes for him. Using Western instruments (contrabass, guitar, strings), sound effects (footsteps, birdcalls), and voices (Cambodian songs, political anthems, spoken words), as well as synthesized sounds and reverb, Marder provides the rich palette from which Panh selects and designs *Exile*'s soundscape.[43]

Raya Morag argues for an interesting interpretation of Panh's disembodied voice—as a strategy he uses to reflect on subject/object positions in which his "present absence" allows him to confront the "rhetoric of utmost objectification."[44] With each film since *S-21*, Panh has retreated further and further from actual places of forced labor, imprisonment, torture, and execution to arrive at this transcendent nonplace that resides within him. "The Lazarean hero is never there where he finds himself . . . because he has lived in a world which is situated nowhere and whose frontiers are not marked out since these are the frontiers of death," as Jean Cayrol writes.[45] Morag proposes his cinematic mission has been to wage war as a survivor with perpetrators in films like *S-21* and *Duch, Master of the Forges of Hell*. She finds the writing of Holocaust survivor Jean Améry as key to understanding the role of resentment in Panh's work. But confronting perpetrators is only one stage of his "mission." Increasingly Panh has turned inward to confront himself in the past and present and to explore "the volatility of time."[46] It seems more likely that in his autobiographical work he is following Cayrol's thoughts on Lazarean memory, which is premised on the notion of a doubled or haunted present in which different times and spaces collide, what Silverman has defined as "palimpsestic memory."[47]

Panh uses language—or more specifically grammar—to permit the beloved dead to remain alive and present for him. Linguistically, past verb tenses dizzyingly shuttle from the completed past (*le passé composé*) to the imperfect or habitual past (*le passé imparfait*). This is how he speaks still with his mother, and their past remains ongoing.[48] Regrettably, this tour de force device is more apparent for French speakers than those reading subtitles, where this subtlety of language and time is untranslatable.

Exile is Panh's most explicit meditation on revolution and its consequences. English subtitles make the complex narration easy to read but not the thoughts inscribed within them: the viewer must work to fathom the ideas here. Panh asks in his synopsis for the film: "What kind of revolution might we wish for? A revolution that lives up to humanity, with respect and understanding? Or an attempt at destruction, the false purity that has seen so many false disciples?"[49] He quotes Mao several times, convinced Mao more than Marx or the Jacobins influenced the Khmer Rouge's ideology and its demented commitment to forging an agrarian utopia overnight, but then he concludes with these rousing words from Robespierre: "Man was made for happiness and freedom but everywhere he is enslaved and miserable. Society's goal is the preservation of his rights, the fulfillment of his being. Everywhere society debases and oppresses him. It's time man was reminded of his true destiny."[50]

This stirring call in defense of human rights cuts to an image that casts a shadow on such revolutionary idealism. A match is struck and reveals in its flickering light a photo, a numbered headshot that eerily resembles those taken of people about to be tortured and executed at S-21 prison. It is probably the photo taken when Panh arrived at the Mairut refugee camp, the image of a boy haunted by the constant specter of death and loss, the child

FIGURE 7.8 Panh checks scene for *Exile* © DBoyle

suddenly grown into a man, an exile. This film more than any other invites the audience into his inner world to understand what it was and still is to be so alone, so hungry, so afraid, and so determined to use his creativity to live as a human being.

Exile has puzzled critics expecting a relatable, chronological narrative told from the viewpoint of a child, like *The Missing Picture*, with its doll-like figurines and dioramas that offer viewers of any age an accessible entry point into the tale of horror that was the Cambodian genocide. Its references to Mao, Robespierre, and Marx seem to fight against such notions. But it may surprise viewers to know that *Exile* delights children, as the sons of two film festival directors in Switzerland and Argentina can attest.[51] Although Panh claims in the film that "exile and childhood can't look each other in the face," this is exactly what happens. In all his films, Panh is reaching out to the young, profoundly aware that 70 percent of the Cambodian population was born after 1979, and they have been taught little about their history. *Exile*'s visuals are appealing to children, inspired one can argue by Antoine de Saint-Exupéry's *The Little Prince*, which is what allows Cambodia's tragic story to be accessible and absorbing for children of all ages and nationalities.

With his ubiquitous kramar wrapped jauntily around his neck, the diminutive Panh in real life resembles the Little Prince, who also sported a signature scarf from the tiny asteroid that was his home. Although he denies it, Panh draws upon elements from the novella for his film's images. For example, there is a scene reminiscent of the Little Prince's three volcanos, a number of equilibrium that recurs throughout the film: three boulders, three clouds, three eggs, three images of the boy in the hut, and so on. In one of the final scenes, the boy plants a field of roses. It was the Little Prince's protective care for the fragile rose that brings him home, a poignant metaphor for Panh's return to Cambodia to remember and honor the dead. Saint-Exupéry's illustrated quest to understand friendship, love, loyalty, honesty, and societal relationships may explain this film's special appeal to a child's imagination. For those who see *Exile* with the heart of a child and the mind of an adult, it reveals the depths of Panh's understanding of childhood and innocence lost.

Exile, the Installation

If *Exile* is Panh's most complex, demanding, and experimental single-channel film to date, his monumental installation seems by contrast direct and deceptively easy to grasp. Elegantly realized, it consists of four circular walls that suggest the enclosure of a camp. Each wall offers different images. Over two hundred beautiful, often tragic photographs of refugees appear on the interior of one wall while much larger photos of the sprawling camps that house them are on the outside. Inside the enclosure is a lashed-together raft with a torn sail at one end and sand at the other end, where the bodice of a nineteenth-century woman's dress is laid out on rocks. Circling two of the facing inner walls is a horizon line presided over by a brilliant sun at one extreme and the moon eclipsing the sun at the other. Designed to be experienced at night, the installation also includes archival film from Cambodia projected onto a metal sculpture of birds that bisects the center. Over all is a soundscape heard through speakers installed above the circular structure.

Essential support for the installation came from the High Commissioner of the United Nations Human Rights Commission (UNHCR), who gave Panh permission to use photographs from their vast archive. The festival director Isabelle Gattiker invited Panh for a month-long artist's residence in the nearby town of Meyrin, where he selected photos and developed his plans, which included securing images and artifacts from local residents who had sought refuge in Geneva during the twentieth and twenty-first centuries. As Gattiker explains, Geneva's tradition of welcoming refugees dates to the sixteenth century when French Huguenots arrived seeking a haven from religious persecution following the St. Bartholomew Day's Massacre. The International Film Festival and Forum on Human Rights (FIFDH) provided expert assistance for construction of a stable, weather-resilient structure for the installation that could be dismantled and reassembled.

Linking the film with the installation are their many shared motifs. Clotheslines of brightly colored shirts hang suspended in the film—in symbolic rejection of the regimented black clothing all were forced to wear by the Khmer Rouge. These shirts hang on one wall in the installation, their cheerful colors and patterns illuminated at nightfall by light bulbs; but only a third are lit, however, honoring those lives extinguished while searching for freedom. Now familiar Khmer Rouge propaganda films are reflected in bowls of water in the film; in the installation, they are projected onto a metal sculpture of birds that bisects the space at its center. Birds appear in the film, too, as predators circling overhead and as two-dimensional cutouts that haunt the boy's dreams. Panh often uses birds in his films, not as figures of freedom or migration, as one might expect, but rather as ill omens or predators that attack the vulnerable and bear witness to the dead.

The installation contains neither Panh's footage nor Marc Marder's music. It is not a narrative film. Its archival images do not require musical accompaniment in this outdoor space where, instead, intermittent explosions and breaking waves provide a subtle soundtrack of war and cataclysm that mixes with the ambient noise of the city.

Panh here steps away from a modernist reliance on narrative to fully embrace the postmodernist role of the archive, which according to some critics has become the dominant symbolic and cultural form.[52] Panh relies on the art of the installation, one of two forms favored by contemporary art practice, and in particular on photography, which along with European colonialism stimulated the nineteenth century's interest in archives. *Exile* is not the first time Panh's fascination with photography and archives coalesced—*France Is Our Mother Country* precedes it. And Panh's involvement in creating and sustaining an archive of Cambodian films and photos has demonstrated his commitment to archives. And then there is his ever-evolving, fascinating, nonlinear archival artwork and teaching platform—his Facebook page.

Exile as an outdoor installation is decidedly nonlinear with its numerous entrances and exits; its curvilinear design offers a symmetrical balancing of elements that are related but different, unequal, essential—horizons dominated by the sun and the moon, old films, archival objects, cheerful shirts old and new, disturbing sounds, and light in darkness. But at the heart of this installation are the photos. Panh believes photographs can do something that news footage fails to achieve—arrest one's gaze so that a dialogue can emerge between viewer and subject. Over two hundred photos selected from the UNHCR archive depict refugees today and the many hardships they endure when forced to flee their homeland and travel on long and dangerous journeys to arrive at makeshift camps where human dignity and life itself are hard to preserve. With these photos, Panh is asking viewers to listen to them. As in the film *Exile*, the installation relies on a charged silence: and it is in the silence that one listens for the heart beats, hushed breathing, muffled cries, and tentative testimonies of refugees, fellow human beings.

Graves without a Name (Les tombeaux sans nom) (2018)

Reviewers pronounced *Graves without a Name* "profoundly moving" (*New York Times*) and "emotionally overwhelming, visually ravishing and intellectually stimulating" (*Hollywood Reporter*).[53] Given the beauty of its images, the poetry of its text, and the depth of its grief, it is an impressive work of mourning, but it is also a complex work whose subject is greater than grief.

Graves is the last film in this autobiographical trilogy. Ten years in the making, *Graves without a Name* invites viewers to witness Panh's daunting search to locate and bury his loved ones and provide them—and himself—elusive peace. His quest led him on a spiritual journey to Buddhist pagodas, traditional mediums, and the land Panh knew as a boy. The film begins with a Buddhist rite in which a monk shaves Panh's head. This is not the first time this rite was enacted in a Panh film, and viewers of his fiction film *Rice People* (1994) will remember when the oldest daughter sees her long and beautiful hair fall to the ground for the funeral of her father. Panh, whose hair is neither long nor abundant, grimaces as his hair falls at the start of an elaborate funeral ritual involving chanting, incense burning, prayers, and burial of a miniature proxy coffin. Later in the film, he meets with soothsayers who perform rituals ranging from a dramatic if reluctant spirit possession to more sedate acts intended to summon the dead. The resurgence today of mediums who channel spirits is a response to the needs of genocide survivors determined to pay their debt to the dead. Panh acknowledged their social role in his earlier fiction film about Cambodian and Vietnamese refugees living in France, *Let the Boat Break, Let the Junk Crack Open* (2001) and his documentary *The People of Angkor* (2003).

Panh hates being filmed and would have preferred to be represented by a figurine like the one he used in *The Missing Picture* (2013), but for *Graves without a Name* his presence was absolutely necessary. So he filmed himself from behind, reflected upside down in water, out of focus, at a great distance or bowed down at the feet of a medium who did not know that the person she had been asked to search for was Panh's father. When she cried out for "my son," her eyes focused on Panh, and he hastily put down his camera and knelt before her as she reached out, tears streaming down her face, to cradle his head. Face hidden, Panh appears impassive but does not hesitate to seize the opportunity of possibly meeting his father once more.

Panh's exhaustive attempts to honor the dead provide the scaffolding for what proves to be a more complex and multilayered film than its title

FIGURE 7.9 Medium in *Graves without a Name* © RPanh / droits réservés

suggests. His quest leads him back to the villages where he once planted rice, dug ditches, and buried countless dead. He revisits the day-to-day lives of "the old people," Pol Pot's agrarian base, who still live and farm in remote villages. He conducted extended interviews in Trum with two elderly men—one is a "base" person; the other, seen wearing a large straw hat, is a former Khmer Rouge cadre and soldier. Their stories link *Graves without a Name* to Panh's documentaries about genocide perpetrators in *S-21: The Khmer Rouge Killing Machine* (2002) and *Duch, Master of the Forges of Hell* (2012). But, having dedicated three films to the big and little perpetrators who executed people at S-21 prison, Panh is no longer focused on Khmer Rouge security sites. Instead, in *Graves*, he pursues the ways "ordinary people" persecuted hundreds of thousands of "new people," who were systematically dehumanized and eliminated in a fashion just as swift and effective as the gassing of Jews in Auschwitz.[54] The two "grandfathers" interviewed soberly reflect on the horrors they witnessed and even facilitated. Their stories will be familiar to those who know about cannibalism practiced ritually or out of hunger during the genocide. The ultimate insult was leaving the dead unburied, abandoned by a roadside to decompose, prey to animals and insects. The Khmer Rouge were determined to "leave no trace," not even of death. The "base people" have tortured memories too. What they say is critical to an understanding of the everyday nature of genocide and the culture of impunity that persists to this day for ordinary perpetrators who live side by side with the people they once tried to destroy. They blend so invisibly within the rural landscape that many critics of Panh's film miss the reality that here too was a perpetrator providing testimony about what happened to people "smashed" by the Khmer Rouge.

The monologues delivered by these soft-spoken, dignified men take place at the base of a large tree. Seen from afar, it dominates the lowland landscape. Panh's narration explains the significance of this tree for him: "Thirty years later I found it again. Nature is an ambiguous grave. And this tree that is so hard, with its secret soul, was a shelter for me." Panh and one of his interlocutors traverse the fields where the tree stands, carrying over their shoulders long bamboo poles with memorial banners attached to them: white pennants known as "white crocodiles" are markers for the dead whereas multicolored flags represent the living.[55] Seen as mere specks on the horizon, Panh and the former Khmer Rouge cadre plant the white crocodiles around the tree, following the traditional way of announcing that someone has died.

Attentive listeners at this juncture will hear an echo of Jean Cayrol's narration for Alain Resnais's film *Night and Fog*, when the narrator says: "Even

FIGURE 7.10 Khmer Rouge guerrilla recalls the past in *Graves without a Name* © RPanh / droits réservés

a simple dirt road may lead to extermination." From the beginning to the very end of *Graves*, Panh questions whether he is dead or alive. "This may be too simple, but I have the idea that I died once already, under the Khmer Rouge, and then was reborn, but with the pain, the death inside me. I have to accept it, this pain, and live with it until the end of my life—my second life."[56] Much like Jean Cayrol's Lazarean man, Panh has "found a way to confront his suffering, to shoulder his solitude, to face up to it."[57]

Before his tree, Panh performs an ersatz funeral ceremony for the ten family members he lost. After completing the cremation, the washed and now purified remains are wrapped and installed in an urn. Following this gesture, Panh provides an exceptional image of the tree reflected upside down in a large crystal globe. It marvelously evokes what Krishna, in the Bhagavad Gita, said about the banyan tree, with its roots reaching skyward and branches reaching down into the earth. It is an image of the material world as a reflection of the spiritual world, the material world being only a shadow of reality. In that shadow there is no reality, but from the shadow we understand that there is substance and reality. It is a lesson dearly learned by Panh.

Although many individuals play critical roles in this film, what remains strongest is the overriding presence of the Cambodian earth, which Panh films using a drone camera for the first time. Whether he is scanning rice paddies like a hungry bird in search of mass graves or racing toward the rapidly setting sun sinking below the distant horizon, he directs the viewer's gaze to the physical locus of Cambodia's pain and suffering and the sense of time passing. Shooting in close-up, he combs the earth with restless fingers that uncover remnants of the dead—a tooth or a bone fragment, scraps of bloodied fabric, dusty buttons—which testify to the anonymous presence of the two million who died in what was known as Democratic Kampuchea. He may not have located his parents' remains, but he has found evidence of unique lives that vanished in the wind. Inspired by a dream, Panh incorporates carved wooden faces in this rural landscape. Whether superimposed on a tree or floating in water, they are reminiscent of the masks in Alain Resnais and Chris Marker's film *Les Statues Meurent Aussi* (*Statues also Die*, 1953), a film that deeply touched Panh when he first saw it as a young refugee. Panh's masks function much like those African sculptures, speaking silently of lost cultures and people almost forgotten, their imagination crushed by colonization, their art forced to become colonial trophies. That film's anticolonial narration said, "These masks fight against death . . . because the familiarity of death leads to the domestication of death . . . to the transmission of death." Music, dramatic ways of filming sculpture to animate their aesthetic force, and a poetic voice-over that reported on their fate provided a model and inspiration for a young man who would later visually, aurally, and critically indict genocidal violence in Cambodia in his films.

Panh populates the Cambodian landscape with photos of his family and of others, like Hout Bophana, who have become totemic figures in Panh's iconography. Every photograph planted in the earth is a reminder of someone's death, of a moment captured that will never return, a memory of the past and of those no longer present. Panh's family photos have become as significant and familiar to his viewers as the images of the dead celebrated by Roland Barthes in *Camera Lucida*.

Graves without a Name is more than a film about mourning and loss; it is proof that Panh has survived, that the Khmer Rouge did not succeed in eliminating him. He is alive on behalf of the land, the people, and the history of a nation still struggling to find inner peace for the living and eternal peace for the dead. He has kept faith with his mother's last words for him before she died: "You must keep walking in life, Rithy. Whatever happens, you have to keep walking."[58] *Il chemine.* He is walking still.

Epilogue

When the historian Peter Maguire first arrived in Phnom Penh in 1994, he wrote his impressions of the city's anarchic and treacherous traffic: "Stoplights were nonexistent; turn signals were not used; driving on the right side of the road was optional; and above all, police were extortionists to be avoided at all costs."[1] I cannot account for the police, but as for the other details, nothing had changed in Phnom Penh since Maguire voiced misgivings about crossing the street.

I was physically and emotionally exhausted after attending the ECCC hearing, so I decided not to return the next day. I was disappointed by my fatigue but realized I needed a break. I wanted to visit the Central Market, an art deco architectural marvel, and judging from the map, it looked like a short walk from my hotel. I called Mr. Lucky to say I would not need his services until the following day. He was not happy to hear I was going for a walk. I strolled along a narrow street without a care, eager to go shopping, something entirely different from my pursuit of Cambodian history. But that history was not going to let go of me. All of a sudden, I found myself flung into the air, violently propelled by invisible forces. I flew in an arc and smashed into the ground, landing hard on my right arm and shoulder and twisting my neck. With the breath knocked out of me, I could do nothing. No one came to my aid. I heard within me a whispering voice, "You wanted to learn about Cambodia's pain and suffering. We can help you with that." After what seemed like forever, I picked myself up and slowly walked back to my hotel. I lay down, hoping I would be OK. When I woke up an hour later, I was unable to move my arm, which was now stiff. This was not good.

I had planned to go to the Bophana Center to have Panh's films transferred to my computer. I slowly climbed the staircase and saw once more Vann Nath's double painting of Bophana on the landing. When I reached the first floor, I found Sopheap Chea, deputy director of the center. He saw my arm and my face, turned ashen, and dashed off. I sat down and quietly began to cry. Within minutes, a crowd of about twenty people had gathered in a wide circle, with Panh standing opposite me in what made me think of the gunfight scene in *High Noon*. It was not a duel, but there was a drama unfolding as I stood up, speechless, cradling my arm, waiting to see what would happen next. He conferred with the person standing beside him. I heard them deciding whether to send me to the hospital. Finally, he sent someone to get the car and drive me to the nearby International Clinic. During this deliberation, I observed what I think it means for him to have his "team" around him, a large group of people utterly devoted to him and to the Bophana Audiovisual Resource Center and its mission. He was more than a CEO; he was a monarch with life-and-death powers over trusty retainers and foreign visitors alike. A sweet young woman drove me to the clinic and waited while the wry Dr. Jean examined me. He had the most exquisitely gentle hands I have ever felt, and as he probed my arm to see if it was broken, he spoke into my ear conspiratorially, "Welcome to Cambodia. Falls, fever, diarrhea. Welcome to Cambodia!" A nurse debrided the wound, poured antibacterial soap on it, and then wrapped the arm tightly. Dr. Jean sent me back to my hotel with pain pills. Lying on my bed under the mesmerizing ceiling fan, I thought of Catherine Deneuve in *Indochine* with her trusty retainer holding her opium pipe as I drifted off to sleep.

My arm was not broken, but it was useless, so the following day I allowed myself a solitary farewell meal at the Foreign Correspondents Club before attending a performance of Cambodian dance at the National Museum. Maguire reported in *Facing Death in Cambodia* that the club was a major hangout for journalists, adventurers, and anyone who was anyone in Phnom Penh. It was an inviting four-story, yellow colonial building on Sisowath Quay with an open-air veranda that overlooked the Tonle Sap and Mekong Rivers. It too was within walking distance, but Mr. Lucky drove me there and fussed over me like an anxious parent whose child had ignored good advice. I enjoyed my dinner of fish amok and lingered over coffee, recalling my visit to Cambodia. Angkor Wat had seemed overpowering in its size and beauty, and like most tourists, I was caught up in the hubbub of souvenir sellers when what I really wanted was unattainable quiet to meditate on the splendor of another time and culture, to admire this symbol of spiritual and earthly power that had inspired some of the Khmer Rouge's worst utopian nightmares. Filtering everything I experienced through the lens of Panh's films and his own story of survival, I was struck by the intense heat at five in the morning when a tour guide collected me to see the sunrise over Angkor Wat's unmistakable triptych of temple towers. How could Panh work in rice paddies for twelve hours day after day under such an unrelenting sun? Siem Reap seemed more cosmopolitan than Phnom Penh, probably because it was organized around luxury hotels, restaurants, and shops that catered to acquisitive, well-heeled tourists. I saw how Cambodians, the true inheritors of this magnificent landmark, were marginalized, much like A'Koy in *The People of Angkor*, who stood aside for rude tourists jostling to take their selfies with the Buddha.

I had expected my time at the ECCC would be a high point of my trip, but it was not. The press were no longer interested in the details of an appeal by two men already found guilty of genocide. Like Panh, I felt there was something missing—a more inclusive definition of their crimes. Panh told Thierry Cruvellier in 2018, when the court ruled that Nuon Chea and Khieu Samphan were guilty of genocide against the Chams and Vietnamese, that he had ceased to feel Cambodian while living under the Khmer Rouge. He was dispossessed of everything—his name, his religious and cultural practice, his family. He felt under attack in his very identity and in his dignity. He asked Cruvellier, "What more did the Chams and Vietnamese suffer than all Cambodians?"[2]

Six years later, I am in the final stages of writing this book. During the intervening years, I interviewed Panh in other cities and watched his prolific work continue to evolve beyond *Exile*, the film he was making while I was in Phnom Penh. Driven by his angels and demons, Panh has continued to use his imagination to create new films, new master classes, a new book, and even a documentary during the COVID-19 pandemic. Working nonstop is how he asserts, "I am alive. The Khmer Rouge did not destroy me." Yet he believes, like such genocide survivors before him as Charlotte Delbo, Primo Levi, and Jean Cayrol, that he died in Democratic Kampuchea, but no one knows it. He is like Sisyphus, who cheated death and as punishment was forced to roll an immense boulder up a hill only for it to roll down every time it neared the top, an action repeated for eternity. Those boulders appear in several guises in *Exile*, and the sight of the last clay figurine in *The Missing Picture* represents the most poignant instance of Panh's mythic task, trying to properly bury the dead in a fathomless grave that can never contain enough earth to cover them. He is the Ferryman of Memories for his family and the two million who died during the Pol Pot years. Making films about this genocide is not Panh's desire; it is his debt to the dead, bringing them back to life if only on film, if only for a moment. He listens to the dead, speaks with the dead. He encourages us to do the same.

Six years after my fall in Phnom Penh, I go twice a week for physical therapy on the arm I thought I had broken. The strength in my right arm has suddenly gone. Pain comes back to haunt one when it will. Fabricio, my therapist, is skilled and compassionate. He unscrews my arm from my shoulder and rotates my forearm at the elbow. At least, that is how it feels. I sometimes cry out in pain as he works on me. Rumi said the cure for pain is in the pain. And Aeschylus, the father of tragedy, who also favored trilogies, said the reward of suffering is experience. Researching and writing this book has been a life-changing experience for me. It has been not only an encounter with Rithy Panh and his films but a collaboration with the dead.

I listen closely for the silent voices that have guided me down unexpected paths to unfamiliar texts, surprising insights, and the depths of Panh's cinema. If this is what it means to be haunted, these welcome ghosts have been with me for many years now, although I confess I am looking forward to letting them go soon to their rest. Jacques Derrida coined the term *hantologie* and promoted his anti-Freudian notion about the merits of melancholia. He concluded *Spectres de Marx* by suggesting that learning to converse with the dead may be the best hope we have: "[The 'scholar' of the future, tomorrow's 'intellectual'] should learn to live by learning not to make conversation with the ghost but to converse with him, with her, to give or return a voice to him, to her, whether this be in oneself, in the other, to the other in the self: spectres are always *there,* even if they don't exist, even if they are no longer, even if they are not yet."[3]

Acknowledgments

I tell my students you can always recognize a film is independent if the credits run nearly as long as the film. Adequate acknowledgment of all the help I received in writing this book would rival its length, too. I am grateful to many institutions, publications, colleagues, students, and friends. I have probably overlooked some names here, and if so, please know that your contributions are woven into this book and inscribed in my heart. First and foremost is my thanks to Rithy Panh, whose extraordinary work inspired this book and more than a decade of research in preparation for writing it. Rithy generously shared copies of all his films and gave me permission to reproduce stills from them. I am grateful to him for answering my questions and for making time for me even when he was under great pressure and in the midst of shooting a film. Differences in language and customs created some big and little misunderstandings, but forbearance prevailed. I earnestly hope this book will help to bring Panh's work to the attention of a wider audience and better distribution for his films worldwide.

Special thanks to John Vink for his patience and generosity during our transatlantic dealings. Vink's photographs provide artful evidence of the chemistry Panh has with his crew and characters when shooting and directing his films. I am honored to have his photo of Panh on the cover of this book. I am enormously grateful for a Calderwood Fellowship at the Mac-Dowell Colony and a writer's residency at the Virginia Center for the Creative Arts. I have also benefited from the opportunity to share my papers on Panh's work with old and new colleagues at Visible Evidence conferences

FIGURE ACK 1.1 Rithy Panh on the set for *The Sea Wall* © John Vink / MAPSimages

in Bochum, Stockholm, Toronto, and Buenos Aires and at other conferences at Monash University in Melbourne and at Hong Kong Baptist
University.

The New School provided me with research and travel funding, a brief
leave of absence from teaching, and gifted graduate assistants who aided
me in many ways. I owe much to them for their editorial insights, helpful
translations, and delightful company: in particular, I thank Victor Torres
Rodriguez, Luigi Leonardo, Rebecca Heidenberg, Lauren Hammersmith,
Anna Schneider, Anya Stewart, and Milos Ciric, among others. I have loved
sharing Panh's films with students, who found their own special connections to his work in our classes on death and media, the documentary film,
and history, memory, and media. I could not have written this without access
to New York University's Bobst Library and the New York Public Library's
research collections. Thanks also go to the Bophana Audiovisual Resource
Center and its devoted staff.

The fellowship of Panh scholarship has grown over the years and become
more diverse and global. I am grateful to the many colleagues I have met—in
person or in print—while on this journey. My one regret is that there was
not enough space to include the bibliography I amassed while researching

this book. I am indebted to all whose writing informed my understanding of Panh's work. In particular I want to acknowledge Vicente Sánchez-Biosca and Raya Morag, whose wisdom and friendship have meant so much.

Many have played an array of supportive roles during this process for which I am deeply grateful: Ann Bienstock, David Chandler, Davy Chou, Gail Collins, Gary Crowdus, Mary Cunnane, Efrén Cuevas, Zlatko Dimitrioska, Isabelle Gattiker, Jill Godmilow, Amir Husak, Alexandra Juhasz, Jonathan Kahana, Deanna Kamiel, Alisa Lebow, Wai Luk Lo, Brenda Longfellow, Denise Marika, Diane Mitchell, Seth Mydans, Kavich Neang, Nick Paterniti, Regula Pickel, Laura Poitras, Christophe Preissing, B. Ruby Rich, Pratap Rughani, Bhaskar Sarkar, Elida Schogt, Noah Shenker, Ann Stoler, Leshu Torchin, Janet Walker, Chi-hui Yang, and Patricia Zimmermann. Warm thanks to friends who read versions of chapters and cheered me on: Anastasia Cleaver, Margaret Diehl, Mary Grein, Kyoko Hirano, Alice Lilly, Aras Ozgün, Miriam Stempler, and Anne Stovell. Finally, special thanks to Rutgers University Press and, in particular, to Nicole Solano, who pursued this book sight unseen, and to the meticulous Michelle Scott and her team at Westchester Publishing Services for wrangling errant details into consistency throughout the text.

I conducted interviews with Rithy Panh via phone on February 28, 2014. I interviewed him in person in Phnom Penh in late June and early July 2015; in Toronto on August 21, 2015; and in Geneva on March 10, 2017. Thanks to *Cineaste* and *CineAction* for permission to include two interviews as Appendices: "Confronting Images of Ideology: An Interview with Rithy Panh," *Cineaste* 39 no. 3 (Summer 2014) and "On a Morality of Filming: A Conversation with Rithy Panh and Deirdre Boyle," *CineAction* 97 (Winter 2016). Earlier versions of some chapters appeared in *Cineaste, Film Quarterly, Framework,* and in *Documentary Testimonies: Global Archives of Suffering,* edited by Bhaskar Sarkar and Janet Walker (New York and London: Routledge, 2009), and in *A Companion to Contemporary Documentary Film,* edited by Alexandra Juhasz and Alisa Lebow (Hoboken, NJ: Wiley-Blackwell, 2020).

Thanks to these publishers for permission to include excerpts from the following:

Letters on Cézanne by Rainer Maria Rilke, edited by Clara Rilke, translated by Joel Agee. Translation copyright © 1985, 2002 by Farrar, Straus, and Giroux. Reprinted by permission of North Point Press, a division of Farrar, Straus, and Giroux. All rights reserved.

Appendix 1

Confronting Images
of Ideology

AN INTERVIEW WITH RITHY PANH BY DEIRDRE BOYLE

We spoke with Rithy Panh while he was in Los Angeles earlier this year for the Academy Awards. What follows are highlights of that laughter-filled telephone interview conducted in English, which includes the participation of one of his long-time collaborators, composer Marc Marder.

> CINEASTE No two films of yours are alike. How do you go about finding the form for the film you are making?
>
> RITHY PANH When I start a documentary film, I do not know what the film is about. I have an idea. For me, the difference between a documentary film and a fiction film is that a documentary is about an idea. I need a lot of time—two or three years. With *S-21*, it took me three years and, by the end, the film focused on the way that cinematography can work with the memory of the body. *The Missing Picture* is another adventure.

Originally published in *Cineaste* 39, no. 3 (Summer 2014): 39–44. Reprinted with the kind permission of *Cineaste*.

I started work on it by following a Khmer Rouge cinematographer and photographer because I wanted to know just how they produced their propaganda images. I am very interested in their footage. You can see behind their images something that sheds light on the ideology of the regime. It is complicated for me to explain. I needed to watch these archival films frame by frame. You know, today we have a lot of images. I don't know what I am looking at sometimes because there's too much. Today everybody can take a picture with their portable phone, tweet it, and put it on Facebook immediately. Everybody can film something. But what is the reality? What is the subjectivity? With these archival films, I need time to sit down and watch frame by frame every image and try to understand the ideology behind the image. I was studying these images when I found this very good sculptor.

Twenty years ago I wanted to make a film about my history, but I could not find a form. I was thinking about making a fiction film, but I did not want to direct actors about how to die and how to kill. I am not somebody like Spielberg who can make a film such as *Schindler's List*. Maybe I would like to do something like him, but I cannot. I lived through genocide. It is very difficult for me to direct a re-creation of it with people. I have been waiting twenty years to find this sculptor and these clay figurines. When I see them, I say, "Yes, I am ready now to make a film about my story. This is a film you cannot make again. You have just one shot, one film."

I'm not someone who makes a film just to make a film. I like teaching people, I like cooking, but if I decide to make a film, I must give to the film a particular effort. I'm not a pretentious man. I just try to bring to my story something very cinematographic, a new reflection on how you can use images.

Maybe I have made only one film in twenty years. [Laughs] I don't want to be a film director specialized on Khmer Rouge killing. I want to be a film director—someone who can talk about that time but not be specialized in it. I need to discover a new form every time. And when the form meets the essentials of the narrative, and they come together, it's good.

With *The Missing Picture*, I had to call Catherine [Dussart], my producer, and tell her that I wanted to make the whole film with clay figurines. [Laughs] At that moment, everybody asked me, "Are you sure? Clay figurines don't move. It's not animation." You know, nobody can see your film except you, the film director. You have to have the trust of your partner and your team. If your team has confidence in you, you can do a great job. I'm very lucky because people believe in my work. So I made one sequence, and I sent it to Mark, to Agnès [Sénémaud, his long-time collaborator], and to Catherine, and I asked them, what do you think? They

FIGURE A1.1 Movie memories in *The Missing Picture* © RPanh / droits réservés

said, "It's great. It's very powerful, but . . . it's not a film! It's only a three-minute sequence." The difficulty then is how to make a one-and-a-half hour film with figurines that do not move. That is the artistic challenge.

You keep in your mind that the music is not fixed yet, and the voice-over does not exist yet; you can introduce archival materials, and you can use—or not use—interviews. I decided very quickly to be much more radical with the form. I will use only clay figurines in the memory footage because the figurines are the missing picture: what I see, what I remember, what is in my memory, or what I would like to see now that does not exist. The Khmer Rouge footage is the image of totalitarianism, the image of the dictatorship, the image of ideology. There must be a confrontation between them in the film.

I think it is terrible for people like Marc Marder, who composes the music, or Christophe Bataille, who writes the narration, because I am always changing the order of the scenes.

CINEASTE What is it like to collaborate with Rithy?

MARC MARDER I worked on Rithy's school film, *Past Imperfect*. We've done eighteen films together now. For *The Missing Picture*, we didn't speak for months. Rithy would send me clips, and I'd send him music—back and forth, back and forth. Then one day I was in Paris, and Rithy called me from Cambodia, and said, "You know the scene at the end when he returns to his village?" Well, I had no script, and I had no idea what was going on in the film, but I just said, "Yes, Rithy." [Laughs]

Working with Rithy is, as he says, like working on one continuous film. I've developed a style of music and a sound he really loves, and we've found a mutual language and way of working together. He has a very fine ear. I make music, he listens, and then he uses it in the film in an appropriate way, although not always the way I would. It's not the typical way of using music in a film. He considers music as a separate art. It's not only film music, it's music music. Music is never an element just supporting an image for Rithy. It's an element that has its own story.

A long time ago someone said to me, "We're doing a film about Cambodia. Would you send us some music." By that time, I'd done quite a few films for Rithy. When they got the music, they said, "That's *not* Cambodian." And I said, "No, it's not Cambodian. It's my music for Rithy Panh."

At the beginning, with *Rice People*, I was trying all kinds of music. I went to Cambodia, and I listened to all kinds of Cambodian folk music. I made a conscious decision to compose in some of the modes that are musically Cambodian. But it couldn't be too ethnic, too folksy. It had to have some distance from the image to tell a different story.

RITHY TO MARC Sometimes you have an image?! I did not give you images! [Laughs] Sometimes I didn't give Marc an image at all. I'd just give him a hint or tell him a story.

MARDER What about the film *Duch, Master of the Forges of Hell*?!! For that film, Rithy just said to me, "There are only two shots in the whole film. Do your music. I'll take care of it." And there is an hour of music in *Duch*.

CINEASTE Rithy, I am very curious to know how you managed to contain your emotions during the three hundred hours you spent interviewing Duch? How did you keep from erupting with rage at the commandant of S-21? You are a master of patience and restraint in that film.

PANH Two days before I started shooting, I had a nightmare and for a week afterward I had nightmares. When you are so close to a perpetrator, the problem is that you discover that behind the killer there is a human being. It's very complex and very disturbing to your mind. I am not a judge. I am here to discover why this person became Duch. We are not born a killer. We become a killer. I tried to understand the mechanism of becoming a killer. You are very near to him, and it's disturbing, very disturbing. Sometimes I lose my control. But it's part of my work on this history. I decided to work on this memory twenty years ago. I will not change my objective, my aim, and I go as far as I can.

CINEASTE Poetry is a constant running through all your films. Is the inclusion of poetry an homage to your father, who loved poems and often quoted them to you, or perhaps a way of countering the oppression of the Khmer Rouge indoctrination slogans?

PANH Yes. Both. You know, totalitarianism tried to erase or wipe out your identity, your name, and your family—and so you must go the other way. You must give a name to a face, you must use images to reveal your identity. When you have very martial music from the Khmer Rouge, sharp like a machete or razor blade, then you must go to Marc's music, to something very poetic. You must set up to fight them. You will use words, you will use poetry, you will use music, you will use light, you will use clay—you will use whatever you have in your hand to fight back. It is very simple in my mind. I put it in each film. The first thing is, you must be free—like Chris Marker, like Shohei Imamura, and like other great film directors. Chris Marker was a poet, an editor, he was everything. Who can classify Chris Marker?! And Imamura—I met him when he was very old, but I had the feeling that he was much younger than me. That is the power of poetics, that is the freedom Imamura used to make his films much more dynamic.

CINEASTE You speak of the figurines in *The Missing Picture* as having a soul. Do you think your history has made you a more spiritual person?

PANH More religious? I don't think so. But maybe more human. My personal story made me who I am today. If it had not been a tragic story, I could have become a politician, a corrupted man, I do not know. [Laughs] But the fact is, I survived because a lot of people decided to help me. They decided to give me their place, and they have made me more humble, made me much more a part of other people. As I said, you are not born a killer and, in the same way, you are not born generous. You have to learn to be generous. We must learn to help people. Making a film is a way to help other people, a way of sharing with other people.

When I teach my students filmmaking, I ask only one thing of them: not to make a film *about* people but to make a film *with* people. When you make a film with people, it means you are with them. If they go to the rice fields, you go with them. If they go out in the rain, you go in the rain. Technically, you can make a film about people. You can film rice cultivators in a rice field by using a zoom lens—there's no need to go into the rice field, you can stay on the road. But this only makes a film about someone not truly with someone.

CINEASTE Can you tell me something about your new documentary project, which I think is now called "Cochinchine"?

PANH You know even more than me. [Laughs] For one year I have been working on it, but I have not even five minutes edited. It's a documentary film. A lot of people think it is very easy to do this: just shoot footage and put a voice-over on it. But if you want to make a good documentary, it is very, very hard, harder than a fiction film. With fiction, you start with a screenwriter, and then you have a script. You can find money, an actor, an actress, and then you find a team. You know where you want to go. But with documentary film, I don't know where I'm going. I have one idea, but what idea will be there at the end, I don't know. This film may be about globalization at the end. Has something changed since colonialism? Maybe. Maybe not. We are still the victims. People are evicted from their land, that is the same. The rich are still the same. I do not know if there is some progress in our life, in our society. So, I don't know what the film is yet.

CINEASTE I look forward to seeing what it will become.

PANH My producer, too!

CINEASTE Are you saying that fiction is easier for you to make than documentary?

PANH Fiction is easier for me to insert myself into, to give my point of view. Documentary is objective, a fact is a fact. But with fiction, it is more comfortable, much easier for a film director to express his politics. I try to use professional actors, but this is hard for me. Actors are nervous. When they are afraid of me, their ego becomes bigger. They defend themselves. An actor puts his image on the film. It's not easy for me to direct an actor, to even talk to actors. Now I know better how to do this. But it was very hard at the beginning, and it's still very hard for me.

CINEASTE You are the first Cambodian director nominated for an Academy Award. How do you feel on the eve of the Oscars ceremony?

PANH I am very happy for two things. One is that Academy members have recognized this kind of film. It's not completely fiction, not completely documentary. It's a little bit an essay film, but it is shot like fiction: you use traveling shots, you use light, you use decoration, you use clay figurines, but it's not fiction. It's a very special kind of film. There is no category for it. Cinema must liberate you, must give you the freedom to express yourself, your point of view, without regard to category. It is the first time that I can recall that the Academy has given recognition to this kind of cinema. That's the first thing.

The second reason I'm happy is because this nomination sends a very strong message to the young film directors in Cambodia. It means that we are alive, that we are here, that we can make a good film, and the Khmer Rouge cannot destroy us. Totalitarianism cannot destroy your imagination. You can stand up now, and you can make a film about your story, your country, your history, your future. Making films is something important for us who live in a country like Cambodia. It's not entertainment. It's a question of whether to live or not to live.

Appendix 2

On a Morality of Filming

A CONVERSATION BETWEEN RITHY PANH AND DEIRDRE BOYLE*

Rithy Panh is Cambodia's leading filmmaker and foremost chronicler of the genocide that decimated his country forty years ago when the Khmer Rouge took power and pursued a draconian scheme to create an agrarian utopia through terror. He has made over 20 award-winning films—both documentary and fiction works—and written several books about them and his experience surviving that genocide. He is best known to English speakers for two documentary films, *S-21: The Khmer Rouge Killing Machine* and *The Missing Picture,* the latter of which won Un Certain Regard at Cannes and was nominated for Best Foreign Language Film at the 86th Academy Awards in 2014. Panh was a special guest of the Visible Evidence conference held in Toronto in August 2015, where he screened *The Missing Picture* at the TIFF cinema and engaged in a discussion of his work with Deirdre Boyle, a documentary scholar and media historian, who had just returned from Phnom

*Originally published in *CineAction*, no. 96 (Winter 2016), 39–44. Reprinted with the kind permission of *CineAction*.

Penh where she had interviewed Panh for a book she is writing about his films. What follows are highlights of that conversation.

DEIRDRE BOYLE One of my colleagues, Leshu Torchin, has written a wonderful essay for *Film Quarterly* about *The Missing Picture*. She begins by making reference to Primo Levi's book, *The Drowned and the Saved*, which begins with a quotation from Coleridge. It's a wonderful association, calling up the way in which you're using the water imagery at the beginning of the film, and how that becomes an important device throughout, an effective wipe between spaces.

For me, it had a very different meaning. It really took me into childhood, and I think it's a kind of universal experience, if you've ever been to the beach as a child in the waves, holding on to the hands of someone who's keeping you safe, and suddenly the wave comes and hits you and you lose their hand, and suddenly, completely, you don't know which end is up and which end is down. It's a terrible experience. I was wondering about the process for you of discovering that image and how you went about using it.

RITHY PANH I remember Jankélévitz[1] talked about this sensation to be drowned again and again. For us, genocide is continuous, you get it for all your life. At the beginning when you come out, you have to fight first to rebuild everything, your capacity to be a human being again, because the process of dehumanization is so strong. It is like you are drowning and you cannot breathe. Psychiatrists call it a panic attack, but it's much more than a psychiatry problem. It's something that you must integrate in yourself when you live. Part of me says, "Don't talk about this again," but another part says, "No, you have to talk about it." I have been making films now for more than 30 years. I respect people who can change their life and not talk about the genocide or remember. Unfortunately for me, it's not possible. I don't feel better after making a film but making it is a necessity, like a process for me to rebuild my humanity.

DEIRDRE We've had several papers here at the conference talking about *The Missing Picture*. The idea of redemption comes up and reclaiming humanity. I think you are not reclaiming your humanity. You are reclaiming the humanity of all those who died. Would you agree?

RITHY Yes. When I make a film, I don't think about philosophy, or about aesthetics. The only thing I focus on is the dignity of people and ethics, some few things that can compose a morality of filming. This element, I have to integrate in myself before filming. When I film, I let things come, I go with that. That's why it takes me a lot of time for each film.

FIGURE A2.1 Panh family before Khmer Rouge emblem © RPanh / droits réservés

DEIRDRE I remember you were telling me that one of the reasons why the figurines were freeing was that you felt you couldn't ask anybody to act the experience that you had. It was an ethical consideration that you couldn't direct actors to experience what you had been through.

RITHY Yes. Maybe one day I could do it, but today, no. I don't know how to ask a fictional perpetrator to kill a victim. I know what happens. I know exactly the gesture, et cetera, but there's something blocked in my mind.

For me they are not really figurines. They are something else: a representation of the people, like a soul. An African mask is not a mask. It is a soul, a spirit. When you go to the temples in Angkor Wat, you have a lot of Buddhas, a lot of statues, but if you put one in the museum here, it's art, just a piece of art, but for us they represent a spirit. With these figurines, I can do things. I can imagine.

DEIRDRE You told me that you make several documentaries, and at the end, there's a culmination of a cycle, and then there's often a fiction film. In your fiction films, you can express your thoughts and feelings, but in the documentaries you must be faithful to the facts.

RITHY Documentary or fiction for me is film. It's subjective. It's something for you to show another person and to show yourself at the same time. I very much like documentary film because you negotiate with reality, with your own reality, with history. When I make documentary, you are so close to your character, but life is very cruel. Sometimes when you shoot somebody very poor, for example, at the beginning you can help them. You can continue to have a relationship with these people, but two years, three years later, they disappear.

Personally, I feel guilty that I have not had success to transform people with this process of filming, to get them out of poverty or prostitution, for example, but I know the film is not made for that. We are not God. We can just show. We can sometimes make small changes, but filming doesn't change the world.

DEIRDRE How have your films been received in Cambodia? Have they been seen widely and have they made changes?

RITHY At the beginning, nobody watched my films. It's normal for people who have just come out from the Khmer Rouge. I make a film about the Khmer Rouge, about the genocide, and it's normal that people don't want to watch it because they want to forget, they want to start a new life.

When I screened a film, sometimes I would see one Cambodian, but little by little, the new generation grew up and wanted to know their history. Now my films are watched by young people, and so the old people now come back and watch my films because their children watch the films, so it's okay.

The films now are available in Cambodia, in pirate copy, or you can see them also at our Bophana Center. Young people want to know what happened, where do they come from, and why their grandparent is not here today.

DEIRDRE Your films have helped to perpetuate consciousness, not just in the mass population but also toward creating a genocide tribunal that's still going on. *S-21*,[2] in particular.

RITHY I don't know exactly, but when I started to make *S-21*, nobody was thinking if there's a necessity to judge the Khmer Rouge or not. It wasn't the right time to talk about a trial. It was a time when people talked a lot about reconciliation. The problem for me is: who do I reconcile with? If you talk about reconciliation, it must be between the victim and perpetrator. If you do not know who the victim is and who is the perpetrator, how can you reconcile? Now most people think that the perpetrators, in a certain way, are also victims. So who am I? If they are victims, who am I?

DEIRDRE That's what Vann Nath says . . .

RITHY Yes, that's Vann Nath.

DEIRDRE . . . in *S-21*.

RITHY You have to work on your memory. It's a long journey.

DEIRDRE I remember reading that Khieu Samphan, who had written his memoir claiming not to have known that there were any mass killings, after seeing *S-21* admitted that, yes, it had happened.

RITHY It's good that he admits it, but he lies. He knew about it.

DEIRDRE He knew. All along.

RITHY Yeah, he knew. He knew it, but it's good the film gave him the possibility to pronounce these words, it's okay.

DEIRDRE I said last night that most English speakers know *S-21*. It's the one film of yours that, until *The Missing Picture*, has gotten attention and has shaken up the way people think about re-enactment in documentary. Fewer people have seen *Duch, Master of the Forges of Hell*, and yet it's as important a film. Can you talk a little bit about your making of that film?

RITHY Maybe we are all interested by horror. I try not to make a horror film, but genocide is horrific. And it captures our attention more.

I think that in *S-21*, for example, that there is much more than just the reenactment. A lot of film directors were influenced by this film, even my friend Joshua Oppenheimer with his *The Act of Killing*, for example. When I made the film, I didn't think about reenactment. I thought about memory. I shot with these people for many months, and most of the time they told me that, "Ah, I forget. It's a long time ago."

One time, I asked one of the chiefs of the guard how many people he killed, for example. He cannot explain this to me. I understand that he cannot tell me the number. I cannot ask how many, or if the first person he killed was a man or a woman. It's very complex, so I worked another way. I tried to ask him the first time he killed, if he remembered the smell.

He said, "Yes, I smelled blood. After, I didn't smell anything. It's just a job." This means that he went there many, many times but he can't tell me if he killed two or three people or five.

Memory is not something fixed. You know it also changes. It's like a photographer's loop, bigger than reality. It transforms everything. There are things that memory keeps in your body. I had a wound and I couldn't walk for a year. I just couldn't stand up. Ten years later, I still felt this pain even though it had already healed.

When I interviewed one of the Khmer Rouge, the guy was my age, so he was in S-21 when he was 13. He could not speak to me. He would just give me a word here, a word there. It's very difficult to understand him, but he made a lot of gestures. I tell him: "You can complete your words by showing me what happened," and it became a re-enactment. I am not asking people to act. I just try to take the memory out of the body, what your body keeps, what your body feels.

I asked him, "You worked at night. Did you have a light or not?" and I tried to create the conditions of what happened for him 25 years ago. If his guard shift was at midnight, I went back to S-21 at midnight. I let him do what he wanted. He just explained to me what happened and it went like that. It's very strange because at the end, he had a big fever, like something came out of his body. A big, big fever. I remember. It was very strange.

DEIRDRE That scene in the film is one that almost everybody writes about and thinks about, and it has so much to do not only with his remembering, his physical remembering, but the way you keep the camera outside of the room. You never cross into the room. Would you say something about that? Also, how did you communicate with your DP (Director of Photography)? Was it Prum Mésar who was the cameraman?

RITHY Yeah, yeah.

DEIRDRE How did that happen?

RITHY We have some code. I touch him [*he reaches out his hand at arm's length*]. First we determine a good distance and a good distance for me is that you can touch your subject. Logically, Mésar must follow him at this distance everywhere. When the guard went inside to beat the prisoner, I don't know why I stopped Mésar, but I just put my hand on his shoulder, and he knew that he had to stop following him.

You must have this kind of ethic in your heart, because when you are filming, things go too fast. I don't know, I see people. I see the prisoners. The room is empty, but I see people, so I just put a hand on Mésar's shoulder. "Don't walk on people. We cannot walk on people who are lying there, who ask for help, who ask for water."

At that moment, I didn't know how important this was, but when I watched the rushes, I understood, okay, you can continue to make the film, because if you followed the guy, that means that you had become a perpetrator yourself.

Making a documentary is like dealing in faith. It's like a religion. I don't practice religion, but I live documentary-making like a faith. If you don't believe, you cannot see people laying on the ground.

Sometimes there's some phenomenon, very rare, but when I film sometimes the birds come. That night birds came, one or two, and after, a family of birds came watching us. Maybe for people it's nothing, but for me, it is the souls of the victims who came here to watch what I'm doing. A very rare bird. When we finished shooting, they flew away.

DEIRDRE Shall we talk about your fiction films?

RITHY I'm not very lucky in fiction films because people love my film three years after it has been released. I say: "I would like you to love it when it is released." But they don't go to see it then. But three or four years later, they say, "Ah, I saw your film. It's amazing." Yes. "Thank you."

I like very much to direct people. Fiction film is a way for me to tell myself that I'm not completely destroyed. I can make a fiction. It means I can imagine, I can transcend, I can direct people, I can think, I'm alive. They cannot destroy me.

DEIRDRE I was thinking today when I was looking at the clip from *The Missing Picture* and saw the figure of your brother flying out to the moon, I was thinking, this is by a man who studied fiction film and there's a memory of Méliès here as well as your experience as a boy watching the Apollo launch and then being punished for telling that story later on. The distinctions between the world of fiction and the world of documentary in our lives are never quite so separate. They coexist in us.

RITHY Yes. It's good. You see, *Nanook* is a fiction film. It's more a fiction film than my documentary film. It's all fiction film in *Nanook*, but we consider it the origin of the documentary.

DEIRDRE Changing the subject for a moment, you've worked with great collaborators. You have your cinematographer, you have Marc Marder as composer, you have wonderful editors. How do you communicate with them? You talked about a code with the cinematographer. I remember you and Marc laughing about how you communicate when you're developing the score for your film. Maybe you could talk about that.

RITHY We were much too serious at the beginning. "Ah, this note must be here!" Now we have changed the idea of how to work. Marc is very good and he is more than a friend. He's like a brother. He started to work with me 30 years ago now. He gives me a lot of liberty, a lot of freedom.

I don't ask him for specific music. Sometimes I ask, "Can you do for me a track like this one?" I cannot read music, but I try to communicate with him with my words or I sing something or I send him some sounds. He has given me permission to edit the music, so sometimes I put 10 music tracks of Marc's together or 20 or only one.

I'm lucky because he allows only me to do that. Most of the time he composes normally for other films. He understands that he must let me do what I want. It's like a sculpture, and I put a sound here and a sound here.

It's the same with Prum Mésar, my DP. I've trained him. In the beginning, we started shooting the film at six in the morning and at midnight he finished cleaning the equipment. From midnight to two, we analyzed the film, and we woke up at six to go to shoot again. That was a very hard time.

We know each other now and I just ask him, "What is the direction of the light?" I ask him to step into the light, and if he feels it's good, it's okay.

DEIRDRE What about the editing? Is it still Marie-Christine Rougerie?

RITHY: Marie-Christine is now retired. Sometimes I ask her to come work with me for one or two weeks like that, just to destroy what I'm doing. She is someone who started editing with the workprint.

DEIRDRE On a Steenbeck.[3]

RITHY For such editors, the perception of time is not the same compared with people who only know how to edit in digital. This kind of editor is disappearing little by little. Time is not the same now with digital editing. We have a lot of technique, good technicians and good IT, but we have lost the notion of time. I watch an Antonioni film. There's one shot, a classic, powerful, beautiful shot, and you just go: "Ah! How can they do that?!" If you watch on TV or in the big cinema now, it's a different rhythm.

DEIRDRE Can we take a question from the audience?

SPEAKER Thank you for your film last night. I was incredibly moved by it and, of course, thought about it late into the evening, and what I was thinking about is exactly what you said. How is it possible, that we go into a trance where in fact they're not figurines anymore, they become people?

I was thinking that one of the elements is your writing, the text, the voice. Just beautiful writing. I'd like you to talk a little bit about how you write, when you write. Do you like to write?

RITHY I don't write, and that's my big problem. I know writing, but I don't want to do it. I don't know if I can continue to make films, for example, because people ask me more and more to write, and I don't want to write. You can't lie to people, but you can lie to a producer from time to time but not three times.

I'm laughing but I am serious. I don't know if they will believe me for the next film to be accepted. "Ah, Rithy Panh, maybe we can give him money because anyway he will do something, so we accept his idea." The world changes, and the TV channels, and the program heads. I am not nostalgic. I accept that the game has changed, but I remember 20 years ago, when you had a subject, you would go to see a producer. "Can you give me three boxes of 16 mm film just to do something?" and you could get it. Now you cannot.

I read a lot of books. I read a lot, a lot, a lot. I go to cinema very rarely. I don't like to go to the theater, but I go sometimes. My source of energy comes from books, from poetry, and from painting and photography.

I have a great admiration for photographers and poets. Just to nourish your imagination and connect it to your subject, and sometimes an idea comes. Sometimes it doesn't come immediately. You must wait. The image is not something that comes to you. You must be patient and you must go to find the image.

The Missing Picture I did in eight months, but I started two years before. When the idea is good, when the story is there, when I am clear, I go very quickly. I have a journal where I take some notes, but I prefer to talk to people.

Everybody knows, the one, the only guy who sees the film is the film director. It's not the DP, it's not the producer, it's not the editor. Only the director knows what his film is. I am a little bit lucky because I made some beautiful films when I was younger, like *The Land of Wandering Souls*, for example. I think it is one of my best films, but people don't talk about this one. *Site 2* is a great film, but people talk only about *S-21* or *The Missing Picture*.

When I started to make films, I was lucky because some producers believed in me and let me do what I needed to do, like Catherine Dussart at CDP. Sometimes she asked me, "Can you show me something?" but that's all. I owe her everything.

PRATAP RUGHANI Thank you so much for your films. They're just so significant for many of us, and also thank you to Deirdre for helping curate this conversation and bring it to our community so meaningfully.

I had a question, or just an area that I'd really appreciate exploring a little bit more, and it's to do with that moment of touch. You described a touch on the shoulder of your camera person and deciding to stay outside of the room and how that seemed like an embodied response rather than a conscious response.

You were saying that you can't have that in your mind and heart just in the moment of directing or of presence, but it's something that's cultivated over a long period. You used the word "dignity" and the word "ethics." I'm just interested to hear more about that. How has your approach been formed through your responses to these events? How have you come to be the shape that you are, if you like, as a director?

RITHY For me, at that moment, I just see people. I see people laying on the floor, the victims. Why do I see that, I don't know, but it happens for me like that. For the documentary filmmaker, you must learn to have a lot of generosity. If you have no generosity, you cannot see things. If your eyes are very like the horse, blinkered, you cannot see.

Generosity, it's not rare in my life and cinema. In my life I am not afraid to go with people. I'm not afraid to offer something to people. This brings you back something like a miracle to keep your eyes open in life. If you do not have generosity, your eyes are always closed because you don't want to see people. You close your eyes and you cross the street. It's okay. You are safe. But if you share something with people, they teach you to keep your eyes open, and when your eyes are open, you can see a lot of things, visible and not visible. You talk about visible evidence, but there's invisible evidence. In this case, it's invisible evidence. Maybe for another film director, it's just an empty room.

IRINA LEIMBACHER I was wondering if you could speak a little bit about your early trajectory, your decision to go to film school, how you developed your earliest visions of what you wanted to see, what you wanted to say, what you wanted to share visually with the rest of the world.

RITHY When I started at l'IDHEC,[4] everybody wanted to make fiction films except me. In the school, you have only three months of documentary practice in three or four years . . . this is nothing.

I liked watching Wiseman or the Maysles or Jean Rouch at the time. I like Wiseman very much, but I was not impressed by some of those films. The first documentary I made for the school, it was catastrophic. Really catastrophic. Shameful. I think that I successfully destroyed it. It was so bad because it misunderstood what documentary film is.

Site 2 is my real first film. I decided I needed to create a good distance, a distance where you can touch your people. You don't need commentary. If you are good, everybody watching your film will understand.

I wanted to go to Site 2[5] but the Thai military didn't want me to go. They kept me outside the camp for months. Every two or three days, I went to see the military in Bangkok. They refused me again and again. I was very naïve. I believed in the UN. I went to see the UN, and I said, "Help me, please, you are the UN." I was really naïve. They didn't help me. They just sat me in a chair, "Wait here. We will help you," but nothing ever happened.

One day I was very angry because I had run out of money. I went back to see the Thai and said, "Maybe I will not make the film, but I will see you, you will be my neighbor. I will see you one day." I went out, and the guy comes after me, "I give you three days." Three days to make *Site 2.*

I went to Site 2. I didn't have a ride to go back. I went to the camp and they have a military post. They kept me there. I could not go inside. When you closed your eyes, you could hear the murmuring of the city. There are 180,000 people inside 5.7 square kilometers. Small place, big town. You cannot see the camp, but you can hear the murmuring. I started to make the film with these sounds, to imagine how people live.

When they gave me the possibility to go back to Site 2, we only had three days. The first day, I did not shoot. It was a situation where I knew I should not do that, but I was young. I did not shoot the first day, but I told my team that, "You can use three boxes of film 12 minutes each, but shoot something that is interesting for you, that you have never seen or something that you can see people fighting to survive or to protect themselves or something like that."

I started to walk in the camp. I met this woman who I think had waited for me for five, six years already. I started to make the first take, and this became the first scene of the film, and we went on like that, and the story kept coming, coming, coming, coming.

We keep our exact distance. We don't change the lens. It's not a rule, but something that I must respect, that you make a film *with* people and not *about* people. When you make a film with people, you must be with them. When they are in the rice field, you are in the rice field. When they are in the water, you will be in the water.

This rule continues today. All my team learn to do that, all my young students. You can go to the website for my center, Bophana Center, B-O-P-H-A-N-A, and you go to One Dollar Project and you see the young students who make seven minute, five minute films about how people can earn one dollar a day and what they can buy, how they can live with one dollar a day.

DEIRDRE Do you want to tell people a little more about the training you do at Bophana?

RITHY Yes. I think that people in Cambodia, now most of them are young people. They are 30 years old and less and they are seventy percent of the population. They don't read books. They read less than one book a year, but they use social media a lot. I don't like this, but I do it. I have Facebook, I have Twitter, I have everything. I follow them, they follow me. I try to understand what kind of language I can use to communicate with them. Now we try to train all the young people to make these films, seven minute films, but with a strong subject of social or political project.

The films we make, we have no chance to broadcast on TV. Of course, TV is like karaoke, but reality is not TV. TV is not reality. Maybe social media can bring reality and reflection together. We must train our young people to use this medium, so we use the internet.

Now these are the subjects in One Dollar. When you are poor, you forget your quality. Most of the time, you don't like yourself, but every human being has some grace, has some quality, a gift that they don't know because they are so poor that they don't see it in themselves. We try to film this grace and to make people understand that even poor, you have something unique that other people do not have. Maybe you can use it to escape from your poverty.

DEIRDRE I just looked at my watch. We have gone way over time, so I want to thank the audience, but especially I want to thank Rithy . . .

RITHY Thank you.

Notes

Chapter 1   Uncle Rithy and the Cambodian Tragedy

1   Rainer Maria Rilke, *Letters on Cézanne*, ed. Clara Rilke, trans. Joel Agee (New York: Northpoint, 2002).

2   Rithy Panh's physical and emotional status at the time of resettlement is not recorded anywhere, and all we know is what he has written about this time in his memoir, *The Elimination*. Linda Son looked at how historical, cultural, and developmental factors affected the way children dealt with the trauma of war, dislocation, and separation from family and home in Cambodia. In particular, she considered how Cambodian culture, with its strong emphasis on the family, might influence how well children developed in the aftermath of war and the refugee camp experience. Depression, PTSD, panic and generalized anxiety, alcohol abuse, personality disorders, and conduct disorders, among others, were some of the problems manifested by adolescent survivors in studies conducted in Southeast Asia, although no consistent pattern emerged across cultures. The most prevalent symptoms included nightmares, depression, somatization, sleeping problems, social problems, fearfulness, anxiety, and antisocial behaviors. Panh's persistent problems with insomnia, panic attacks, and fearfulness presumably date from this period of his life. His dislike of psychiatry may also date from this time. He would have been grilled in psychiatric interviews, when his fitness for resettlement in France was being evaluated. In an interesting study, *Unaccompanied Children: Care and Protection in Wars, Natural Disasters, and Refugee Movements*, there is a chapter on Cambodia in the 1970s and another on issues of separation, trauma, and intervention for unaccompanied children in refugee centers. Of particular interest is discussion of the situation that governed Rithy Panh's own evacuation when, as an orphan and a minor under the age of eighteen, he was resettled in France. Statistics do not exist on just how many children made their way to refugee camps and to eventual resettlement during the Pol Pot years, but some venture to estimate that only 1 in 10 children succeeded in their bid to escape. Rithy Panh was one of these,

1 of 638 children resettled to France between 1973 and 1984. Linda Son, "Understanding the Psychological Impact of War Trauma and the Refugee Camp Experience on Cambodian Refugee Children in Site Two" (PhD diss., Harvard University, Graduate School of Education, 1994); Everett M. Ressler, Neil Boothby, and Daniel J. Steinback, eds., *Unaccompanied Children: Care and Protection in Wars, Natural Disasters, and Refugee Movements* (New York: Oxford University Press, 1988), 89–112, 153–73.

3 Rithy Panh, "Cambodia: A Wound That Will Not Heal," *UNESCO Courier*, December 1999, 30.

4 Panh, "Cambodia," 30.

5 Rithy Panh with Christophe Bataille, *The Elimination, A Survivor of the Khmer Rouge Confronts His Past and the Commandant of the Killing Fields*, trans. John Cullen (New York: Other Press, 2012), 5–6.

6 Nicolas Bauche and Dominique Martinez, "Entretien avec Rithy Panh: Mon entreprise dépasse celle d'un cinéaste," *Positif*, October 2013, 34–38.

7 Panh, *Elimination*, 5–6.

8 "J'aime le cinéma depuis peu," *Cahiers du Cinéma*, CNC issue, 2005, 4.

Chapter 2   The Return

1 Jonathan Spence, "In China's Gulag," *New York Review of Books*, August 10, 1995.

2 "Aux abords des frontières" (1987) is available in the Bibliothèque du film, BiFi Archives, as cited in Sylvia Blum-Reid, *East-West Encounters: Franco-Asian Cinema and Literature* (London: Wallflower, 2003), 158n3.

3 Hannah Arendt, "We Refugees" (1943), in *Altogether Elsewhere: Writers on Exile*, ed. Marc Robinson (London: Faber and Faber, 2007), 110–19.

4 Michèle Halberstadt, "Entretien avec Rithy Panh," *L'Avant-Scène Cinéma* 435 (October 1994): 1–3.

5 Arendt, "We Refugees," 264.

6 Blum-Reid, *East-West Encounters*, 158n3.

7 All the camps supported the noncommunist resistance of the Khmer People's National Liberation Front (KPNLF). Vietnamese refugees, including boat people, were also housed at the camp. By 1988 a new educational assistance program for primary school was launched, and by early 1989 the school system at Site 2 consisted of fifty primary schools plus three middle schools and high schools, serving students and illiterate adults.

8 Lindsay Cole French, "Enduring Holocaust, Surviving History: Displaced Cambodians on the Thai-Cambodian Border, 1989–1991" (PhD diss., Harvard University Department of Anthropology, 1994).

9 Readers curious about the situation of Cambodian refugees at the mercy of bandits, smugglers, and political opportunists might consult Michael Vickery, "Refugee Politics: The Khmer Camp System in Thailand," in *The Cambodian Agony*, ed. David A. Ablin and Marlowe Hood (Armonk, NY: M. E. Sharpe, 1987), 293–331; William Shawcross, *The Quality of Mercy: Cambodia, Holocaust, and Modern Conscience* (New York: Simon and Schuster, 1984), 302–27. Both writers describe the circumstances affecting Cambodian refugees when Panh was in the Mairut camp awaiting reunion with his family in France.

10 "On a Morality of Filming: A Conversation between Rithy Panh and Deirdre Boyle," *CineAction* 97 (2016): 39–44.

11 "On a Morality of Filmmaking," 44.

12 Bertrand Bacqué and Barbara Levendangeur, "Entretien avec Rithy Panh," Festival Visions du Reél de Nyon, November 2005, quoted in Alain Freudiger, "Festival Visions du Réel de Nyon 2006, Gros plan sur le cinema de Rithy Panh," *Décadrages*, 8–9, 2006, 138. http://decadrages.revues.org/294. "J'ai realizé ce film de manière instinctive, sans vraiment réfléchir, dans l'urgence, et il est devenu la matrice de mon oeuvre—où l'on retrouve bien sûr le travail sur la mémoire, mais aussi la quête d'une juste distance physique avec les personnages la decision de laisser la parole aux autres sans ajouter d'explication, le désir de filmer un territoire unique" (author's translation).

13 Rithy Panh, "*La parole filmée. Pour vaincre la terreur*," booklet accompanying DVDs, 2000 (text originally appeared in *Communications*, Editions du Seuil), 39.

14 Panh, "*La parole filmée*," 39.

15 Panh, "*La parole filmée*," 23.

16 VGIK, the Russian State University of Cinematography, located in Moscow, is the world's oldest film school and was founded in 1919 by Lev Kuleshov and Vladimir Gardin.

17 Samuel Lelièvre, "Enjeu interprétatifs de la féminité dans l'écriture de Souleymane Cissé," *Cinémas*, 11, no. 1 (Autumn 2000): 61–76.

18 Panh, "*La parole filmée*," 39.

19 An earlier film based on the novel and faithful to Ahmad's original setting was made by the popular Malaysian actress Sarimah, and it won the best film award at the Malaysian Film Festival in 1983. Panh has never seen this film, following his practice of never viewing prior films based on a novel or short story that he has adapted for the screen.

20 Blum-Reid, *East-West Encounters*, 109.

21 "Interview with Rithy Panh," conducted in 1997, published in Blum-Reid, 127.

22 Bidou was a graduate from the INSAS (Institut Supérieur des Arts du Spectacle, Brussels) and started as a filmmaker. He then moved into politics after 1968 but continued to produce documentary films between 1971 and 1981. He was associated with Atelier Varan. In 1987 he created JBA Production and started producing documentaries made by young directors from developing countries. Blum-Reid, 119.

23 Danielle Dumas, "Les risques du métier, Entretien avec J. Bidou," *L'Avant-Scène Cinéma* 435 (October 1994): 75–77 (author's translation).

24 The scenario includes visual directions, but when questioned about the shot-by-shot details, Panh explained that they had been added after the film was finished, probably by the journal, and were not part of a shooting script. Interview with author, Geneva, March 10, 2017.

25 Derek Elley, "Review: 'Rice People,'" *Variety*, May 30, 1994. https://variety.com /1994/film/reviews/rice-people-12004369.

26 Halberstadt, "Entretien avec Rithy Panh," 1–3 (author's translation).

27 Blum-Reid, *East-West Encounters*, 125–26.

28 Notable among the French crew is cinematographer Jacques Bouquin and the editing team of Andrée Daventure and Marie-Christine Rougerie, the latter of whom would become Panh's principal editor until her retirement.

29 "Look Back in Pain: Rithy Panh Talks to Bruno Jaeggi and Martial Knaebel" (1994), *Cinemaya* 24, 44–47, as quoted in Blum-Reid, *East-West Encounters*, 109.

30 For more on Cambodian theatrical forms, see chapter 7 on *The Burnt Theater*.

31 Halberstadt, "Entretien avec Rithy Panh," 2.

32 Blum-Reid, *East-West Encounters*, 109.

33 From the script for "Aux abords des frontières."

34 Halberstadt, "Entretien avec Rithy Panh," 3.

35 Blum-Reid, *East-West Encounters*, 122.

36 In addition, LaSept/Cinema contributed 1.1 million francs, CNC contributed 1.06 million francs, Ecrans du Sud 150,000 francs, and Channel Four 380,000 francs (sales abroad). *Ecran Total* 57 (November 30, 1994), as quoted in Blum-Reid, 160.

37 "La très belle part du film c'est son materialisme, cette manière de nous attacher aux gestes du travail: peiner derrière la charrue se courber pour le repiquage." ("The most beautiful part of the film is its materialism, this manner of attaching us to the gestures of work—to labor behind the plough, to bend down for planting" [author's translation]). Gérard Lefort, *Libération*, quoted in "La Presse de Cannes," *L'Avant-Scène Cinéma* 435 (October 1994): 68

38 *L'Avant-Scène Cinéma* includes a selection of brief quotes about the film by writers from *L'Humanité, Le Quotidien, Le Monde, Le Soir, Le Figaro, France-Soir, Libération, Le Nouvel Observateur, Studio, Nice-Matin, Sud-Ouest, Le Quotidien du Médecin, Réform* and *L'Avant-Scène*, 67–69.

39 Dumas, "Les risques du métier," 76.

40 Blum-Reid, *East-West Encounters*, 127.

Chapter 3   The Khmer Rouge

1 Arthur and Joan Kleinman, "The Appeal of Experience; The Dismay of Images: Cultural Appropriations of Suffering in Our Times," in *Social Suffering*, ed. Arthur Kleinman, Veena Das, and Margaret Lock (Berkeley: University of California Press, 1997), 17.

2 Readers will find answers to their questions about the Cambodian genocide in books by eyewitnesses like François Ponchaud, Laurence Picq, and François Bizot; by historians like David Chandler and Ben Kiernan; by journalists like William Shawcross, Elizabeth Becker, Nic Dunlop, and Peter McGuire; by foreign policy and human rights specialists like Samantha Power; and in the films of John Pilger, Adrien Maben, Annie Goldson, Thet Sambath, and Rob Lemkin, to name only a few.

3 David P. Chandler, "Seeing Red: Perceptions of Cambodian History in Democratic Kampuchea," in *Revolution and Its Aftermath in Kampuchea: Eight Essays*, ed. David P. Chandler and Ben Kiernan (New Haven, CT: Yale University Press, 1983), 35.

4 Ben Kiernan, *Blood and Soil: A World History of Genocide and Extermination from Sparta to Darfur* (New Haven, CT: Yale University Press, 2007), 540–41.

5 David P. Chandler, *A History of Cambodia*, 4th ed. (Boulder, CO: Westview, 2008), 229–32.

6 "Lemkin Defines Genocide," https:// www.genocidewatch.com/what-is-genocide. The genocide convention Lemkin crafted, which was finally adopted by the United Nations in 1948, offered a somewhat narrower definition. Some historians and political analysts prefer the broader term *crimes against humanity* to describe the slaughter of Cambodians by the Khmer Rouge because, as Philip Short argues in *Pol Pot: Anatomy of a Nightmare*, the Khmer Rouge did not set out to exterminate a national, ethnic, racial, or religious group; they conspired to enslave people, and this is a crime against humanity. Philip Short, *Pol Pot: Anatomy of a Nightmare*

(New York: Henry Holt, 2004), 446. Readers may wish to navigate among the various concepts of genocide, politicide (killings of people in groups targeted because of organized political opposition), democide (state mass murder), and crimes against humanity. *Genocide* is the term Rithy Panh uses, and throughout this book, I defer to Panh's understanding that it is the correct term when discussing what happened in Cambodia.

7   Samantha Power, *"A Problem from Hell"—America and the Age of Genocide* (New York: Harper Perennial, 2002), 90. The Pulitzer Prize–winning author is a lawyer, human rights specialist, and former U.S. ambassador to the United Nations during the Obama administration.

8   Timothy Snyder, *Black Earth: The Holocaust as History and Warning* (New York: Duggan Books, 2015), 339.

9   Chandler, *History of Cambodia*, 244–45. See also Paul Thomas Chamberlin, *The Cold War's Killing Fields: Rethinking the Long Peace* (New York: Harper Collins, 2018), 304.

10   Kiernan, *Blood and Soil*, 545–46.

11   Short, *Pol Pot*, 74.

12   Short, *Pol Pot*, 148–49.

13   Kiernan, *Blood and Soil*, 544.

14   Short, *Pol Pot*, 39.

15   Chandler, *History of Cambodia*, 246–47.

16   Kiernan, *Blood and Soil*, 544–45.

17   Chamberlin, *The Cold War's Killing Fields*, 301–2.

18   Sophal Ear, "The Khmer Rouge Canon, 1975–1979: The Standard Total Academic View on Cambodia" (PhD diss., University of California, Berkeley, 1995), 15, http://www.csua.berkeley.edu/~sophal.

19   James Pringle, "Sihanouk Adapts to 'Austere Life,'" *Washington Post*, July 19, 1973, A18, as quoted in Power, *"Problem from Hell,"* 93.

20   Power, *"Problem from Hell,"* 92.

21   William Shawcross, *Sideshow: Kissinger, Nixon and the Destruction of Cambodia* (New York: Simon and Schuster, 1979), 153.

22   Power, *"Problem from Hell,"* 92–93.

23   Peter Kerr, "Lon Nol, 72, Dies; Led Cambodia in Early 1970s," *New York Times*, November 18, 1985.

24   Chamberlin, *Cold War's Killing Fields*, 351.

25   Chamberlin, *Cold War's Killing Fields*, 329.

26   Other films have attempted to realistically depict the arrival of the Khmer Rouge: the first was the harrowing documentary from David Munro and the investigative journalist John Pilger, *Year Zero: The Silent Death of Cambodia* (1979), and the most recent, Angelina Jolie's narrative film *First They Killed My Father* (2018), based on a survivor's childhood memories of that time, which was filmed in Khmer and produced by Panh.

27   Spalding Gray, *Swimming to Cambodia* (New York: Theater Communications Group, 1985), 48–52. Spalding Gray was cast in the minor role of the U.S. consul in Joffé's film *The Killing Fields*. Gray's theatrical performance of his monologue about making the film in Thailand and Hollywood is the basis of the book. Jonathan Demme's film of *Swimming to Cambodia* was released in 1987 and rereleased in 2013.

28   William Shawcross, *Quality of Mercy: Cambodia, Holocaust and Modern Conscience* (New York: Simon and Schuster, 1984), 14.

29 Rithy Panh and Christophe Bataille, *The Elimination: A Survivor of the Khmer Rouge Confronts His Past and the Commandant of the Killing Fields*, trans. John Cullen (New York: Other Press, 2012).

30 Boreth Ly, *Traces of Trauma: Cambodian Visual Culture and National Identity in the Aftermath of Genocide* (Honolulu: University of Hawai'i Press, 2020), 77.

31 Ly, *Traces of Trauma*, 64–65.

32 François Ponchaud, *Cambodia Year Zero*, trans. Nancy Amphoux (New York: Holt, Rinehart and Winston, 1977), 192. The Jesuit missionary Ponchaud spent ten years living in Cambodia and was forced to leave with the last convoy of foreigners on May 8, 1975. He returned to France, where he worked with Cambodian refugees and was one of the first to report on the atrocities being committed there. His book was vigorously contested by pro-revolutionary leftists who dismissed the validity of the testimony of refugees and defended the Khmer Rouge against Western "propaganda." In the end, Ponchaud's efforts at documenting the experiences of genocide survivors met with acceptance and respect. Unfortunately, his call for international condemnation of the Khmer Rouge regime was heard but not heeded. Ponchaud gave testimony at the Extraordinary Chambers in the Courts of Cambodia in Phnom Phenh in 2013 in Case 002 against the Khmer Rouge leaders Khieu Samphan and Nuon Chea.

33 Rejection of the testimonies given by refugees fleeing the Cambodian genocide was led by leftist Western academics who championed the revolution over the refugees. Chief among them was Noam Chomsky, who, with his collaborator Edward S. Hermann, denounced Ponchaud's research, first in an article for *The Nation* (June 25, 1977) and later in *After the Cataclysm: Postwar Indochina and the Reconstruction of Imperial Ideology* (1979). William Shawcross countered their assertions of Western press propaganda with "Cambodia: Some Perceptions of a Disaster," in *Revolution and Its Aftermath in Kampuchea: Eight Essays*. Chomsky, who has never visited Cambodia, claimed authority over the facts and has never admitted his mistakes or apologized. See also Ear, "The Khmer Rouge Canon."

34 Chandler, *History of Cambodia*, 255–57.

35 Chandler, *History of Cambodia*, 259.

36 Rithy Panh, *La parole filmée, Pour vaincre la terreur,* booklet with DVDs, 19–20.

37 Short, *Pol Pot*, 248.

38 Laurence Picq, *Beyond the Horizon: Five Years with the Khmer Rouge*, trans. Patricia Norland (New York: St. Martin's Press, 1989), as quoted in Short, *Pol Pot*, 318.

39 Hannah Arendt, *On Violence* (New York: Harcourt Brace & World, 1960), 53–55, as quoted in Elizabeth Becker, *When the War Was Over: Cambodia and the Khmer Rouge Revolution* (New York: Public Affairs, 1998), 209–10.

40 Kiernan, *Blood and Soil*, 549.

41 Chandler, *History of Cambodia*, 260.

42 Chandler, *History of Cambodia*, 260–62.

43 Ponchaud, *Cambodia Year Zero*, 55–56, 58–59.

44 Chandler, *History of Cambodia*, 264.

45 Chandler, *History of Cambodia*, 269.

46 Ly, *Traces of Trauma*, 67.

47 Chandler, *History of Cambodia*, 266–69.

48 Kiernan, *Blood and Soil*, 553.

49 Becker, *When the War Was Over*, 293.

50 Shawcross, *Sideshow*, 369.

51 Chandler, *History of Cambodia*, 276.

52 David P. Chandler, *Brother Number One: A Political Biography of Pol Pot*, rev. ed. (Chiang Mai, Thailand: Silkworm Books, 2000), 158.

53 Chandler, *Brother Number One*, 159.

54 Bringing the surviving leaders of the Khmer Rouge to justice would have to wait until 2007 when, after years of debate and opposition, the joint UN- and Cambodian-sponsored tribunal, the Extraordinary Chambers of the Courts of Cambodia, was convened in Phnom Penh. See chapter 4.

55 Chandler, *Brother Number One*, 161.

56 Gray, *Swimming to Cambodia*, 52. When Gray wrote *Swimming to Cambodia*, Pol Pot was still living along the Cambodian-Thai border. He died April 15, 1998. After having ordered the death of Son Sen and all his household, Pol Pot was put under house arrest by the Khmer Rouge, and a show trial was organized by Ta Mok denouncing Pol Pot for this mass murder. Ironically it was this killing and not the genocide of nearly two million Cambodian people that finally brought him face-to-face with judicial review. Although his death was officially attributed to heart failure, the American journalist Nate Thayer, who was present both at the trial and his funeral, suggested it was more likely suicide.

57 Kiernan, *Blood and Soil*, 554.

Chapter 4   Perpetrators and Survivors

1 Different figures have been offered to account for those who died at S-21 and the few who survived. The ECCC judgment of Duch noted that there were 12,273 prisoners, but no children were registered, and many records were lost or incomplete. David Chandler estimates that 17,000 were killed. Five children were left behind and found by the Vietnamese. Seven adults were long thought to be the only survivors, but others have surfaced, not wishing to reveal their identities, and so the likely number of survivors was 23.

2 Explanation sent to the author by Panh in an email dated June 4, 2022. *Santebal* was a compound term that combined the words *santisuk* (security) and *nokorbal* (police). Thierry Cruvellier, *The Master of Confessions: The Making of a Khmer Rouge Torturer*, trans. Alex Gilly (New York: Harper Collins, 2014), 44.

3 David Chandler, *Voices from S-21: Terror and History in Pol Pot's Secret Prison* (Berkeley: University of California Press, 1999), 4.

4 Raya Morag prefers to call the coerced confessions of S-21 victims "testimonies" since they were not admissions of guilt but rather statements imposed by torture and bore little relationship to actual crimes committed by those seized for execution by Santebal. Raya Morag, *Perpetrator Cinema: Confronting Genocide in Cambodian Documentary* (London and New York: Wallflower Press, 2020), 92–93.

5 Françoise Sironi, "The Psychological Evaluation of Duch, a Criminal against Humanity in Cambodia," in *The Scene of the Mass Crime: History, Film, and International Tribunals*, ed. Christian Délage and Peter Goodrich (New York: Routledge, 2013). Françoise Sironi, one of two court-appointed psychiatrists who evaluated Duch, interviewed him over many hours and learned about his life, his relationship with Democratic Kampuchea's totalitarian personality, and the goals he pursued on behalf of Angkar. Her conclusions about what happened at S-21 are based on what Duch—an unreliable witness at best—told her and are presented here as one version of the truth.

6　Chandler, *Voices from S-21*, 3.

7　Chandler, 145.

8　Panh told Noy Thrupkaew that his uncle, who had been attending college in Oklahoma, was called back by Pol Pot to "help build the country," and when he arrived, he was taken straight from the airport to S-21. He never revealed under torture that he had a wife and children, thus keeping his family safe. Panh chooses to recall him in times of peace: "He made beautiful omelettes," Rithy remembers. "I never let them break what was good for me before the war." See Noy Thrupkaew, "Speak, Memory," *American Prospect*, July 30, 2004.

9　It was screened at the Venice Film Festival and was the top award winner at the 1996 International Documentary Film Festival in Marseille. *Bophana, a Cambodian Tragedy* has yet to be subtitled in English; however, a transcript of the film in English was published in *Manoa* 16, no. 1 (2004): 108–26.

10　Rithy Panh, "Cambodia: A Wound That Will Not Heal," *UNESCO Courier* 52, no. 12 (December 1999): 31.

11　Some claim she abandoned her son, but this interpretation seems doubtful. She was the only member of her family able to work and needed childcare while earning the wages to support them. Her younger sister looked after the boy. Assumptions about abandonment do not fit her character and do not mesh with her portrait in Becker and Panh's stories.

12　Elizabeth Becker, *When the War Was Over: Cambodia and the Khmer Rouge Revolution* (New York: Public Affairs, 1998), 212–25.

13　Rithy Panh, *La parole filmée, Pour vaincre la terreur*, booklet for "Le Cinéma de Rithy Panh" DVDs, 8. Also published in *Communications* (Paris: Editions du Seuil, 2000). The neurologist and writer Oliver Sacks confirms these views. Sacks observed: "Extreme interrogation—outright physical and mental torture—has been used to extract political 'confessions,' but the deeper intentions may be to brainwash, to effect a genuine change of mind, to fill it with implanted . . . memories." See "Speak, Memory," *New York Review of Books*, February 21, 2013.

14　Chandler, *Voices from S-21*, 110–12.

15　Rithy Panh, "*Bophana, a Cambodian Tragedy*" (screenplay), *Manoa* 16, no. 1 (2004): 115.

16　Panh, "*Bophana*," 116.

17　Chandler, *Voices from S-21*, 141.

18　James Burnet, "Autour de Rithy Panh," *La parole filmée, Pour vaincre la terreur*, booklet for "Le Cinéma de Rithy Panh" DVDs, 44.

19　Vicente Sánchez-Biosca, "Bophana's Image and Narrative: Tragedy, Accusatory Gaze, and Hidden Treasure," in *The Cinema of Rithy Panh: Everything Has a Soul*, ed. Leslie Barnes and Joseph Mai (New Brunswick, NJ: Rutgers University Press, 2021).

20　Cambodian names when Latinized are often spelled differently. For example, Houy is also written as Huy in other texts. For non-Khmer speakers, it is also difficult to determine the surname or family name of a Cambodian and the gender.

21　Nicholas Bauche and Dominique Martinez, "Entretien avec Rithy Panh: Mon entreprise dépasse celle d'un cinéaste," *Positif*, October 2013, 34–38.

22　Panh, "*Bophana*," 122–24.

23　Even historians were pleased to have such confirmation. When François Roux told David Chandler that Duch had read his book on S-21 and had praised its accuracy, Chandler was gratified by his approval.

24　Anne Elizabeth Moore, "'A Very Small Satisfaction': Oscar-Nominated Rithy Panh on Cambodia's Missing Pictures," *Truthout*, March 2, 2014.

25 Christian Delage, *Caught on Camera: Film in the Courtroom from the Nuremberg Trials to the Trials of the Khmer Rouge* (Philadelphia: University of Pennsylvania Press, 2014), 231.

26 Joram Ten Brink and Joshua Oppenheimer, *Killer Images: Documentary Film, Memory and the Performance of Violence* (London and New York: Wallflower, 2012), 243–55.

27 Interview with Panh in Jean-Marie Barbe's documentary film, *Uncle Rithy (Oncle Rithy)* (Ardèche Images Production, 2008), 94 min.

28 Ten Brink and Oppenheimer, *Killer Images*, 249.

29 William Guynn, *Unspeakable Histories: Film and the Experience of Catastrophe* (New York: Columbia University Press, 2016), 183–84.

30 Peter Maguire, *Facing Death in Cambodia* (New York: Columbia University Press, 2005), 125.

31 First Run Features' press packet for *S-21: The Khmer Rouge Killing Machine* (2003).

32 Dominick LaCapra, *History and Memory after Auschwitz*. (Ithaca, NY: Cornell University Press, 1998), 41.

33 First Run Features' press packet for *S-21*.

34 Ten Brink and Oppenheimer, *Killer Images*, 248.

35 Leslie Camhi, "The Banal Faces of Khmer Rouge Evil: How Can Torturers Seem So Ordinary?," *New York Times*, May 16, 2004, 24.

36 Camhi, "Banal Faces," 24.

37 Paul Ricoeur, "Histoire et mémoire," in *De l'histoire au cinema*, ed. Antoine Baecque and Christian Délage (Paris: Complexe, 1998), 20.

38 Robert Davis, "Review of *S21: The Khmer Rouge Killing Machine*," *Errata*, March 29, 2004, http://www.erratamag.com/archives/2004/03/s21_the_khmer_r .html#comments (italics added).

39 Bessel A. van der Kolk and Onno van der Hart, "The Intrusive Past: The Flexibility of Memory and the Engraving of Trauma," in *Trauma: Exploration in Memory*, ed. Cathy Caruth (Baltimore: Johns Hopkins University Press, 1995), 158–82.

40 Panh, "Cambodia."

41 Van der Kolk cites Janet's *L'Etat Mentales Hystériques* and Freud's *Inhibitions, Symptoms, and Anxiety*. Van der Kolk and van der Hart, "Intrusive Past," 166–67.

42 Rowena Santos Aquino, "Necessay F(r)ictions: Reenactment, Embodied Historiography, and Testimony" (PhD diss., University of California, Los Angeles, 2011), 156.

43 Sotheara Chhim, "Baksbat (Broken Courage): The Development and Validation of the Inventory to Measure Baksbat, a Cambodian Trauma-Based Cultural Syndrome of Distress," *Culture, Medicine and Psychiatry* 36 (2012): 640–59. See also Gay Becker, Yewoubdar Beyene, and Pauline Ken, "Memory, Trauma, and Embodied Distress: The Management of Disruption in the Stories of Cambodians in Exile," *Ethos* 28, no. 3 (2000): 320–45.

44 Boreth Ly, *Traces of Trauma: Cambodian Visual Culture and National Identity in the Aftermath of Genocide* (Honolulu: University of Hawai'i Press, 2020), 16–17.

45 Ly, *Traces of Trauma*, 34.

46 Susan J. Brison, "Trauma Narratives and the Remaking of the Self," in *Act of Memory: Cultural Recall in the Present*, ed. Mieke Bal, Jonathan Crewe, and Leo Spitzer (Dartmouth, NH: Dartmouth College, 2000), 40, as quoted by Boreth Ly, "Of Performance and the Persistent Temporality of Trauma: Memory, Art, and Visions," *East Asia Cultures Critique* 16, no. 1 (Spring 2008): 128. Memories of traumatic events, both great and small, are often evoked by body language, images, words, sounds, and silence; trauma continues to haunt one.

47 Panh dedicated his film *Que la barque se brise, que la jonque s'entrouvre* to the psychiatrist Richard Rechtman. See Rechtman's book with Didier Fassin, *The Empire of Trauma: An Inquiry into the Condition of Victimhood* (Princeton, NJ: Princeton University Press, 2009); and *Living in Death: Genocide and Its Functionaries*, trans. Lindsay Turner (New York: Fordham University Press, 2022).

48 Prime Minister Hun Sen suggested they "dig a hole and bury the past." Seth Mydans, "Cambodian Leader Resents Punishing Top Khmer Rouge," *New York Times*, December 29, 1998, 1.

49 Khieu Samphan, *L'histoire récente du Cambodge et mes prises de position* (Reflection on Cambodian history up to the era of Democratic Kampuchea) (Paris: L'Harmattan, 2004).

50 Associated Press, "Former Khmer Rouge Leader Admits Genocide," *New York Times*, December 30, 2003.

51 Seth Mydans, "Cambodia Arrests Former Khmer Rouge Head of State," *New York Times*, November 20, 2007, http://www.nytimes.com/2007/11/20/world/asia/20cambo.html?ref=asia&pagewanted=print.

52 Panh, "Cambodia."

53 René Char, *Hypnos*, trans. Mark Hutchinson (Calcutta: Seagull, 2014), 8.

54 Hannah Arendt, *Eichmann in Jerusalem: A Report on the Banality of Evil* (New York: Viking, 1964).

55 The name Kaing Guek Eav has been Latinized in various forms, but this is the spelling most used today. He possessed a string of aliases: Yun Cheav, Kang Cheav, Kaing Yun Cheav, Doan, and Hang Pin. He is best known by his nom de guerre within the Khmer Rouge, Comrade Duch.
　　As the first defendant before the ECCC, Duch attracted the attention of many writers as well as filmmakers. More has been written about him and his trial than about Pol Pot and the other leaders of Angkar. Rithy Panh's memoir, *The Elimination*, is in large measure a postmortem reflection on the making of his film with Duch. Panh claimed writing it saved him: "After hours of rushes, I had to find words to get by. Words freed me and helped me find peace." It is the first text readers will want to consult after viewing this film and before seeing Panh's autobiographical film *The Missing Picture*. Readers interested in knowing more about Duch are recommended to the following texts: François Bizot, *Facing the Torturer*, trans. Charlotte Mandell and Antoine Audouard (New York: Alfred A. Knopf, 2012); François Bizot, *The Gate*, trans. Euan Cameron, (New York: Vintage Books, 2004); Cruvellier, *Master of Confessions*; Nic Dunlop, *The Lost Executioner: A Journey to the Heart of the Killing Fields* (New York: Walker, 2005); Alexander Laban Hinton, *Man or Monster? The Trial of a Khmer Rouge Torturer* (Durham, NC: Duke University Press, 2016); Marcel Lemonde et Jean Reynaud, *Un Juge Face Aux Khmers Rouge* (Paris: Editions du Seuil, 2013); and Christophe Peschoux and Haing Kheng Heng, *Itinerary of an Ordinary Torturer: Interview with Duch, Former Khmer Rouge Commander of S-21* (Chiang Mai, Thailand: Silkworm, 2015).

56 Rithy Panh, *The Elimination: A Survivor of the Khmer Rouge Confronts His Past and the Commandant of the Killing Fields*, trans. John Cullen (New York: Other Press, 2012), 255.

57 Y-Dang Troeung and Madeleine Thien, "'To the Intellectuals of the West': Rithy Panh's *The Elimination* and Genealogies of the Cambodian Genocide," *TOPIA: Canadian Journal of Cultural Studies* (March 2016): 155–71.

58 This chapter's scope precludes analysis of the many reasons why Cambodia has hidden or otherwise attempted to deny its traumatic past under the Khmer Rouge. Competing political interests from within and outside the country have struggled over the importance and necessity of examining this troubled time. The efforts of many have ultimately led to the creation of the international criminal tribunal that, however much it has been criticized for lax legal standards, time-consuming preliminaries, and extravagant cost, has undertaken a national as well as international search for truth and reconciliation. The efforts of filmmakers and journalists like Panh have played an important role in this process. Anyone interested in following the trial records for cases before the ECCC, will find them online at Extraordinary Chambers in the Courts of Cambodia, homepage, accessed June 26, 2022. https://www.eccc.gov.kh/en.

59 Sebastian Strangio, *Hun Sen's Cambodia* (New Haven, CT: Yale University Press, 2014), 235–67. See also Craig Etcheson, *After the Killing Fields: Lessons from the Cambodian Genocide* (Westport, CT: Praeger, 2005).

60 Pol Pot died in 1998 before the ECCC was convened. He had already been convicted of crimes against humanity in a show trial conducted by the People's Republic of Kampuchea. In 1998 the Khmer Rouge put him under house arrest for the slaughter of Son Sen and his family; he was convicted of these murders but not the genocide of nearly two million Cambodians during the Khmer Rouge regime. His death was attributed to natural causes, but some suspected suicide; others, poisoning. All remaining members of the Central Committee were arrested and placed on the list for trial before the ECCC. While awaiting his case to come forward, Ieng Sary died and his wife, Ieng Thirith, who had been receiving medical treatment for dementia, was excused from further participation. She too has since died. Only Nuon Chea and Khieu Samphan stood trial and were convicted of crimes against humanity and genocide and sentenced to life in prison. Nuon Chea died in August 2019. Khieu Samphan is the last man standing.

61 Panh, *Elimination*, 5.

62 Nicolas Bauche and Dominique Martinez, "Entretien avec Rithy Panh: Mon entreprise dépasse celle d'un cineaste," *Positif*, October 2013, 34–38.

63 For more on Panh's collaboration with the novelist Christophe Bataille on their book, *The Elimination*, which combined Panh's memories with his reflections about interviewing Duch, see chapter 8.

64 Panh, *Elimination*, 255.

65 Panh, *Elimination*, 200.

66 *Chronicle of a Summer* (1960) by Jean Rouch and Edgar Morin was the first film to present a Holocaust survivor recounting concentration camp experiences (at Auschwitz-Birkenau) for the camera. Marceline Loridan carried a portable audio recorder in her oversized handbag and, while walking in the Place de la Concorde, whispered into a microphone her painful memories. Panh was clearly influenced by Rouch's film and taught documentary classes for Rouch's Atelier Varan in Phnom Penh, a model he would borrow when designing classes for his documentary students at the Bophana Audiovisual Resource Center in Phnom Penh. He became a close friend of Marceline Loridan Ivens.

67 Guynn, *Unspeakable Histories*, 174–75.

68 Panh, *Elimination*, 33.

69 Cruvellier, *Master of Confessions*, 1–2.

70 Joël Isselé, "Entretien avec Rithy Panh," *L'Autre Voie* 9 (2013): (author's translation).

71 Counterparts to Santebal include the Soviet NKVD, the East German Stasi, the Central Case Examination Group in China, the American FBI, and British MI5. Like them, Santebal was a national security apparatus, but unlike its counterparts, it had no central policy-making office and no foreign or domestic agents. For more information, see Chandler, *Voices from S-21*.

72 It is estimated there were 20,000 killing fields throughout Cambodia.

73 Readers familiar with Holocaust literature may know the writer Stéphane Hessel, who recited poems to himself while he was being tortured at Buchenwald. Panh discloses this in *The Elimination*, noting how disturbing it was for him to see Duch reading Hessel's poetry. Duch ultimately asked Hessel to testify on his behalf at his trial, a calculated risk that proved disastrous to his cause. Panh makes no reference to any of this in the film, instead maintaining his tight focus on Duch in the minimalist space of interrogation that Panh created for their meetings.

74 Apparently Saloth Sar (a.k.a. Pol Pot) was also fond of de Vigny's poetry. Ly, *Traces of Trauma*, 66.

75 Françoise Sironi was a cofounder of the Primo Levi Center in Paris, which specialized in psychotherapy and the care and support of victims of torture and political violence. She is considered a pioneer in bridging differences between psychotraumatology and ethnopsychiatry, one of the new wave of French mental health professionals who rejected approaches linked to colonial psychiatry's racism and rejection of cultural singularity. Appointed an expert for the ECCC, she developed a "geopolitical" method of assessment for her psychological evaluation of Comrade Duch. See Fassin and Rechtman, *Empire of Trauma*, 240–41.

76 Sironi, "Psychological Evaluation of Duch," 131–53.

77 Vicente Sánchez-Biosca, "The Perpetrator's *Mise-en-Scène*: Language, Body, and Memory in the Cambodian Genocide," *Journal of Perpetrator Research* 2, no. 1 (2018): 88.

78 Cruvellier, *Master of Confessions*, 210–11.

79 The documentary scholar Vicente Sánchez-Biosca persuaded Panh to watch the film with him, discussing his frame composition and editing scene by scene, exploring how Panh's cinematic choices—such as keeping Duch in the frame along with his staff and his victims—succeeded in emphasizing the unrepentant sinner at Duch's core.

80 Susan Sontag, *Regarding the Pain of Others* (New York: Farrar, Straus & Giroux, 2003), 60–61.

81 Panh, *Elimination*, 77.

82 Sánchez-Biosca, "Perpetrator's *Mise-en-Scène*," 54.

83 Panh, *Elimination*, 113–14.

84 Cruvellier, *Master of Confessions*, 34.

85 Cruvellier, *Master of Confessions*, 216.

86 Apparently Duch believed Pol Pot was responsible for the burglary attack on Duch's home that killed his wife and maimed one of his hands. It was after that incident that Duch turned to Christianity as his refuge.

87 Florent Papin, "Rithy Panh: 'I Was Afraid That the Khmer Rouge Would Use the Court as a Platform,' Nonfiction.fr, January 12, 2012, https://www.nonfiction.fr/article-5402-rithy-panh-jai-eu-peur-que-les-khmers-rouges-se-servent-du-tribunal-comme-dune-tribune.htm.

88　Panh had been appalled by the court's alleged "neutral images" during the trial. He criticized the way the ECCC's filming of the trial focused solely on the speaker. He repeatedly offered to film the trial himself but was refused because they feared his filming would not be neutral. He tried to give them advice on camera setups, which they also rejected. He offered to train people to show them how the Nuremberg trials and the Eichmann trials were filmed. He even proposed that France send the film director of the infamous Klaus Barbie (the Butcher of Lyon) trial. But the court rejected all his offers, content to capture the speaker only. The only editing by the court was done live during the recording. "There are times when the accused disagrees, gets up, shakes his head. It's important when he shakes his head, when he's not looking at the victims; it's important when he cries, when he smiles. But we'll never see him," Panh angrily told Florent Papin. Over time, Panh's frustrations subsided and were replaced with a more philosophical outlook. He approved of the installation of the tribunal in Phnom Penh, not in The Hague, so that Cambodians could see and hear. And beyond the trials, there was the pedagogy of the rule of law, on what a court is and on what justice is. More than one hundred thousand people attended the Duch trial, not to mention all those who came to the traveling screenings organized by the Bophana Audiovisual Resource Center in partnership with the court. All of this had pedagogical value.

89　Troeung and Thien, "'To the Intellectuals,'" 155–71.

90　Tuol Sleng means "hill of the sleng tree," which was the name of the land where S-21 was built. Tuol Sleng was chosen by the Vietnamese as the name for the entire S-21 compound in 1980 when they turned the buildings into a museum of genocide. For more information about S-21, see Chandler, *Voices from S-21.*

91　Martine Guyot-Bender, "Review of *Duch: le maître des forges de l'enfer*," *French Review* 86, no. 3 (2013): 627–28.

92　Richard Rechtman, "A propos de *Duch, le maître des forges de l'enfer*: reconstitution de la scène du crime," *Etudes* 415 (2011): 1–2.

93　Alexandra Del Perra and Agence France-Presse, "Filmmaker Rithy Panh Says Unmoved by Death of Khmer Rouge Torturer," *Jakarta Press*, September 3, 2020.

94　Rithy Panh, "Nath, tu es parti trop tôt," in *Cambodge, Le Génocide Effacé*, ed. Pierre Gayard and Soko Phay-Vakalis (Paris: Editions Nouvelles Cécile Defaut, 2013).

95　Associated Press, "Former Khmer Rouge Leader Admits Genocide," *New York Times*, December 30, 2003. See also Mydans, "Cambodia Arrests Former Khmer Rouge Head of State."

96　Deirdre Boyle, "Trauma, Memory, Documentary: New Forms of Re-enactments in Two Films by Rithy Panh and Garin Nugroho," in *Documentary Testimonies: Global Archives of Suffering*, ed. Baskar Sarkar and Janet Walker (New York: Routledge, 2009). See also Deirdre Boyle, "Shattering Silence: Traumatic Memory and Reenactment in Rithy Panh's *S21: The Khmer Rouge Killing Machine*," *Framework* 50, no. 1–2 (Spring–Fall 2009): 95–106.

97　Hayden White, "The Modernist Event," in *The Persistence of History: Cinema, Television, and the Modern Event*, ed. Vivian Sobchack (London: New York: Routledge, 1996), 36.

98　A genocidaire is a person who commits mass murder of defenseless people under the authority of a state, army, or militant group of some sort. The French word is generally used in English to refer to participants in the Rwandan genocide. Otherwise, the English term generally used is *perpetrator*, but this is not very nuanced. Rechtman's English translator Lindsay Turner uses *genocidaire* because it provides a way to discuss an individual's genocidal actions even outside of any genocide. It is worth considering as a better substitute for *perpetrator* in English texts. Rechtman, *Living in Death*, 204n9.

99 Rechtman, *Living in Death*, 129, 190–91.

Interlude

1 There are far too many places to visit to experience the horrors of the Khmer Rouge era. In 2019, the *Phnom Penh Post* reported on a popular tourist destination in the mountains of Phnom Sampov—"killing caves" where people had been thrown off cliffs by the Khmer Rouge. Visitors are guided to Pka Sla Cave, Chest Pounding Cave, and the Bat Cave, where it is estimated 10,000 victims were executed. Child guides claim they "take time from their studies" to tell tourists the history of the caves. But, like A'Koy in *The People of Angkor*, child guides rarely attend school because they must work to support their families, a transgenerational continuation of abuses committed by the Khmer Rouge. Raksmey Hong, "Former 'Killing Caves' Become a Sobering Tourist Destination," *Phnom Penh Post*, August 21, 2019.

2 Rithy Panh and Amandine Scherrer, "Filmer pour voir. Ombres et lumières sur le genocide Khmer. Entretien avec Rithy Panh." *Cultures et Conflits* 17, no. 1 (2015): 145–55. https://cairn.info/revue-cultures-et-conflits-2015-1-page-145.htm.

3 Nick Paterniti, "Never Forget: Life after the Khmer Rouge Genocide." *GQ*, July 1, 2009, https://www.gq.com/story/cambodia-khmer-rouge-nick-paterniti/.

4 Rithy Panh with Christophe Bataille, *The Elimination: A Survivor of the Khmer Rouge Confronts His Past and the Commandant of the Killing Fields*, trans. John Cullen (New York: Other Press, 2012), 3.

5 Panh, *Elimination*, 169.

6 Erin Handley, "'We Did Not Exterminate Our People': Defiant Khieu Samphan Gives Final Statements at Khmer Rouge Tribunal," *Phnom Penh Post*, June 23, 2017.

7 James F. Moyers, "Film and the Public Memory: The Phenomena of Nonfiction Film Fragments," *Contemporary Aesthetics* 5 (2007), https://digitalcommons.risd.edu/liberalarts_contempaesthetics.

Chapter 5   After the Wars

1 Mahmoud Darwish, *In the Presence of Absence*, trans. Sinan Antoon (New York: Archipelago Books, 2011), 84–85.

2 The Khmer Rouge proclaimed 1975 the Year Zero, a new era without family, religion, education, culture, and all familiar social and political realities.

3 Sylvie Blum-Reid, "Interview with Rithy Panh," in *East-West Encounters: Franco-Asian Cinema and Literature* (New York: Wallflower, 2003), 124.

4 Boreth Ly, "Screening the Crisis in Monetary Masculinity in Rithy Panh's *One Night After the War* and *The Burnt Theatre*," in *Film in Contemporary Southeast Asia: Cultural Interpretation and Social Intervention,* ed. David C. L. Lim and Hiroyuki Yamamoto (London: Routledge, 2012), 54–55.

5 Ly, "Screening the Crisis," 57–58.

6 Ly, "Screening the Crisis," 60.

7 Godfrey Cheshire, "Review: *One Evening After the War*," *Variety*, May 20, 1998.

8   "C'est faute d'aimer que l'on songe à la distance. Que la barque se brise, que le jonque s'entrouvre. . . . On arrive à Ceylan sur leur épaves si le désir d'y arriver vous domine."

9   Rithy Panh, *The Elimination: A Survivor of the Khmer Rouge Confronts His Past and the Commandant of the Killing Fields*, trans. John Cullen (New York: Other Voices, 2012), 20–21.

10 Christine Chartier, "Interview with the Director: *Que la barque se brise, que la jonque s'entrouvre,*" *Arte*, August 15, 2006.

11 Panivong Norindr, "The Sounds of Everyday Life in Rithy Panh's Documentaries," *French Forum* 35, no. 2–3 (Spring–Fall 2010): 181–90.

12 Rithy Panh, *"La parole filmée. Pour vaincre la terreur,"* booklet accompanying DVDs, 2000.

13 Chi-hui Yang, "Documentary, other spaces and the infrastructural migration route: Rithy Panh and Ursula Biemann," master's thesis, San Francisco State University, 2011. http://htl.handle.net/10211.3/116490.

14 David Chandler, *A History of Cambodia*, 4th ed. (Boulder, CO: Westview, 2008), 298–300.

15 Leslie Barnes, "Objects of Pleasure: Epistephilia and Sex Workers in Rithy Panh's *Le Papier ne peut pas s'envelopper la braise,*" *French Cultural Studies* 26, no. 1 (2015): 56–65.

16 Norindr, "Sounds of Everyday Life," 188.

17 *L'arrière-fond de cette douleur sociale est l'histoire même du Cambodge, confronté à la blessure toujours ouverte des années khmers rouges, à la culture de l'impunité comme au désir effréné de la consommation, qui se traduit par la course à l'argent et à la corruption: « Le signe évident de la fêlure sociale apparaît dans l'exploitation économique et politique du corps et de l'esprit. Les pères-soldats morts au combat laissent des enfants-ouvriers ou, pire, prostitués."* Rithy Panh and Louise Lorentz, *Le papier ne peut pas envelopper la braise* (Paris: Grasset, 2007), 9.

18 Panh and Lorentz, *Le papier*, 17.

19 An edited version of the film was made for the U.S. public television series *Wide Angle* in 2002; it is shorter by several minutes and has a voice-over narration spoken with little sensitivity in a film effectively stripped of Panh's aesthetic. Most of the credits pertain to the PBS series staff. Viewers would be well advised not to watch this edited version of a powerful film and hope that the original, full-length version with English subtitles and no voice-over will be released for distribution in English-speaking countries.

20 Panivong Norindr, "The Fascination for Angkor Wat and the Ideology of the Visible," in *Expressions of Cambodia: The Politics of Tradition, Identity, and Change*, ed. Leakthina Chau-Pech Ollier and Tim Winter (London: Routledge, 2006), 66–67.

21 Norindr, "Fascination for Angkor Wat," 68.

22 Apsaras were beautiful and graceful goddesses who diverted the gods with their songs and dances.

23 Panh, *La parole filmée*, 28.

24 Ly, "Screening the Crisis," 64.

25 Robert Turnbull, "A Burned-Out Theater: The state of Cambodia's Performing Arts," in *Expressions of Cambodia: The Politics of Tradition, Identity, and Change*, ed. Leakthina Chau-Pech Ollier and Tim Winter (London: Routledge, 2006), 133–49. See also Robert Turnbull, "Staring Down Horrors of the Khmer Rouge," *International Herald Tribune*, Paris edition, April 6, 2007, 8.

26 Not long after King Sihamoni was crowned, he promised to restore the theater as a public entity under the Ministry of Culture, but days later, Hun Sen's government announced the theater and the land around it would be sold to a telecommunications company and the theater disbanded. Kith Meng announced he would build a television tower and conference hall on the site. The artists squatting in the theater expected to be relocated outside the capital with little access to shops, schools, or pagodas. Turnbull, "Burned-Out Theater," 144–45.

27 Catherine Diamond, "Emptying the Sea by the Bucketful: The Dilemma in Cambodian Theater," *South Asian Journal* 20, no. 2 (Autumn 2003): 147–78.

28 Turnbull, "Burned-Out Theater," 148–49.

Chapter 6   Colonialism

1 Dina Sherzer, "Introduction," in *Cinema, Colonialism, Postcolonialism: Perspectives from the French and Francophone World*, ed. Dina Sherzer (Austin: University of Texas Press, 1996), 5–6.

2 Michael Guillen, "*TIFF08: Un Barrage Contre le Pacifique (The Sea Wall)*, Interview with Rithy Panh," *Screen Anarchy*, September 25, 2008, https://screenanarchy. com/2008/09/tiff08-un-barrage-contre-le-pacifique-the-sea-wallinterview-with-rithy-panh.html.

3 Only Cochinchina (now South Vietnam) was a full-status colony; the other nations were protectorates but nonetheless functioned as colonies under the umbrella of French Indochina.

4 The Viet Minh was a communist-dominated nationalist movement, formed in 1941, that fought for Vietnamese independence from French rule. Members of the Viet Minh later joined with the Vietcong.

5 John Tully, *France on the Mekong: A History of the Protectorate in Cambodia, 1863–1953* (London: University Press of America, 2002), xxii–xxiii.

6 Tully, *France on the Mekong*, xxii–xxv.

7 Nicola Cooper, *France in "Indochina": Cultural Representations* (New York: Oxford University Press, 2001), 29.

8 Tully, *France on the Mekong*, 487–88.

9 Antoine de Baecque, "In Cambodia, Cinema Is Medicine," *Liberation*, October 5, 2005.

10 The civilizing mission was a political rationale for colonization purporting to facilitate the modernization and Westernization of Indigenous peoples.

11 Barbara Creed and Jeanette Hoorn, "Memory and History: Early Film, Colonialism and the French Civilizing Mission in Indochina," *French History and Civilization*, vol. 4 (2011), 225. https://h-france.net/rude/vol4/.

12 Creed and Hoorn, "Memory and History," 236.

13 Tom Gunning, "Early Cinema as Global Cinema: The Encyclopedic Ambition," *Early Cinema and the "National,"* ed. Richard Abel, Giorgio Bertellini, and Rob King (Bloomington: Indiana University Press, 2016), 11–16.

14 Duras, in *The Sea Wall*, speaks about the influence of colonial propaganda on her parents:

> Occasionally on Sunday, she [Ma] stopped to gaze at the colonial propaganda posters in front of the town hall. "Enlist in the Colonial Army!" said some. And others: "Young People, a Fortune awaits you in the Colonies!" The picture usually showed a Colonial couple, dressed in white, sitting in rocking chairs

under banana trees while smiling natives busied themselves around them. She married a schoolmaster who was as sick as she was of life in the northern village and victimized as she was by the maunderings of Pierre Loti and his romantic description of exotic lands. The consequence was that, shortly after their marriage, they made out a joint application to be sent, as teachers, to that great Colony then known as French Indo-china. (Marguerite Duras, *The Sea Wall*, trans. Herma Brifault [New York: Farrar, Straus and Giroux, 1952], 17)

15 Panivong Norindr, "Enlisting Early Cinema in the Service of 'La Plus Grande France,'" in *Early Cinema and the "National,"* ed. Richard Abel, Giorgio Bertellini, and Rob King (Bloomington: Indiana University Press, 2016), 111–12, 116. Norindr analyzes an influential early text, *Le Cinéma colonisateur*, written in 1916 by the Pathé-Frères agent Gérard Madieu, whose premise is not an unapologetic endorsement of colonialism but rather a pragmatic vision that provides a qualified and complex treatment of how it should be achieved. Norindr also offers astute analysis of ambivalence in a Lumière film shot by Constant Girel, *Coolies of Saigon*, which can be read as either an endorsement of the benefits of French colonialism or an irrefutable record of the cruel treatment of natives in Indochina at the turn of the century. He notes that analysis of early films reveals that the work performed by the natives and captured on film offers a more accurate image of the French imperial nation-state and how early film practitioners conceived and imagined the potential of cinema. See also Jacques Scherrer, "*La Trace Lumière*: Early Cinema and Colonial Propaganda in French Indochina," in *Le Cinématographe, nouvelle technologies du XXe siècle*, ed. André Gaudreault, Catherine Russell, and Pierre Vérnoneau (Lausanne: Payot Lausanne, 2004), 329–37.

16 *La France est Notre Patrie* is rather curiously translated as *France Is Our Mother Country*. *Patrie*, a masculine noun, is more commonly translated as "country" or "homeland," either of which would be a better choice for this film. The term *patrie* leads to thoughts of patriarchy and paternalism, not motherhood. Too often translations of Panh's films into English leave much to be desired.

17 Paula Amad, *Counter-Archive: Film, the Everyday, and Albert Kahn's Archives de la Planète* (New York: Columbia University Press, 2010). Kahn's archive was part of his humanitarian mission, "the work of mutual comprehension of peoples and international rapprochement" that obsessed him until his death. The aim of the Archives de la Planète was to promote international understanding and world peace, a utopian belief that the newest art form could help bring it about. Films made between 1908 and 1931 were as short as Lumière films and as long as ninety minutes, unedited, and never intended for the public.

18 The BBC series, *The Wonderful World of Albert Kahn*, is a ten-part series that includes the episode "Far East: Expedition to Empires." The series is available on DVD.

19 Allison J. Murray Levine, "Film, Propaganda and Politics: *La France est un empire, 1939–1943*," *Contemporary French Civilization* 40, no. 1 (2015): 71–91. *La France est un empire* was a prime example of colonial documentaries in the late thirties. It was completed during the Vichy regime and includes films by the directors Gaston Acelle (North Africa), Hervé Missir (Asia), George Barois (Madagascar and Somalia), Raymond Méjat (Guyana and Antilles), and André Persin (Black Africa). Murray explains how French documentary filmmakers navigated shifting political waters during the Vichy regime and adapted the content of colonial rhetoric to suit the times. It afforded a certain view of racial harmony and respect for cultures that builds to a nationalistic and militaristic climax. D'Agraives, a staunch supporter of

imperial France, submitted a film proposal in 1939 and completed the film after the outbreak of war; it was then shepherded through the Vichy censorship process in 1940 and banned in 1943. Panh borrows liberally from the films, which assert how troubled and diseased precolonial nations were rescued by French medicine, religion, schools, economic infrastructure, agricultural innovation, and roads, railroads, and air routes. The film is available on DVD.

20 Anonymous, DOXA Film Festival, Vancouver, Canada, May 2015.

21 Siegfried Forster, "Le cinéaste Rithy Panh montre pourquoi 'La France est notre patrie,'" *Asie-Pacifique*, May 6, 2015.

22 Poppy McPherson, "Glimpses of Cambodia's French Past," *The Diplomat*, May 5, 2015.

23 Research has uncovered the possibility that this classic representation of colonial condescension toward the poor may have alternate meanings. The ladies in white tossing local coins suggests the French custom of tossing candies and coins along with wishes for good fortune, fertility, and fun to children at celebrations, much like the way people toss rice at a bridal couple. As the historians Creed and Hoorn indicate, French intercultural communications were often complex and not necessarily as they might appear a century later.

24 Penny Edwards, "Womanizing Indochina: Fiction, Nation and Cohabitation in Colonial Cambodia, 1890–1930," in *Domesticating the Empire: Race, Gender, and Family Life in French and Dutch Colonialism*, ed. Julia Clancy-Smith and Frances Gouda (Charlottesville: University Press of Virginia, 1998), 117.

25 Creed and Hoorn, "Memory and History," 233.

26 Creed and Hoorn, "Memory and History," 235. See also Kathryn Robson and Jennifer Yee, eds., *France and "Indochina": Cultural Representations* (New York: Lexington Books, 2005).

27 McPherson, "Glimpses."

28 McPherson, "Glimpses."

29 Michelle Vachon, "Film Shows Indochina through Colonizer's Eyes," *Cambodia Daily*, May 9, 2015.

30 Kent Jones, "*Hiroshima, mon amour*: Time Indefinite," essay written for a booklet accompanying the 2003 release of the Criterion Collection DVD of the film. https://www.criterion.com/search#stq=time+indefinite.

31 In *Uncle Rithy* (*Oncle Rithy*), by Jean-Marie Barbe (Ardèche Images Productions, 2008), 94 min.

32 Guillen, "TIFF08."

33 An earlier film based on Duras's *The Sea Wall* was made in 1958, directed by René Clément and shot in Thailand. It takes liberties with Duras's story. Although the performances from actors like Jo Van Fleet, Anthony Perkins, Anna Magnani, Alida Valli, and Nehemiah Persoff were well received, the film itself was poorly reviewed. Panh never views other films based on literature he has adapted for the screen.

34 Marie Dieudonné, Duras's mother, acquired the *concessionnat* Prey Nop in Kampot in 1916. The letters written by the mother in the novel are close to those Duras's mother wrote to the cadastral agents.

35 "Interview with Rithy Panh," press package for *The Sea Wall*, 2008 (author's translation).

36 Panivong Norindr, *Phantasmatic Indochina: French Colonial Ideology in Architecture, Film, and Literature* (Durham, NC: Duke University Press, 1996), 107.

37 "Interview with Michel Fessler," press package for *The Sea Wall*, 2008 (author's translation).

38 "Interview with Rithy Panh," press package for *The Sea Wall*.

39 Norindr, *Phantasmatic Indochina*, 107–8. Norindr writes about the way influential poststructuralist critics favored Duras's more abstract writing, shifting discussion toward self-reflexive textual questions and away from political issues raised by her work. He believes influential critics like Julia Kristeva failed to recognize the interdependency of personal drama and political events. He writes, "By subsuming the political under the realm of the intersubjective, Kristeva dehistoricizes, not unlike humanist critics, Duras's work," 108.

40 Norindr, *Phantasmatic Indochina*, 130. Norindr concludes his essay on Duras's Indochinese trilogy by asserting that "Duras negotiates the physical and symbolic geographies of Indochina in too ambivalent a fashion to support and sustain a coherent critical position." Panh would probably disagree. Like her, he frequently resorts to ambivalence in his films and is no stranger to its uses. Curiously, Duras's adolescence in Cambodia took many by surprise when Panh's film was released. Few knew she had lived in Cambodia as well as Vietnam. The first book devoted to her time there is by Luc Mogenet, *Marguerite Duras au Cambodia*, and available from Publikam.

41 Norindr, *Phantasmatic Indochina*, 108.

42 Cooper, *France in "Indochina,"* 122–23.

43 Norindr, *Phantasmatic Indochina*, 124.

44 Cadastre is the register of property showing the extent, value, and ownership of land for taxation.

45 David Del Testa, "Automobiles and Anomie in French Colonial Indochina," in *France and "Indochina": Cultural Representations*, ed. Kathryn Robson and Jennifer Yee (Lanham, MD: Lexington Books, 2005), 68.

46 Dina Sherzer, "Race Matters and Matters of Race: Interracial Relationships in Colonial and Postcolonial Films," in *Cinema, Colonialism, Postcolonialism: Perspectives from the French and Francophone World*, ed. Dina Sherzer (Austin: University of Texas Press, 1996), 246.

47 "Interview with Rithy Panh," press packet for *The Sea Wall*.

48 "Interview with Rithy Panh."

49 Jean-Marie Barbe, *Uncle Rithy* (*Oncle Rithy*) (2008).

50 *Uncle Rithy* (2008), citing a passage in Panh's film, *Souleymane Cissé*.

51 "Interview with Isabelle Huppert," bonus feature on DVD of *The Sea Wall*, CinéMoi TV.

52 Norindr, *Phantasmatic Indochina*, 132–35.

53 Florence Jacobowitz, "Review of *Un barrage contre le Pacifique/The Sea Wall*," *CineAction* 76 (March 22, 2009). https://link.gale.com/apps/doc/A194486562 /AONE?u=nysl_oweb&sid=googleScholar&xid=4d02701e.

54 In his 2008 review for *Screen Daily*, Howard Feinstein compared Panh's adaptation of *The Sea Wall* with Régis Wargnier's 1992 Academy Award–winning *Indochine*. He found Wargnier's film—which starred Catherine Deneuve as a glamorous landowner—"overblown, brushed with a varnish that disguised the realities of imperialism in tropical climes." Feinstein praised Panh's fearlessness in revealing "the worms in a gorgeous world of lush palms and attractive rice paddies in what might otherwise be construed as paradise." https://www.screendaily.com/features /the-sea-wall/4040752.article.

55 Gérard Grugeau, "Entretien avec Rithy Panh: Le cinéma peut-il envelopper la braise?" *24 Images* 153 (2011): 58–65.

Chapter 7   Remembering the Past, Mourning the Dead

1 James F. Moyer, "Film and the Public Memory: The Phenomena of Nonfiction Film Fragments," *Contemporary Aesthetics* 5 (2007), https://digitalcommons.risd.edu /liberalarts_contemporaryaesthetics.

2 Anonymous, "TIFF Tokyo International Film Festival Event Report: Master of the Documentary Challenges Kenzaburô Ôe's Masterpiece," October 25, 2011.

3 *Le Monde* wrote: "This is a great text, humble in tone and with universal import. We greet it today in the tradition of Jean Hatzfeld [acclaimed French journalist noted for his coverage of the Bosnian war and the genocide in Rwanda]. For his part, Rithy Panh takes his place among those rare figures who have shared Vladimir Jankélévitz's conviction: 'It's not enough to be sublime, one must be faithful and serious.'" Strand Releasing press kit for *The Missing Picture* at the Cannes Film Festival.

4 François Ekhajzer, "Rithy Panh vit dans la mort, c'est un rescapé, Christophe Bataille écrivain," *Télérama*, October 9, 2013.

5 François Ekhajzer, "Au Cambodge, les âmes d'argile de Rithy Panh," *Télérama*, April 10, 2013.

6 Rosa Ellen, "Rithy Panh: The Director on Cannes Glory and Haunted Life," *Phnom Penh Post*, May 31, 2013. See also Nicolas Bauche and Dominique Martinez, "Entretien avec Rithy Panh: Mon entreprise dépasse celle d'un cinéaste," *Positif,* October 2013, 34.

7 Bauche and Martinez, "Entretien avec Rithy Panh," 34–38.

8 Florence Colombani, "Rithy Panh: 'The Unconsciousness of Childhood Saved Me from the Khmer Rouge,'" *Le Point*, March 10, 2013.

9 Poppy McPherson and Vandy Muong, "Sculpting an Oscar Nominee," *Phnom Penh Post*, March 3, 2014.

10 Sheerly Avni, "Rithy Panh Talks Oscar-Nominated 'The Missing Picture,'" *Indiewire*, March 19, 2014.

11 Colombani, "Rithy Panh."

12 Tobias Grey, "A Cultural Conversation with Rithy Panh: Cambodia's Oscar Contender," *Wall Street Journal*, February 25, 2014.

13 Ada Tseng, "Clay Souls: Interview with *The Missing Picture* Director Rithy Panh," *Asia Pacific Arts*, June 3, 2013, https://adatseng.com/2013/06/05/ cannes-2013-interview-with-rithy-panh/.

14 Vicente Sánchez-Biosca, "Challenging Old and New Images Representing the Cambodian Genocide: *The Missing Picture* (2013)," *Genocide Studies and Prevention: An International Journal* 12, no. 2 (2018): 140–64; Nick Bradshaw, "Memories of Murder: Rithy Panh on *The Missing Picture*," *Sight and Sound*, June 5, 2017, https://www.bfi.org.uk/news-opinion/sight-sound-magazine/interviews /memories-murder-rithy-panh-missing-picture.

15 Norodom Sihanouk, dir., *Apsara* (Khemara Pictures, 1966), 150 min. Bopha Devi trained as a dancer from the age of five. The Apsara Dance was choreographed for her by Queen Kosamak. Like other members of the royal family, Bopha Devi escaped Cambodia during the Pol Pot years. When she returned in the early nineties, she worked to revive traditional dance and became director of the Royal Ballet and Minister of Culture and Fine Arts. She died in 2019.

16 This is not the first time a boy's love for an apsara plays a pivotal role in one of Panh's films. A'Koy in *The People of Angkor* confides his longing for his lost mother to an apsara at Baphuon. Many of Panh's films include children as incidental characters—the family of daughters in *Rice People*, the kite flyer in *Site 2*, the string-cup telephone talkers in *The Land of Wandering Souls*—as well as principal characters: the mute boy in *One Year after the War*, A'Koy in *The People of Angkor*, and A'Pang in *Farm Catch*. Children not only allow Panh to incorporate aspects of his own childhood in his films; they help to engage younger audiences born after the genocide with his stories. This is especially true in *Exile*.

17 Jacques Prévert's poetry influenced many post–World War II French artists, including singers like Yves Montand and Edith Piaf. He also wrote scenarios for cinema, such as the classic *Les Enfants du Paradis*, including many animated films for children. His poetry is taught in French language classes around the world to this day.

18 Griselda Pollock and Max Silverman, eds., *Concentrationary Art: Jean Cayrol, the Lazarean and the Everyday in Post-War Film, Literature, Music and the Visual Arts* (New York: Berghahn Books, 2019).

19 Richard Rechtman, "The Survivor's Paradox: Psychological Consequences of the Khmer Rouge Rhetoric of Extermination," *Anthropology and Medicine* 13, no. 1 (April 2006): 1–11.

20 The voice-over is spoken in French by Randal Douc, who played M. Jo in *The Sea Wall*. Douc's mellifluous voice is a key element in the film, which is apparent when compared with the English language version. Jean-Baptiste Phou's voice is clear but lacks the grace Douc's voice possesses. Perhaps more significantly, the English language translation lacks the poetry of Bataille's French text.

21 In his afterword to *Charlotte Delbo, Oeuvres et Engagements*, Panh praised her book *The Measure of Our Days*, which he first read while preparing his film *S-21: The Khmer Rouge Killing Machine*.

22 Charlotte Delbo, *Auschwitz and After*, trans. Rosette C. Lamont, with introduction by Lawrence L. Langer (New Haven, CT: Yale University Press, 1995), x–xi, 267.

23 Sánchez-Biosca, "Challenging Old and New," 149, 153.

24 Rithy Panh, *La parole filmée, Pour vaincre la terreur*, a booklet accompanying DVDs, 2000 (text originally appeared in *Communications*, Editions du Seuil), 24–25.

25 François Ekchajzer, "'Rithy Panh vit dans la mort, c'est un rescapé,' Christophe Bataille, écrivain," *Télérama*, September 10, 2012, https://www.telerama.fr/festival-de-cannes/2016/exil-de-rithy-panh-la-si-belle-presence-de-l-absence,142347.php/.

26 Rechtman, "Survivor's Paradox."

27 Bradshaw, "Memories of Murder."

28 Readers are especially recommended to the following texts on *The Missing Picture*: Leshu Torchin, "Mediation and Remediation: *La Parole Filmée* in Rithy Panh's *The Missing Picture (L'Image Manquante)*," *Film Quarterly* 68, no. 1 (Fall 2014): 32–14; Jennifer Cazenave, "Earth as Archive: Reframing Memory and Mourning in *The Missing Picture*," *Cinema Journal* 57, no. 2 (Winter 2018): 44–65; Raya Morag, "The Survivor-Perpetrator Encounter and the Truth Archive in Rithy Panh's Documentaries," in *Post-1990 Documentary: Reconfiguring Independence*, ed. Camille Deprez (Edinburgh: Edinburgh University Press, 2015), 97–111. See also Sánchez-Biosca, "Challenging Old and New."

29 Hannah Arendt, "We Refugees" (1943), in *Altogether Elsewhere, Writers on Exile,* ed. Marc Robinson (London: Faber & Faber, 1984), 110–19.

30 Giorgio Agamben, "We Refugees," trans. Michael Rocke, *Symposium: A Quarterly Journal in Modern Literature* 49, no. 2 (1994): 114–19.

31 Nic Dunlop, *The Lost Executioner: A Journey to the Heart of the Killing Fields* (New York: Walker, 2005), 205.

32 François Ekchajzer, "'Exil' de Rithy Panh: la si belle presence de l'absence," *Télérama,* May 13, 2016, http://www.telerama.fr/festival-de-cannes/2016/exil-de -rithy-panh-la-si-belle-presence-de-l-absence.142347.php; Jean-Claude Raspiengeas, "La stèle des âmes mortes," *La Croix,* May 14, 2016, http://www.la-croix.com/article /imprimer/Culture/Cinema/La-stele-des-ames-mortes-2016-05-14-1200760157; Élisabeth Chardon, "Rithy Panh, partageur d'exil," *Le Temps,* Geneva, March 11, 2017, 24–25; Frédéric Burnand, "L'élégie de Rithy Panh dans un monde régressif," SwissInfo, March 17, 2017, https://www.swissinfo.ch/fre/ fifdh_exil—l-%C3%A9l%C3%A9gie-de-rithy-panh-face-%C3%A0-un-monde- r%C3%A9gressif/43035590.

33 Clarence Tsui, writing for *The Hollywood Reporter,* conceded *Exile* was "daunting for the historically uninitiated" but "relentlessly mesmerizing and thought-provoking." He predicted *Exile* might not be able to secure the same string of international theatrical and home releases as Panh's *The Missing Picture* (http://www .hollywoodreporter.com/review/exile-exil-cannes-review-892975). Ben Kenigsberg, writing for *Variety,* liked the film but found *Exile* not as accessible as *The Missing Picture* and likely to be received as a footnote to the earlier film (https://variety.com /author/ben-kenigsberg). Lee Marshall agreed, writing for *Screen Daily* that the film was suited to an arthouse niche but added it "never looks anything less than ravishing" (www.screendaily.com/reviews/exile-cannes-review/5103866.article). The inattentive Daniel Kasman, writing for *Mubi Notebook,* mistakenly attributed the time span of the film to the period following the Khmer Rouge era, referred to nonexistent potato fields, substituted the filmmaker René Clair for poet René Char, and considered the boy a Cambodian Everyman, not Panh's doppelgänger (https:// mubi.com/notebook/posts/cGannes-2016-rithy-panh-s-exile). The myopic Jasmin Valjas gave the film one star in her review for a UK online publication, The Upcom- ing, mistaking the narrator Randal Douc for the actor Sang Nan. She liked nothing about the film, dismissing it for its "tedious voice over," "mishmash of archival footage and mannered fiction scenes," "overly artsy and metaphoric mise-en-scene," and "cross-genre experimentation that eventually becomes quite uncomfortable" (www.theupcoming.co.uk/2016/05/13/cannes-film-festival-2016-exil-exile-review).

34 Rithy Panh, "Synopsis" for *Exile,* press kit for the Cannes Film Festival, May 2016.

35 Susan Sontag, *Regarding the Pain of Others* (New York: Farrar, Strauss, and Giroux, 2003), 89.

36 I was in Phnom Penh during the shooting of *Exile,* and I got to see the creation of several sets, some of which required as much as a week to be configured for the next scene. Panh's team were seasoned professionals and, like Panh, perfectionists. I observed how his alter ego Son Mang possessed amazing endurance, lying motionless in a fetal position for long periods of time while final details were resolved and lighting adjusted before Panh, who kept out of the way until he was called, gave his approval and the shot could be made.

37 Alessandro Marazzi Sasson, "Q&A: Rithy Panh on *Exile* and Dignity," *Phnom Penh Post,* March 4, 2017.

38 Rithy Panh with Christophe Bataille, *The Elimination: A Survivor of the Khmer Rouge Confronts his Past and the Commandant of the Killing Fields*, trans. John Cullen (New York: Other Press, 2012), 247.

39 Max Silverman, *Palimpsestic Memory: The Holocaust and Colonialism in French and Francophone Fiction and Film* (New York: Berghahn Books, 2013), 46.

40 Gaston Bachelard, *The Poetics of Space*, trans. Maria Jolas (Boston: Beacon, 1964), 229.

41 Panh, *Elimination*, 91.

42 Film narration.

43 Benoît Basirico, "Interview Marc Marder: Une Rélation de Confiance avec Rithy Panh," *Cinezik*, Cannes, May 14, 2016, on YouTube (www.cinezik.org/).

44 Morag, "Survivor-Perpetrator Encounters," 97–111.

45 Silverman, *Palimpsestic Memory*, 40, quoting Cayrol, "Lazarus among Us," in Pollock and Silverman, *Concentrationary Art*.

46 Raya Morag, *Perpetrator Cinema: Confronting Genocide in Cambodian Documentary* (New York: Wallflower Press, 2020).

47 Pollock and Silverman, *Concentrationary Art*, 11.

48 It is perhaps worth noting that Panh's very first film, his graduation thesis from l'IDHEC, was titled *Le passé imparfait*.

49 Rithy Panh, "Synopsis" for *Exile*, Cannes Film Festival.

50 Maximilien Robespierre, "Discourse on the Constitution (printed by order of the Jaobins, 10 May 1793)," as quoted in the film *Exile*.

51 Sassoon, "Q&A."

52 Ernst van Alphen, *Staging the Archive: Art and Photography in the Age of New Media* (London: Reaktion Books, 2014), 7–9.

53 Glenn Kenny, "Review: *Graves without a Name*: An Improbable Quest in Cambodia," *New York Times,* April 14, 2020, https://www.nytimes.com/2020/05/14/movies/graves-without-a-name-review.html?searchResultPosition=1; Clarence Tsui, "Film Review: *Graves without a Name*|Venice 2018," *The Hollywood Reporter,* August 29, 2018, https://www.hollywoodreporter.com/movies/movie-reviews/graves-a-name-les-tombeaux-sans-noms-film-review-venice-2018-1136600/.

54 Thierry Cruvellier, "Rithy Panh: Living the Experience of Genocide in Body and Soul," JusticeInfo.Net, November 27, 2018, https://www.justiceinfo.net/en/39596-rithy-panh-living-the-experience-of-genocide-in-body-and-soul.html.

55 The White Crocodile is a powerful and auspicious symbol in the Khmer otherworld. He was present at Cambodia's birth and is believed to have been put in charge of controlling the current of the Mekong River. He appears when the Cambodian people are at a crossroads and was rumored to appear in March 1970 before Lon Nol's coup, which abolished the monarchy and ushered in a period of war. See Elizabeth Becker, *When the War Was Over: Cambodia and the Khmer Rouge Revolution* (New York: Public Affairs, 1986, 1998), 114.

56 Bradshaw, "Memories of Murder."

57 Cayrol, "Lazarus among Us," 31.

58 Panh, *Elimination*, 143.

Epilogue

1 Peter Maguire, *Facing Death in Cambodia* (New York: Columbia University Press, 2005), 18.

2 Thierry Cruvellier, "Rithy Panh: Living the Experience of Genocide in Body and Soul," JusticeInfo.net, November 27, 2018, https://www.justiceinfo.net/en/39596 -rithy-panh-living-the-experience-of-genocide-in-body-and-soul.html.
3 Jacques Derrida, *Spectres de Marx: L'Etat de la dette, le travail du deuil et la nouvelle Internationale* (Paris: Galilée, 1994), 279. As quoted by Colin Davis in *Haunted Subjects: Deconstruction, Psychoanalysis and the Return of the Dead* (New York: Palgrave MacMillan, 2007), 76.

Appendix 2

1 Vladimir Jankélévitz, a French philosopher and musicologist.
2 S-21 was the notorious secret prison where it is estimated that more than 14,000 Cambodians were tortured, interrogated, and executed. Today, S-21 prison is known as the Tuol Sleng Museum of Genocide. In 2002, Panh made *S-21: The Khmer Rouge Killing Machine*. In Cambodia, the film was a catalyst in sparking a historical and judicial reckoning about the genocide.
3 A Steenbeck is a flatbed 16mm or 35mm analog film editing machine.
4 L'IDHEC, the Institut des Hautes Études Cinématographiques, is now known as La Fémis, and remains France's premier school for the training of filmmakers. It is located in Paris.
5 Site 2 was a large refugee camp on the Thai-Cambodian border.

Films and Books by Rithy Panh

Feature Films

1988—*Le passé imparfait*

1989—*Site 2* (92 min.)

1991—*Souleymane Cissé* (for the TV series *Cinéma de notre temps*) (53 min.)

1992—*Cambodia, between War and Peace* (*Cambodia, entre guerre et paix*) (65 min.)

1994—*Rice People* (*Les gens de la rizière, Neak Sre*) (125 min.)

1996—*Bophana, a Cambodian Tragedy* (*Bophana, une tragédie Cambodgienne*) (60 min.)

1997—*One Evening after the War* (*Un soir après la guerre*) (108 min.)

1999—*The Land of Wandering Souls* (*La terre des âmes errantes*) (60 min.) (an edited version was broadcast for the PBS series *Wide Angle* in 2002)

2001—*Let the Boat Break, Let the Junk Crack Open* (*Que la barque se brise, que la jonque s'entrouvre*) (87 min.)

2002—*S-21: The Khmer Rouge Killing Machine* (*S-21, La machine de mort Khmère Rouge*) (101 min.)

2003—*The People of Angkor* (*Les gens d'Angkor*) (90 min.)

2005—*The Burnt Theater* (*Les artistes du théâtre brûlé*) (82 min.)

2006—*Paper Cannot Wrap Up Embers* (*Le papier ne peut pas envelopper la braise*) (90 min.)

2008—*The Sea Wall* (*Un barrage contre le Pacifique*) (156 min.)

2011—*Farm Catch* (*Gibier d'élevage*) (91 min.)

2012—*Duch, Master of the Forges of Hell* (*Duch, Le maître des forges de l'enfer*) (110 min.)

2013—*The Missing Picture* (*L'image manquante*) (92 min.)

2015—*France Is Our Mother Country* (*La France est notre patrie*) (60 min.)

2016—*Exile* (*Exil*) (77 min.)

2018—*Graves without a Name* (*Les tombeaux sans noms*) (115 min.)

2020—*Irradiés* (88 min.)
2022—*Everything Will Be OK* (98 min.)

Books

La Paix avec les morts, Rithy Panh and Christophe Bataille (Paris: Grasset, 2019)
L'Image manquante, Rithy Panh with Christophe Bataille (Paris: Grasset, 2013)
The Elimination: A Survivor of the Khmer Rouge Confronts His Past and the Commandant of the Killing Fields, Rithy Panh with Christophe Bataille, translated by John Cullen (New York: Other Press, 2012)
Le papier ne peut pas envelopper la braise, Rithy Panh and Louise Lorentz (Paris: Grasset, 2007)
La Machine Khmère Rouge: Monti Santésok S-21, Rithy Panh and Christine Chaumeau (Paris: Flammarion, 2003)

Index

Academy Awards, 6, 13, 172, 197, 202
Act of Killing, The (Oppenheimer), 207
actualités, 140
Adorno, Theodor, 176
Aeschylus, 192
Agamben, Giorgio, 173
A'Koy, 70, 127–130, 191, 228n1, 235n16
ambiguity, 7, 131–132, 144–145, 167
ambivalence, 150, 231n15, 233n40
American war. *See* Vietnam War
Améry, Jean, 179
Angkar (the Organization): A'Pang's
    indoctrination, 159; Bophana as traitor
    to, 67–69; CPK hidden within, 49;
    and Duch, 221n5, 224n56; loyalty to, 53;
    reads confessions, 87; unraveling with
    Vietnamese invasion, 16; villagers and, 81
Angkor Wat, 2; archival images, 30; before
    colonialism, 190–191; benefit from
    colonialism, 139; in *Cambodia, between
    War and Peace,* 29–30; influence on Pol
    Pot, 42; opposes Legendre claims, 142,
    145; in *People of Angkor,* 127–128; spirit
    realm, 205
Antonioni, Michelangelo, 210
A'Pang, 159
Apsara dance, 166, 234n15
apsaras, 129, 229n22
Arbeit macht frei, 62

archival films: in *Cambodia, between War
    and Peace,* 28; and colonialism, 139,
    141–143; and ideology, 198, 232n23;
    memories of childhood, 169; and "new"
    people, 166
archive, postmodernist role of, 182
Archives de la Planète. *See* Kahn, Albert
Arendt, Hannah: on banality of evil, 82, 98; on
    normalized actions, 82–83, 98; on refugees,
    16, 172–173; on rule by terror, 53–54
Atelier Varan, 24, 117, 217n22
Aux abords des frontières (Near the
    borders), 15, 34, 216n2

Bachelard, Gaston, 177
baksbat (broken courage), 80
Bangsokol, Requiem for Cambodia, 13
Barbe, Jean-Marie, 152
bar girl, 108, 112, 125
Barnes, Leslie, 122
Bashō, Matsuo, 175
Bataille, Christophe: author of *Annam,* 163;
    collaboration on *Elimination,* 6, 163;
    on *Duch,* 162; first encounter with Panh,
    162–163; intertitles for *France Is Our
    Mother Country,* 142; narration for *Exile,*
    176; narration for *Missing Picture,* 170,
    235n20; remarks by Panh, 199
Battambang province, 52, 163